T0321843

FOUNDATIONS OF REAL-TIME COMPUTING:
Scheduling and Resource Management

THE KLUWER INTERNATIONAL SERIES
IN ENGINEERING AND COMPUTER SCIENCE

REAL-TIME SYSTEMS

Consulting Editor

John A. Stankovic

REAL-TIME UNIX SYSTEMS: *Design and Application Guide,*
B. Furht, D. Grostick, D. Gluch, G. Rabbat, J. Parker, M. McRoberts,
ISBN: 0-7923-9099-7

FOUNDATIONS OF REAL-TIME COMPUTING: *Formal
Specifications and Methods,* A. M. van Tilborg,
ISBN: 0-7923-9167-5

FOUNDATIONS
OF
REAL-TIME COMPUTING:

SCHEDULING
AND
RESOURCE MANAGEMENT

edited by

André M. van Tilborg
Gary M. Koob
Office of Naval Research

KLUWER ACADEMIC PUBLISHERS
Boston/Dordrecht/London

Distributors for North America:
Kluwer Academic Publishers
101 Philip Drive
Assinippi Park
Norwell, Massachusetts 02061 USA

Distributors for all other countries:
Kluwer Academic Publishers Group
Distribution Centre
Post Office Box 322
3300 AH Dordrecht, THE NETHERLANDS

Library of Congress Cataloging-in-Publication Data
Foundations of Real-Time Computing: Scheduling and Resource
        Management / edited by Andre M. van Tilborg, Gary M. Koob
                p.   cm. -- (The Kluwer international series in engineering and
        computer science ; 0141. Real-time systems)
                "Preliminary versions of these papers were presented at a workshop
        ...sponsored by the Office of Naval Research in October 1990 in
        Washington D. C." -- Foreword.
                Includes bibliographical references and index.
                ISBN 0-7923-9166-7
                1. Real-time data processing.   I. van Tilborg, Andre M. 1953 -
        . II. Koob, Gary M., 1958 -   . III. United States. Office of
        Naval Research. IV. Series: Kluwer international series in
        engineering and computer science ; SECS 0141. V. Series:
        Kluwer international series in engineering and computer science.
        Real-time systems.
                QA76.54.F68   1991   91-3540
                004'.33--dc20

Printed on acid-free paper.

Printed in the United States of America

Contents

FOREWORD

This volume contains a selection of papers that focus on the state-of-the-art in real-time scheduling and resource management. Preliminary versions of these papers were presented at a workshop on the foundations of real-time computing sponsored by the Office of Naval Research in October, 1990 in Washington, D.C. A companion volume by the title *Foundations of Real-Time Computing: Formal Specifications and Methods* complements this book by addressing many of the most advanced approaches currently being investigated in the arena of formal specification and verification of real-time systems. Together, these two texts provide a comprehensive snapshot of current insights into the process of designing and building real-time computing systems on a scientific basis.

Many of the papers in this book take care to define the notion of *real-time* system precisely, because it is often easy to misunderstand what is meant by that term. Different communities of researchers variously use the term *real-time* to refer to either *very fast* computing, or *immediate* on-line data acquisition, or *deadline-driven* computing. This text is concerned with the very difficult problems of scheduling tasks and resource management in computer systems whose performance is inextricably fused with the achievement of *deadlines*. Such systems have been enabled for a rapidly increasing set of diverse end-uses by the unremitting advances in computing power per constant-dollar cost and per constant-unit-volume of space. End-use applications of deadline-driven real-time computers span a spectrum that includes transportation systems, robotics and manufacturing, aerospace and defense, industrial process control, and telecommunications.

As real-time computers become responsible for managing increasingly sensitive applications, particularly those in which failures to satisfy deadline constraints can lead to serious or even catastrophic consequences, it has become more important than ever to develop the theoretical foundations that ensure the *predictability* of real-time computing system behavior. Of course, the general problem of scheduling resources optimally is NP-hard, and the addition of deadline timing constraints offers no relief from that fact of life. Somewhat surprisingly, however, research over the past few years has demonstrated that there are many practical, sometimes subtle and counter-intuitive, techniques that can be used to extract both predictable performance from real-time systems, and also better overall ability to satisfy deadlines. The papers in this volume offer a vivid portrayal of the cutting-edge research in this topic being pursued by ONR investigators, and the exciting advances that have been achieved within the last few years.

The chapters in this volume are arranged so as to lead the reader through a reasonably structured sequence of real-time problem descriptions and solution approaches, although any given chapter is self-contained and can be profitably studied without prior familiarity with previous chapters. Chapters 1-4 present descriptions of relatively broad attacks on real-time scheduling problems by several leading research groups. Chapter 5 then focuses on the rationale and advantages of rate monotonic scheduling, while Chapter 6 considers real-time scheduling in transaction systems. In Chapter 7, the real-time aspects of concurrency control in database systems are examined. Chapter 8 offers the notion of *imprecise computation* as an alternative to the more common strategy of trying to guarantee the deadlines of real-time tasks without considering how such tasks might be modified in tight circumstances. Chapters 9, 10 and 11 round out this volume by describing experimental scheduling research focused on cache memory management, practical scheduling mechanisms for a multiprocessor testbed, and real-time deadlock avoidance algorithms.

This book is suitable for graduate or advanced undergraduate course use when supplemented by additional readings that place the material contained herein in fuller context. In addition, this text is an excellent source of ideas and insights for the rapidly growing community of real-time system practitioners who want to design and build their systems on scientifically validated underpinnings.

From its first scientifically notable roots in the early 1970s, the discipline of deadline-driven real-time resource management is truly now beginning to emerge as a robust, credible, and important research discipline. It is our hope that the present volume will convey the many important ideas and results so painstakingly devised by the real-time scheduling research community to as wide an audience as possible, and that the insights contained herein will catalyze the discovery of even deeper foundations of real-time computing.

André M. van Tilborg
Gary M. Koob

Arlington, Virginia
March, 1991

CHAPTER 1

Fixed Priority Scheduling Theory
for Hard Real-Time Systems[1]

John P. Lehoczky[2], Lui Sha[3], J. K. Strosnider[4] and Hide Tokuda[5]
Carnegie Mellon University
Pittsburgh, PA 15213-3890

Abstract

This paper summarizes recent research results on the theory of fixed priority scheduling of hard real-time systems developed by the Advanced Real-Time Technology (ART) Project of Carnegie Mellon University. The Liu and Layland theory of rate monotonic scheduling is presented along with many generalizations including an exact characterization of task set schedulability, average case behavior and allowance for arbitrary task deadlines. Recent research results including the priority ceiling protocol which provides predictable scheduling when tasks synchronize and the deferrable and sporadic server algorithms which provide fast response times for aperiodic tasks while preserving periodic task deadlines are also presented.

1   Introduction

Real-time computer systems are used for the monitoring and control of physical processes. Unlike general purpose computer systems, the dynamics of the underlying physical process place explicit timing requirements on individual tasks which must be met in order to insure the

---

[1]Sponsored in part by the Office of Naval Research under contract N00014-84-K-0734, in part by the Naval Ocean Systems Center under contract N66001-87-C-0155, and in part by the Systems Integration Division of IBM Corporation under University Agreement Y-278067.
[2]Department of Statistics
[3]Software Engineering Institute and School of Computer Science
[4]Department of Electrical and Computer Engineering
[5]School of Computer Science

correctness and safety of the real-time system. Historically, hand-crafted techniques were used to insure the timing correctness by statically binding task executions to fixed slots via timelines. This *ad hoc* approach tended to result in systems which were not only expensive to develop, but also extremely difficult and costly to upgrade and maintain. The Advanced Real-Time Technology (ART) Project at Carnegie Mellon University has been developing algorithmic-based scheduling solutions for real-time computing that guarantee individual task execution times in multi-tasking, interrupt driven environments. Unlike earlier time-line scheduling approaches, the scheduling theory developed by the ART Project ensures the timing correctness of real-time tasks without the costly handcrafting and exhaustive testing associated with the use of timelines. Furthermore, this algorithmic-based scheduling approach is designed to support dynamic, process-level reconfiguration, an important approach to achieving high system dependability with limited hardware resources.

Embedded real-time systems must schedule diverse activities to meet the timing requirements imposed by the physical environments. While this may be a difficult problem, the real-time system developer works in a controlled enviroment, and typically has the advantage of knowing the entire set of tasks that are to be processed by the system. An algorithmic-based scheduling methodology allows the developer to combine task characterization data with its associated timing requirements to determine through the use of formulas whether or not the task set is schedulable. This capability readily lends itself to automation allowing the system developer not only to quickly determine the timing correctness of current processing requirements, but also to be able to assess the timing impact of future system upgrades and modifications. The scheduling theory makes the timing properties of the system *predictable*. This means that one is able to determine analytically whether the timing requirements of a task set will be met, and if not, which task timing requirements will fail.

The Advanced Real-Time Technology Project of Carnegie Mellon University has been developing and testing a theory of predictable hard real-time scheduling based on fixed priority scheduling algorithms. An important aspect of the project is the development of a real-time operating system, ARTS, and a real-time tool set, both developed by H. Tokuda

[23, 24]. The ARTS operating system supports the scheduling theory described in this paper, and it provides a vehicle by which the theory is tested and improved. A second important aspect is the relationship with the RMARTS (Rate Monotonic Analysis for Real-Time Systems) Project in the CMU Software Engineering Institute. RMARTS Project leaders J. Goodenough and L. Sha and their co-workers have been instrumental in applying rate monotonic theory to major U. S. government projects, in transitioning the theory developed to the user community and in addressing the Ada language implications of the scheduling theory being developed [13].

The ART Project research is built on the seminal paper by Liu and Layland [7] which introduced the *rate monotonic scheduling algorithm*, the optimal fixed priority scheduling algorithm for periodic tasks. Over the last several years many generalizations of this algorithm have been derived, which address practical problems that arise in the construction of actual real-time systems. These include problems of transient overload and stochastic execution times, scheduling mixtures of periodic and aperiodic tasks, and task synchronization among others.

In this paper we review the basic Liu and Layland results and present some of the recent results obtained by ART project researchers. The paper is organized as follows. In Section 2, we present the Liu and Layland theory of rate monotonic scheduling. Section 3 presents an exact schedulability criterion for the rate monotonic algorithm, its average case behavior and new results for the case of variable task deadlines. Section 4 discusses the problem of task synchronization and introduces the priority ceiling protocol. Section 5 contains a discussion of the aperiodic task scheduling problem and introduces two attractive solutions: the sporadic server algorithm and the deferrable server algorithm. Section 6 describes other generalizations of the theory and current research.

2   The Liu and Layland Analysis

The problem of scheduling periodic tasks was first addressed by Liu and Layland in 1973 [7]. They considered both fixed priority and dynamic priority scheduling algorithms, but we discuss only their analysis of fixed priority algorithms. The Liu and Layland analysis was derived under several assumptions:

A1: Tasks are periodic, are ready at the start of each period, have deadlines at the end of the period and do not suspend themselves during their execution.

A2: Tasks can be preempted, and the overhead for context swapping and task scheduling is ignored.

A3: Tasks are independent, i.e., there is no task synchronization and tasks have known, deterministic worst-case execution times.

Even though these assumptions are very stringent, Liu and Layland were able to derive very important results. Their paper provides a firm foundation upon which to build a more comprehensive theory of hard real-time system scheduling, one which addresses practical problems such as task synchronization, stochastic task execution times and scheduling mixtures of periodic and aperiodic tasks. We next present Liu and Layland's major results on fixed priority scheduling.

Consider a set of n periodic tasks, $\tau_1, \ldots, \tau_n$. Each task is characterized by four components (C_i, T_i, D_i, I_i), $1 \leq i \leq n$ where

$$
\begin{aligned}
C_i &= \text{deterministic computation requirement of each job of } \tau_i, \\
T_i &= \text{period of } \tau_i, \\
D_i &= \text{deadline of } \tau_i, \\
I_i &= \text{phasing of } \tau_i \text{ relative to some fixed time origin.}
\end{aligned}
$$

Each periodic task creates a stream of jobs. The jth job of τ_i is ready at time $I_i + (j-1)T_i$, and the C_i units of computation required for each job of τ_i have a deadline of $I_i + (j-1)T_i + D_i$. Liu and Layland assumed $D_i = T_i$. Such a task set is said to be *schedulable* by a particular scheduling algorithm provided that all deadlines of all the tasks are met under all task phasings if that scheduling algorithm is used.

Liu and Layland proved three important results concerning fixed priority scheduling algorithms. Consider first the longest response time for any job of a task τ_i where the response time is the difference between the task instantiation time $(I_i + kT_i)$ and the task completion time, that is the time at which τ_i completes its required C_i units of execution. If a fixed priority scheduling algorithm is used and tasks are ordered so that τ_i has higher priority than τ_j for $i < j$, then

Theorem 2.1 (Liu and Layland)

The longest response time for any job of τ_i occurs for the first job of τ_i when $I_1 = I_2 = \ldots = I_i = 0$. $\square$

The case with $I_1 = I_2 = \ldots = I_n = 0$ is called a *critical instant*, because it results in the longest response time for the first job of each task. Consequently, this creates the worst case task set phasing and leads to a criterion for the schedulability of a task set.

Theorem 2.2 (Liu and Layland)

A periodic task set can be scheduled by a fixed priority scheduling algorithm provided the deadline of the first job of each task starting from a critical instant is met using the scheduling algorithm. $\square$

Liu and Layland went on to characterize the optimal fixed priority scheduling algorithm, the *rate monotonic* scheduling algorithm. The rate monotonic scheduling algorithm assigns priorities inversely to task periods. Hence, τ_i receives higher priority than τ_j if $T_i < T_j$. Ties are broken arbitrarily. Here the optimality of the rate monotonic scheduling algorithm means that if a periodic task set is schedulable using some fixed priority scheduling algorithm, then it is also schedulable using the rate monotonic scheduling algorithm. We summarize this as

Theorem 2.3 (Liu and Layland)

The rate monotonic scheduling algorithm is optimal among all fixed priority scheduling algorithms for scheduling periodic task sets with $D_i = T_i$. $\square$

It is interesting to note that the rate monotonic scheduling algorithm considers only task periods, not task computation times or the importance of the task. Liu and Layland went on to offer a worst case upper bound for the rate monotonic scheduling algorithm, that is a threshold U_n^* such that if the utilization of a task set consisting of n tasks, $U = C_1/T_1 + \cdots + C_n/T_n$, is no greater than U_n^*, then the rate monotonic scheduling algorithm is guaranteed to meet all task deadlines. They accomplished this by studying full utilization task sets. These are task sets which can be scheduled by the rate monotonic algorithm under critical instant phasing; however, if the processing requirement C_i of any single task τ_i, $1 \leq i \leq n$, were increased, a deadline of some task would be missed. They then identified the full utilization task set with smallest utilization, and this utilization became the worst case upper bound. The result is given by

Theorem 2.4 (Liu and Layland)
A periodic task set $\tau_1, \tau_2, \ldots, \tau_n$ with $D_i = T_i$, $1 \leq i \leq n$, is schedulable by the rate monotonic scheduling algorithm if

$$U_1 + \cdots + U_n \leq U_n^* = n(2^{1/n} - 1), \, n = 1, 2, \ldots . \quad \Box$$

The sequence of scheduling thresholds is given by $U_1^* = 1$, $U_2^* = .828$, $U_3^* = .780$, $U_4^* = .756, \ldots, U_\infty^* = U^* = ln\,2 = .693$. Consequently, any periodic task set can be scheduled by the rate monotonic algorithm if its utilization is no greater than .693.

3   Extensions of the Liu and Layland Theory

The worst case bound of .693 given in Theorem 2.4 is respectably large; however, Theorem 2.4 is quite pessimistic. Randomly generated task sets are often schedulable by the rate monotonic algorithm at much higher utilization levels even assuming worst case phasing. It is also important to derive a more exact criterion for schedulability that can be used in more general circumstances. We first consider the situation in which the task deadlines need not be equal to the task periods. This problem was initially considered by Leung and Whitehead [6] in 1982. They introduced a new fixed priority scheduling algorithm, the *deadline monotonic* algorithm, in which task priorities are assigned inversely with respect to task deadlines, that is τ_i has higher priority than τ_j if $D_i < D_j$. They proved the optimality of the deadline monotonic algorithm when $D_i \leq T_i$, $1 \leq i \leq n$.

Theorem 3.1 (Leung and Whitehead)
For a periodic task set $\tau_1, \ldots, \tau_n$ with $D_i \leq T_i$, $1 \leq i \leq n$, the optimal fixed priority scheduling algorithm is the *deadline monotonic* scheduling algorithm. A task set is schedulable by this algorithm if the first job of each task after a critical instant meets its deadline. $\Box$

Theorem 2.4 was generalized by Lehoczky and Sha [4], Peng and Shin [8] and Lehoczky [2] for the case in which $D_i = \Delta T_i$, $1 \le i \le n$ and $0 < \Delta \le 1$. In this case, the rate monotonic and deadline monotonic scheduling algorithms are the same. We have the following generalization of Theorem 2.4.

Theorem 3.2 (Lehoczky, Sha, Peng and Shin)
A periodic task set with $D_i = \Delta T_i$, $1 \le i \le n$ is schedulable if

$$U_1 + \cdots + U_n \le U_n^*(\Delta) = \begin{cases} n((2\Delta)^{1/n} - 1) + (1 - \Delta), & \frac{1}{2} \le \Delta \le 1 \\ \Delta & 0 \le \Delta \le \frac{1}{2} \end{cases} \quad \square$$

An exact analysis of the schedulability of a task set using a fixed priority scheduling algorithm was presented by Lehoczky, Sha and Ding [5] for the case in which $D_i \le T_i$, $1 \le i \le n$ and by Lehoczky [2] for the case of arbitrary deadlines. Under critical instant phasing, $\sum_{j=1}^{i} C_j \lceil \frac{t}{T_j} \rceil = W_i(t)$ gives the cumulative demand for processing by tasks τ_j, $1 \le j \le i$ during $[0, t]$. Using Theorem 2.2, task τ_i meets all its deadlines if its first job meets its deadline under critical instant phasing. This occurs if $W_i(t) = t$ at some time t, $0 \le t \le D_i$, the deadline of the first job of τ_i. Equivalently, this job will meet its deadline if and only if there is a t, $0 \le t \le D_i$, at which $W_i(t)/t \le 1$. We summarize this in the following theorem.

Theorem 3.3 (Lehoczky, Sha and Ding)
Let a periodic task set $\tau_1, \tau_2, \ldots, \tau_n$ be given in priority order and scheduled by a fixed priority scheduling algorithm using those priorities. If $D_i \le T_i$, then τ_i will meet all its deadlines under all task phasings if and only if

$$\min_{0 \le t \le D_i} \sum_{j=1}^{i} \frac{C_j}{t} \left\lceil \frac{t}{T_j} \right\rceil \le 1.$$

The entire task set is schedulable under the worst case phasing if and only if

$$\max_{1 \le i \le n} \min_{0 \le t \le D_i} \sum_{j=1}^{i} \frac{C_j}{t} \left\lceil \frac{t}{T_j} \right\rceil \le 1. \quad \square$$

The criterion given in Theorem 3.3 is not difficult to compute. The sum is a piecewise continuous decreasing function of t. Consequently, to find the minimum, one needs only to consider the points of discontinuity, namely the values of t which are multiples of any of $T_1, T_2, \ldots, T_{i-1}$ and D_i. Only a subset of these multiples needs to be checked.

The criterion given by Theorem 3.3 also provides a simple way of showing that the rate monotonic scheduling algorithm can schedule task sets up to 100% utilization when $D_i = T_i$ and the periods are harmonic. Suppose that T_i/T_j is an integer for $1 \leq j \leq i$. Then letting $t = T_i$,

$$\sum_{j=1}^{i} \frac{C_j}{T_i} \left\lceil \frac{T_i}{T_j} \right\rceil = \sum_{j=1}^{i} \frac{C_j}{T_i} \frac{T_i}{T_j} = \sum_{j=1}^{i} \frac{C_j}{T_j} = U_1 + \cdots + U_i .$$

Consequently, τ_i will be schedulable if all higher priority tasks have periods which evenly divide T_i and $\sum_{j=1}^{i} U_j \leq 1$. If the periods are completely harmonic, that is if T_i/T_j is an integer, $1 \leq j \leq i$, $1 \leq i \leq n$, then all tasks are schedulable provided $U_1 + \cdots + U_n \leq 1$. We summarize as

Theorem 3.4

If a task set $\tau_1, \ldots, \tau_n$ is scheduled using the rate monotonic algorithm and T_j evenly divides T_i for $1 \leq j \leq i$, then τ_i meets all its deadlines if and only if $U_1 + \cdots + U_i \leq 1$. If T_j evenly divides T_i for all $j \leq i$, $1 \leq i \leq n$, then the task set is schedulable if and only if $U_1 + \cdots + U_n \leq 1$. $\square$

The criterion also gives a means of determining the average case behavior of the rate monotonic scheduling algorithm. The analysis was presented in Lehoczky, Sha and Ding [5] and assumed that task periods were chosen independently from a probability distribution with cumulative distribution function (c.d.f.) F_T and task computation requirements were chosen independently from a probability distribution with c.d.f. F_C. Task computation times are then scaled by a common factor k, and k is increased to the point at which a task deadline is first missed. The corresponding utilization for this critical value of k is called the *breakdown utilization*. The breakdown utilization for the task set characterized by $(C_1, T_1), \ldots, (C_n, T_n)$ is given by the formula

$$U_{BD}^{(n)} = \sum_{i=1}^{n} \frac{C_i}{T_i} \Big/ \max_{1 \le i \le n} \min_{0 \le t \le D_i} \sum_{j=1}^{i} \frac{C_j}{t} \left\lceil \frac{t}{T_j} \right\rceil .$$

The breakdown utilization is a complicated function of the random variables $C_1, \ldots, C_n$ and $T_1, \ldots, T_n$; however, if n is large and all these random variables are independent, then $U_{BD}^{(n)}$ converges to a constant. This limiting value was characterized by Lehoczky, Sha and Ding [5] and is given by the following theorem.

Theorem 3.5 (Lehoczky, Sha and Ding)

Suppose a random task set is generated with $C_1, \ldots, C_n$ independent with c.d.f. F_C, $T_1, \ldots, T_n$ independent with c.d.f. F_T and the Cs and Ts are independent. Suppose also $D_i = \Delta T_i$ with $0 < \Delta \le 1$. Then as $n \to \infty$

$$\lim_{n \to \infty} U_{BD}^{(n)} = E(1/T) \Big/ \sup_{0 < \alpha < 1} \inf_{0 < s < \Delta F_T^{-1}(\alpha)} \int_0^\alpha \frac{1}{\alpha} \left\lceil \frac{s}{F_T^{-1}(u)} \right\rceil du \qquad \Box$$

The asymptotic characterization given in Theorem 3.5 is further explored in [5]. In general it is shown that when periods are drawn from a uniform distribution with a sufficiently wide range of values, the breakdown utilization will generally be in the 88% to 92% range. Surprisingly, however, if periods are chosen according to a uniform $(1, 2)$ distribution and n is large, then the breakdown utilization converges to the Liu and Layland lower bound of .693. This occurs because the full utilization task set having smallest utilization derived by Liu and Layland consists of n tasks having equal utilization and periods nearly uniformly distributed over (1,2). Thus the random task set is very likely to be close to the Liu and Layland worst-case task set as n becomes large.

The worst case bound of .693 and the average case values of .88 are sufficiently large that the rate monotonic scheduling algorithm should provide a satisfactory solution in the simple cases thus far discussed. Unfortunately, in more complicated situations, the bounds can be much lower. This occurs in the distributed scheduling case where tasks must use several resources and have an end-to-end deadline. Consider the following examples.

Example 1

Suppose we have two periodic tasks, both of which must first use resource 1 followed by resource 2. Let task 1 have period T and computation requirement C_{11} and C_{12} respectively on these two resources. Suppose task 2 also has period T. If $C_{11} + C_{12} = T$, then task 1 cannot be interrupted or it will miss its deadline. If these two tasks have the same phasing, then if task 2 has an arbitrarily small processing requirement on each resource, either task 1 or task 2 must miss its deadline. The utilization on resource i can be made arbitrarily close to C_{1i}/T for $i = 1, 2$. These utilizations sum to 1, thus the worst case *total* utilization on the two resources at most 1. The minimum of the two resource utilizations is at most 0.5. Similar examples show that this quantity drops to $1/3$ if we consider 3 resources and becomes $1/r$ for r resources. It is important to note that this task set cannot be scheduled by *any* scheduling algorithm, even using variable priorities. Consequently, the low levels of schedulable utilization achieved in this case are a consequence of the multiprocessor or distributed context, not the poor performance of the rate monotonic algorithm. □

Example 2

Consider three periodic tasks for which $D_i = T_i$. Each uses resource 1 followed by resource 2 and has the following characteristics

Task	Time on Resource 1	Time on Resource 2	Period	U_1	U_2
1	.5	ε	2	.25	0
2	.5	ε	2.5	.20	0
3	$1.0 + \varepsilon$	.5	3.5	.28	.14
				.73	.14

For any $\varepsilon > 0$ the above task set cannot be scheduled by the rate monotonic algorithm. This follows because starting with a critical instant, τ_3 is processed on resource 1 during $[1,2]$ and $[3, 3 + \varepsilon]$, so τ_3 will finish no earlier than $3.5 + \varepsilon$ and therefore misses its deadline. The utilizations are given for the two resources for the only schedulable case, $\varepsilon = 0$. The utilization of resource 1 is below the Liu and Layland bound for three tasks (.780), and the utilization of resource 2 is painfully low. Two solutions are possible. First, one can change the priority order, for example by inserting intermediate deadlines for tasks on each resource and using the deadline monotonic algorithm. Second, one can allow more time than a single period for each task to complete its required processing. The latter approach leads to a situation in which task deadlines can be longer than task periods □

The case in which task deadlines can be longer than task periods is different from the cases presented thus far. In particular Theorem 2.2 and 2.3 are no longer true, so a new characterization of the schedulability of a task set must be determined. The problem is more complicated than the case in which all task deadlines are shorter than the corresponding task periods, because a job of τ_i may have to wait for the completion of an earlier job of τ_i in addition to waiting for higher priority tasks. This problem was studied by Lehoczky [2], and we present some results from that work. First, however, consider the following example due to Ye Ding.

Example 3
Let $n = 2$ with $C_1 = 52, T_1 = 100, D_1 = 110$ and $C_2 = 52, T_2 = 140, D_2 = 154$. Here $D_1/T_1 = D_2/T_2 = 1.1$, so both the rate monotonic and deadline monotonic scheduling algorithms accord highest priority to τ_1. With this priority assignment, the task set is not schedulable. Task 1 will be processed during $[0, 52], [100, 152]$ and $[200, 252]$. The first job of task 2 will be completed at time 156 and will miss its deadline at 154. If one were to accord the highest priority to τ_2, then it would be processed during $[0, 52], [140, 192]$ and $[280, 332]$. This means the first job of τ_1 will finish at 104, the second at 208 and the third at 260 at which time the processor will become idle. The three task 1 response times are 104, 108 and 60 respectively. Each meets its deadline, thus in [2] it is shown that the task set can be scheduled with this non-rate-monotonic priority assignment. It should also be pointed out that the response time of the second job is longer than for the first, thus the deadlines of all the jobs in the busy period must be checked. If one considered only the first job of task 1, one would draw the erroneous conclusion that $D_1 = 104$ would be sufficient for the task set to be schedulable with this priority ordering. □

Example 3 shows that neither the rate monotonic nor the deadline monotonic scheduling algorithms are optimal for scheduling periodic tasks when deadlines can exceed period lengths. Recently, Shih, Liu and Liu [16] considered the situation in which periodic deadlines are deferred. They defined the *modified rate monotonic algorithm* and proved certain optimality properties. In this paper, however, we restrict attention to the rate monotonic algorithm. To develop an exact schedulability criterion for a fixed priority scheduling algorithm, we require the concept of a *level-i busy period*.

Definition

A level-i busy period is a time interval [a,b] within which jobs of priority i or higher are processed throughout [a,b] but no jobs of level i or higher are processed in $(a - \epsilon, a)$ and $(b, b + \epsilon)$ for sufficiently small $\epsilon > 0$. $\square$

We illustrate the level-i busy period by a very simple example. Intuitively, from the perspective of a priority level $i + 1$ job, the processor is busy with higher priority work during a level-i busy period.

Example 4

Consider the case of $n = 2, C_1 = 26, T_1 = 70, C_2 = 62, T_2 = 100, U = .9914$. Let τ_1 have highest priority in accordance with the rate monotonic algorithm. We ignore the deadlines for the moment. Assuming that both tasks are initiated at time 0, one can find the level-2 busy period to be [0, 694]. The table below gives the response times of τ_2 jobs during this busy period.

Arrival time of τ_2 job	Completion Time	Response Time
0	114	114
100	202	102
200	316	116
300	404	104
400	518	118
500	606	106
600	694	94

Task τ_1 will meet all of its deadlines provided $D_1 \geq 26$ or $\Delta_1 = D_1/T_1 \geq$ .371. The longest response time for τ_2 occurs for the fifth job of τ_2 during the busy period. Consequently, all deadlines of τ_2 will be met provided

$D_2 \geq 118$ or $\triangle_2 = D_2/T_2 \geq 1.18$. The non-monotonic behavior of the response times of task 2 illustrates that all response times must be checked for all jobs processed during the busy period. □

We have the following generalization of Theorem 2.1 given by Lehoczky [2],

Theorem 3.6 (Lehoczky)
The longest response time for a job of τ_i occurs during a level-i busy period started at a critical instant, $I_1 = \cdots = I_i = 0$. □

Theorem 3.3 can also be generalized to provide an exact criterion for schedulability. To do this, we generalize the workload function arising in that theorem to

$$W_m(k, x) = \min_{t \leq x} \left(\left(\sum_{j=1}^{m-1} C_j \left\lceil \frac{t}{T_j} \right\rceil + kC_m \right) / t \right).$$

The quantity $\sum_{j=1}^{m-1} c_j \lceil \frac{t}{T_j} \rceil + C_m$ gives the total cumulative processor demands made by all jobs of $\tau_1, \ldots, \tau_{m-1}$ and the first job of τ_m during $[0, t]$ assuming critical instant phasing. Jobs associated with task $\tau_{m+1}, \ldots, \tau_n$ can be ignored, because these jobs have lower priority than τ_m and can be preempted. The first job of τ_m will meet its deadline if and only if this quantity is less than or equal to t for some $t \leq D_m$, because at such a time the processor will have completed all C_m units of required execution and all required higher priority execution time. Indeed, the smallest value of t for which $\sum_{j=1}^{m-1} C_j \lceil \frac{t}{T_j} \rceil + C_m = t$ is the time at which this job is completed. In addition, the level-m busy period which started at time 0 will end with the completion of the first job of τ_m if there is no more processing at level m or higher to be done.

These two conditions can be reexpressed as $W_m(1, D_m) \leq 1$ for deadline fulfillment of the first job of τ_m and $W_m(1, T_m) < 1$ for the end of the level-m busy period. If $W_m(1, D_m) \leq 1$ but $W_m(1, T_m) \geq 1$, then the first job of τ_m meets its deadline, but the busy period continues beyond T_m, because there is additional work at level m from later jobs of τ_m yet to be done. One must now consider the second job of τ_m. This can be done by replacing τ_m by τ'_m having computation requirement $2C_m$ and deadline $T_m + D_m$. Thus the second deadline is satisfied if and only if $W_m(2, T_m + D_m) \leq 1$. If $W_m(2, 2T_m) \geq 1$, additional jobs of τ_m must be checked. If we define $N_m = \min\{k \mid W_m(k, kT_m) < 1\}$, then exactly N_m task τ_m jobs are part of the level-m busy period. Note that N_m is finite, because the total processor utilization is assumed to be less than 1. Schedulability of τ_m is determined by

$$\max_{k \leq N_m} W_m(k, (k-1)T_m + D_m) \leq 1.$$

One must check that each of the tasks in the task set is schedulable, thus we require the above inequality to hold for each $m, 1 \leq m \leq n$, that is

$$\max_{1 \leq m \leq n} \max_{k \leq N_m} W_m(k, (k-1)T_m + D_m) \leq 1.$$

Lehoczky [2] also presents a generalization of Theorems 2.4 and 3.2 to give the worst case scheduling bounds when task deadlines may be different from task periods. We consider only the case in which task deadlines are a constant factor Δ of the corresponding task periods, $D_i = \Delta T_i, 1 \leq i \leq n$. We separate the analysis into two cases, first when Δ is an integer and second when Δ is not an integer.

Theorem 3.7 (Lehoczky)

If the rate monotonic scheduling algorithm is used to schedule a periodic task set with $D_i = \Delta T_i$ and $\Delta = 1, 2, \ldots$, then if the task set utilization $C_1/T_1 + \cdots + C_n/T_n$ is less than $U_n^*(\Delta)$, the task set is schedulable where

$$U_n^*(\Delta) = \begin{cases} n\left((\Delta + 1)^{1/n} - 1\right) = n\left(2^{1/n} - 1\right), & \Delta = 1, \\ \Delta\left((n-1)\left((\frac{\Delta+1}{\Delta})^{1/(n-1)} - 1\right)\right), & \Delta = 2, 3, \ldots. \end{cases}$$

As $n \to \infty$

$$U_n^* \to U^*(\Delta) = \Delta \log_e\left(\frac{\Delta + 1}{\Delta}\right), \quad \Delta = 1, 2, \ldots. \quad \square$$

The scheduling bound is much more complicated when Δ is not an integer. We summarize the asymptotic bound given in

Theorem 3.8 (Lehoczky)

Given the framework of Theorem 3.7 with $\Delta \in [k, k+1]$, $k = 0, 1, \ldots$,

$$U_\infty^* = \begin{cases} (k+1)\log_e(\Delta/S(k+1)) - k\log_e((\Delta - S)/k) + (k+1)S - k \\ \qquad \text{if } k \leq \Delta \leq k+1 - 1/(k+2) \\ (k+1)\log_e((k+2)\Delta/(k+1)^2) + (k+1) - \Delta \\ \qquad \text{if } k+1 - 1/(k+2) \leq \Delta \leq k+1 \end{cases}$$

where S is the smallest root of

$$S^2 - S[\Delta + (2k+1)/(k+1)] + \Delta = 0. \quad \square$$

For example

$$U_\infty^* = \begin{cases} \Delta & \Delta \in [0, \frac{1}{2}] \\ \log_e(2\Delta) + 1 - \Delta & \Delta \in [\frac{1}{2}, 1] \\ 2\log_e(\Delta/2S) - \log_e(\Delta - S) + 2S - 1 & \Delta \in [1, \frac{5}{3}] \\ 2\log(\frac{3}{4}\Delta) + 2 - \Delta & \Delta \in [\frac{5}{3}, 2] \end{cases}$$

where S is the smallest root of $S^2 - (\Delta + \frac{3}{2})S + \Delta = 0$.

A graph of the worst case utilization bound is given in Figure 1 for $\Delta \in [0, 5]$. A blown up version is given for $\Delta \in [\frac{1}{2}, 2]$ in Figure 2. It is interesting to observe the irregular behavior between the integer arguments. The "S-Shape" behavior suggest that the most significant increases in the worst case upper bound for schedulable utilization come in the middle of an interval $[k, k+1]$ rather at the integer values themselves where the curve is flat.

4 Task Synchronization

In the previous sections, the tasks being scheduled were assumed to be independent and to be completely preemptable. Consequently, there could never be a case in which *priority inversion* occurs, that is when a high priority task is ready to execute but is blocked by the execution of a lower priority task. For example, if tasks require the use of nonpreemptable resources or access shared data, then a lower priority task's use of such a resource or such data can block a high priority task from executing. There are many well-known methods for task synchronization including semaphores, locks and monitors; however, a straightforward use of these synchronization primitives can lead to unbounded periods of priority

Figure 1:

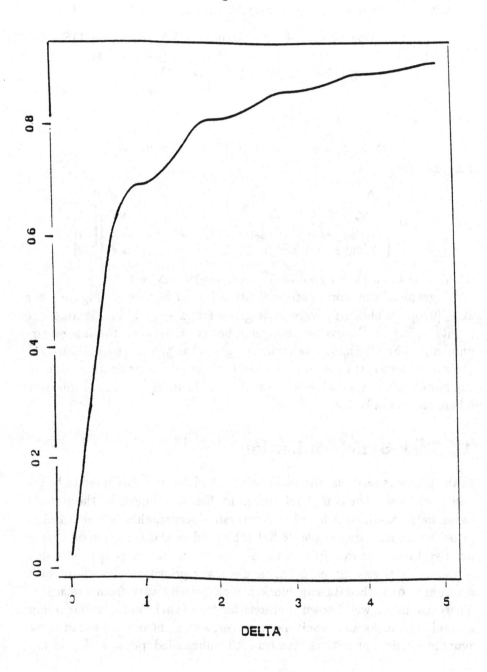

Figure 2:

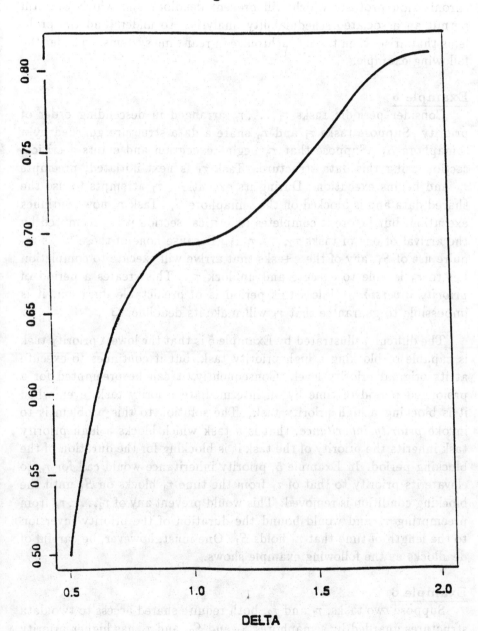

DELTA

inversion and even deadlock. Some care is needed to develop a task synchronization protocol which will prevent deadlock and which will still permit an associated schedulability analysis. To understand the problems that arise when tasks synchronize in real-time systems, consider the following example.

Example 5

Consider periodic tasks $\tau_1, \ldots, \tau_n$ arranged in descending order of priority. Suppose tasks τ_1 and τ_n share a data structure guarded by a semaphore S_1. Suppose that τ_n begins execution and enters a critical section using this data structure. Task τ_1 is next initiated, preempts τ_n and begins execution. During its execution, τ_1 attempts to use the shared data and is blocked on the semaphore S_1. Task τ_n now continues execution, but before it completes its critical section it is preempted by the arrival of one of tasks $\tau_2, \ldots, \tau_{n-1}$. Because none of these tasks require use of S_1, any of these tasks that arrive will execute to completion before τ_n is able to execute and unblock τ_1. This creates a period of *priority inversion*. Unless this period is of predictable duration, it is impossible to guarantee that τ_1 will make its deadline. □

The difficulty illustrated by Example 5 is that the lowest priority task is capable of blocking a high priority task, but it continues to execute at its original priority level. Consequently, it can be preempted for a prolonged period of time by an intermediate priority task, even when it is blocking a high priority task. The solution to this problem is to invoke *priority inheritance*, that is a task which blocks a high priority task inherits the priority of the task it is blocking for the duration of the blocking period. In Example 5, priority inheritance would call for τ_n to elevate its priority to that of τ_1 from the time τ_1 blocks on S_1 until the blocking condition is removed. This would prevent any of $\tau_2, \ldots, \tau_n$ from preempting τ_n and would bound the duration of the priority inversion to the length of time that τ_n holds S_1. One must, however, be careful of deadlocks as the following example shows.

Example 6

Suppose two tasks, τ_1 and τ_2, both require shared access to two data structures guarded by semaphores S_1 and S_2, and τ_1 has higher priority than τ_2. Suppose τ_1 and τ_2 have the following sequence of operations:

$$\tau_1 : \{\ldots P(S_1)\ldots P(S_2)\ldots V(S_2)\ldots V(S_1)\ldots\}$$
$$\tau_2 : \{\ldots P(S_2)\ldots P(S_1)\ldots V(S_1)\ldots V(S_2)\ldots\},$$

If τ_2 executes $P(S_2)$ and is preempted by τ_1, then if τ_1 executes $P(S_1)$, a deadlock is created. The only practical solution to this problem is to prevent τ_1 from executing $P(S_1)$ to prevent the deadlock. □

One way of solving the potential deadlock problem illustrated by Example 6 is to define the *priority ceiling* of a semaphore.

Definition
The priority ceiling of a semaphore is defined as the priority of the highest priority task that may lock this semaphore. The priority ceiling of a semaphore S_j, denoted by $C(S_j)$, represents the highest priority that a critical section guarded by S_j can execute, either by normal or inherited priority. □

The *priority ceiling protocol* was defined in Sha, Rajkumar and Lehoczky [12] and is given next.

Definition (Priority Ceiling Protocol, [12, p. 1180])
1. Job J, which has the highest priority among the jobs ready to run, is assigned the processor, and let S^* be the semaphore with the highest priority ceiling of all semaphores currently locked by jobs other than job J. Before job J enters its critical section, it must first obtain the lock on the semaphore S guarding the shared data structure. Job J will be blocked and the lock on S will be denied, if the priority of job J is not higher than the priority ceiling of semaphore S^*.[1] In this case, job J is said to be blocked on semaphore S^* and to be blocked by the job which holds the lock on S^*. Otherwise, job J will obtain the lock on semaphore S and enter its critical section. When a job J exits its critical section,

---
[1]Note that if S has been already locked, the priority ceiling of S will be at least equal to the priority of J. Because job J's priority is not higher than the priority ceiling of the semaphore S locked by another job, J will be blocked. Hence, this rule implies that if a job J attempts to lock a semaphore that has been already locked, J will be denied the lock and blocked instead.

the binary semaphore associated with the critical section will be unblocked and the highest priority job, if any, blocked by job J will be awakened.

2. A job J uses its assigned priority, unless it is in its critical section and blocks higher priority jobs. If job J blocks higher priority jobs, J *inherits* P_H, the highest priority of the jobs blocked by J. When J exits a critical section, it resumes the priority it had at the point of entry into the critical section. That is, when J exits the part of a critical section, it resumes its previous priority. Priority inheritance is transitive. Finally, the operations of priority inheritance and of the resumption of previous priority must be indivisible.

3. A job J, when it does not attempt to enter a critical section, can preempt another job J_L if its priority is higher than the priority, inherited or assigned, at which job J_L is executing. □

The priority ceiling protocol has many properties, but we single out the three most important for consideration.

Theorem 4.1 (Sha, Rajkumar and Lehoczky)
The priority ceiling protocol prevents deadlocks. □

Theorem 4.2 (Sha, Rajkumar and Lehoczky)
Under the priority ceiling protocol, a job J can experience priority inversion for at most the duration of one critical section. □

To give a schedulability analysis using the rate monotonic scheduling algorithm in conjunction with the priority ceiling protocol, we define B_k, $1 \leq k \leq n$, the longest duration of blocking that can be experienced by τ_k. Note $B_n = 0$, because τ_n is assumed to have lowest priority and hence cannot experience a priority inversion. Once these blocking terms have been determined, they can be used to generalize Theorem 3.3.

Theorem 4.3 (Sha, Rajkumar and Lehoczky)
A set of n periodic tasks with $D_i = T_i$ using the priority ceiling protocol can be scheduled by the rate monotonic algorithm for all task phasings if the following conditions are satisfied:

$$\frac{C_1}{T_1} + \cdots + \frac{C_i}{T_i} + \frac{B_i}{T_i} \leq i(2^{1/i} - 1), 1 \leq i \leq n. \qquad \square$$

A less restrictive sufficient condition is given by

Theorem 4.4 (Sha, Rajkumar and Lehoczky)

A set of n periodic tasks with $D_i = T_i$ using the priority ceiling protocol can be scheduled by the rate monotonic algorithm for all task phasings if

$$\max_{1 \leq i \leq n} \min_{0 \leq t \leq T_i} \left(\sum_{j=1}^{i} \frac{C_i}{t} \left\lceil \frac{t}{T_j} \right\rceil + \frac{B_i}{t} \right) \leq 1. \qquad \square$$

Theorem 4.4 gives a sufficient condition for the schedulability of a task set in which task synchronization is done using the priority inheritance protocol, and this gives a fairly complete solution for the real-time task synchronization problem in uniprocessors. This problem becomes much more complicated in the multi-processor case. Rajkumar, Sha and Lehoczky [11] developed extended priority ceiling protocols for multi-processors using message passing architectures. Rajkumar [9] has further generalized the priority ceiling protocol to be applicable in the shared memory multi-processor case. Finally, the optimal real-time synchronization protocol called the *semaphore control protocol* was defined and analyzed in [9]. The thesis by Rajkumar [9] contains a wealth of information on real-time synchronization.

5 Aperiodic Task Scheduling

In this section, we address another important practical problem that arises in real-time system scheduling, namely the scheduling of mixtures of periodic and aperiodic tasks. There are some traditional approaches to this problem, for example, (1) allowing the aperiodic tasks to interrupt the periodic tasks and run to completion, (2) establish a polling server to provide a private resource for the exclusive use of the aperiodic tasks and (3) force the aperiodic tasks to background service at a priority level lower than all the periodic tasks. Approaches (1) and (3) are unsatisfactory, because they either jeopardize the hard deadlines of the periodic tasks (1) or they provide very poor response times for the aperiodic tasks. The polling approach is a major improvement, but it is rather inflexible in that it offers regular service to a stream of tasks whose demand for that service is irregular. Significant improvements can be obtained by modifying the polling server to be more flexible by allowing it to serve aperiodic tasks on demand rather than at periodic times. The amount of service provided must be controlled so that the deadlines of the periodic tasks are still met; however, the analysis presented in Sections 2 and 3 can be used to achieve this goal.

The basic concept of an aperiodic server is to provide a resource for the exclusive use of aperiodic tasks which can be used on demand. To provide fast aperiodic response times, that resource should be given as high a priority as possible. The size of the resource and its replenishment must be carefully controlled to ensure that the periodic deadlines are not missed, for example, if a burst of aperiodic requests were to arrive during a short time span. Two different types of aperiodic servers have been defined: the *deferrable server* (Strosnider [20]) and the *sporadic server* (Sprunt [19]). These two server algorithms are similar in spirit but differ in their replenishment algorithms.

The deferrable server (DS) algorithm creates a periodic server task τ_1 with C_1 units of execution and priority defined by the rate monotonic priority associated with the server's period T_1. The periodic server task, hereafter referred to as the Deferrable Server (DS) task, is a special purpose task created to provide high priority execution time for aperiodic tasks. The DS task has the entire period, T_1, within which to use its C_1 units of execution time at priority P_1 to service aperiodic tasks. If at the end of the period T_i any portion of the C_1 run-time has not been used, then it is discarded. The DS task's capacity, C_1, is renewed at the beginning of each server period. Assigning the DS task the highest priority (by giving it a period no longer than the shortest periodic task period) allows us to introduce guaranteed response times for high priority aperiodic tasks as well as enhancing the responsiveness of the soft deadline aperiodic class. Both of these capabilities are provided while maintaining guaranteed response time performance for periodic tasks. The possibility that the DS task execution can be deferred until the end of its period where it could be immediately followed by a DS task execution from the next period necessitates the development of a new schedulability analysis to determine conditions on the size of the DS task which will ensure that all periodic tasks meet their deadlines. A full characterization of the bounds is provided by Strosnider [20]. The DS algorithm has successfully been applied to both processor scheduling [3] and local area network scheduling [21, 22].

The use of a DS task to provide fast aperiodic response times results in lower levels of schedulable utilization than if an ordinary periodic task were used as a server. Furthermore, the analysis has been carried out only when the DS task has the highest priority. The sporadic server algorithm avoids the schedulable utilization penalty and can be implemented at any priority level. Similar to the DS algorithm, the sporadic server (SS) algorithm creates a relatively high priority task for servicing aperiodic tasks. This server preserves its execution capacity until an aperiodic request occurs. That request can receive immediate service by using some or all of the remaining SS execution capacity, so if there is sufficient capacity remaining, the aperiodic request can be serviced to completion immediately. Unlike the DS algorithm, the SS algorithm has a more sophisticated replenishment policy. The execution allotment is replenished using two rules defined in [19, p. 21]. Suppose the SS executes at priority level P, then

1. If the server has execution time available, the replenishment time, RT, is set when priority level P becomes active. If, on the other hand, the server capacity has been exhausted, then RT cannot be set until the SS's capacity becomes greater than zero and P is active. In either case, the value of RT is set equal to the current time plus the period of the SS.

2. The amount of execution time to be replenished can be determined when either the priority level of the SS, namely P, becomes idle or when the SS's available execution time has been exhausted. The amount to be replenished at RT is equal to the amount of server execution time consumed since the last time at which the status of P changed from idle to active.

The important consequences of the SS algorithm replenishment policy are: (1) the SS can be treated just like an ordinary periodic task in a schedulability analysis, and (2) several sporadic servers can be defined at different priority levels to handle different aperiodic streams. These are summarized by the following theorems:

Theorem 5.1 (Sprunt, Sha and Lehoczky)

A periodic task set that is schedulable with a task τ_i, is also schedulable if τ_i is replaced by a sporadic server with the same period and execution time. □

Theorem 5.2 (Sprunt)

Given a real-time system composed of soft-deadline aperiodic tasks and hard deadline periodic tasks. Suppose the soft-deadline aperiodic tasks are serviced by a polling server that starts at full capacity and executes at the priority level of the highest priority periodic task. If the polling server is replaced by a SS having the same period, execution time and priority, the SS will provide high-priority aperiodic service at times earlier than or equal to the times the polling server would provide high priority aperiodic service. □

Example 7

As an example of the aperiodic response time improvements possible using the DS and SS algorithm, consider the results of the following set of simulation experiments. Ten different periodic task sets were chosen at random, each set having ten periodic tasks. A period of 55 units was selected to be the minimum period for each periodic task set. The maximum periods for the task sets ranged from 210 to 2,310 units. The relative phasing of task periods within each task set was chosen at random. For each periodic task set, a periodic load of 60% was selected. The aperiodic task components for these experiments were chosen as follows. The aperiodic task arrival times were modeled using a Poisson arrival process, and the aperiodic task service times were modeled using an exponential service time distribution. The mean aperiodic service time for these experiments was chosen to be 1% of the minimum periodic task period, or .55 units. Five aperiodic streams of varying traffic intensity were chosen to span the range of resource utilization unused by the periodic tasks from a total load just above the periodic task load up to a total load of 90%.

The background, polling, DS, and SS algorithms were simulated for each of the combinations described above. The period of each aperiodic server was chosen to be the longest period such that the rate monotonic priority of the server would be the highest priority in the system. Thus, the aperiodic server period was set equal to the minimum periodic task period (55). The execution time of each aperiodic server was chosen to be the maximum value at which the periodic task set remained schedulable using the exact test. This strategy gives the largest server execution time at the highest priority level for a rate monotonic priority assignment. The average server sizes over the ten tasks for the polling, DS and SS servers were 33%, 28% and 33% respectively.

The average response time performance data for a mean aperiodic service time is summarized in Figure 3 for background, polling, DS, and SS algorithms. The y-axis represents average response time; the bottom scale represents the total periodic and aperiodic load; and the top scale shows the mean aperiodic interarrival time. Each data point is an average of the ten average response times for the ten different periodic task sets simulated. An additional curve, the M/M/1 curve, is also plotted on these graphs. The M/M/1 curve represents the ideal response time for the aperiodic tasks that would be obtained if the periodic tasks were not present. Since a low response time is desired, the lower the curve for a particular algorithm is on the graph, the better is its response time performance.

Referring to the graph in Figure 3, one can see that the DS and SS algorithms effectively eliminate the interference of the periodic tasks for aperiodic loads up to approximately 20%. The response time performance for the background and polling algorithms is much worse. For background aperiodic service, this is due to the typically large intervals between background service opportunities. Although polling is an improvement over background aperiodic service, its performance is worse than that of the DS and SS algorithms, because aperiodic tasks typically have to wait for the start of the poller's period before receiving any service. The good response time performance of the DS and SS algorithms is due to the ability of these algorithms to preserve their capacity for aperiodic task execution until needed by aperiodic tasks. This allows these algorithms to provide immediate service to most aperiodic requests. The DS and SS algorithms perform as well as the ideal M/M/1 response time for aperiodic loads up to about 20% and offer an order of magnitude improvement in average response time for the aperiodic tasks. Above this range, the response time performance of these algorithms diverges from the ideal M/M/1 case, because at these high loads, the server's capacity is often exhausted, forcing some aperiodic tasks to be

Figure 3:

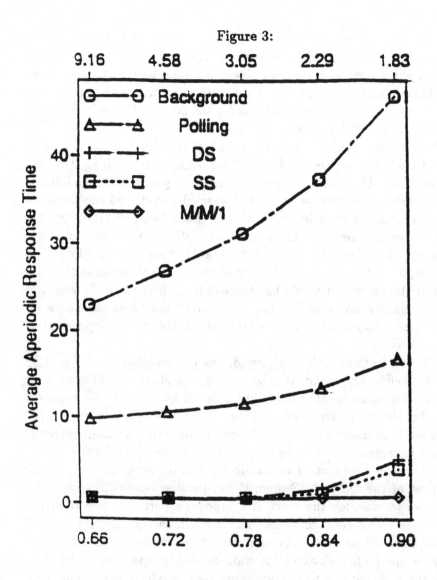

Total Load

Periodic Load = 0.60, Mean Aperiodic Service Time = 0.5

serviced as background tasks. The slight difference in response time performance between the DS and SS algorithms primarily is due to the difference in server size of 5%. □

Strosnider [20] and Sprunt [19] go on to study a wealth of issues related to aperiodic scheduling using the DS and SS algorithms including: processor and Local Area Network application studies, integrated hard deadline aperiodic service, soft deadline aperiodic response time prediction, incorporation of the priority ceiling protocol, and a comprehensive performance analysis.

6 Further Generalizations

Sections 3, 4 and 5 have described a set of new results for fixed priority scheduling of periodic tasks developed by the ART project. These results greatly generalize the original Liu and Layland analysis. Moreover, Section 4 shows how to achieve predictable scheduling of tasks that synchronize, while Section 5 gives results on the efficient scheduling of mixtures of periodic and aperiodic tasks. ART project researchers have developed many other results that address practical problems arising in the scheduling of real-time systems. These include

- Analyzing the loss in schedulable utilization due to a limit in the number of distinct priority levels, for example, in communication scheduling [4],

- Ensuring that the most important tasks meet their timing requirements in cases of transient overload when not all deadlines can be met [14],

- Extending the priority inheritance protocol to a multiprocessor environment [9,11],

- Extending the processor scheduling theory to communication subsystems [20, 21, 22],

- Developing a theory of predictable mode changes [15],

ART Project researchers continue to work on developing a fixed priority scheduling theory for hard real-time systems. The project is now primarily concerned with: (1) extending the fixed priority scheduling theory to the distributed system case in which threads have end-to-end deadlines, (2) the integration of scheduling theory and fault tolerance to develop a theory of hard real-time system dependability, and (3) the development of the scheduling theory in the context of hardware and software standards and the transitioning of this technology to the user community.

References

[1] Bettati, R. and Liu, J.W.S., "Algorithms for end-to-end scheduling to meet deadlines," Report No. UIUCDCS-R-90-1594, Department of Computer Science, University of Illinois.

[2] Lehoczky, J.P., "Fixed priority scheduling of periodic task sets with arbitrary deadlines," *Proceedings of the 11th IEEE Real-Time Systems Symposium*, December 1990, 201-209.

[3] Lehoczky J. P., Sha, L. and Strosnider, J. K., "Enhanced aperiodic responsiveness in hard real-time environments," *Proceedings of the 8th IEEE Real-Time Systems Symposium*, December 1987, 261-270.

[4] Lehoczky, J.P., and Sha, L., "Performance of real-time bus scheduling algorithms," *ACM Performance Evaluation Review*, 14, 1986.

[5] Lehoczky, J.P., Sha, L. and Ding, Y., "The rate monotonic scheduling algorithm: exact characterization and average case behavior," *Proceedings of the 10th IEEE Real-Time Systems Symposium*, December 1989, 166-171.

[6] Leung, J. and Whitehead, J., "On the complexity of fixed-priority scheduling of periodic, real-time tasks," *Performance Evaluation*, 2, 1982, 237–50

[7] Liu, C.L. and Layland, J.W., "Scheduling algorithms for multiprogramming in a hard real-time environment," *JACM*, 20, 1973, 460–61.

[8] Peng, D-T. and Shin, K.G., "A new performance measure for scheduling independent real-time tasks," Technical Report, Real-Time Computing Laboratory, University of Michigan, 1989.

[9] Rajkumar, R., "Task synchronization in real-time systems," Ph. D. Dissertation, Department of Electrical and Computer Engineering, Carnegie Mellon University, 1989.

[10] Rajkumar, R., Sha, L. and Lehoczky, J.P., "On countering the effects of cycle-stealing in a hard real-time environment," *Proceedings of the 8th IEEE Real-Time Systems Symposium*, December 1987, 2–11.

[11] Rajkumar, R., Sha, L. and Lehoczky, J.P., "Real-time synchronization for multiprocessors," *Proceedings of the 9th IEEE Real-Time Systems Symposium*, December 1988, 259-269.

[12] Sha, L., Rajkumar, R. and Lehoczky, J. P. , "Priority inheritance protocols: An approach to real-time synchronization," *IEEE Transactions on Computers*, Vol **39**, 1990, 1175-1185.

[13] Sha, L. and Goodenough, J., "Real-time scheduling theory and Ada," *Computer*, **23** No. 4, 1990, 53–62.

[14] Sha, L., Lehoczky, J.P. and Rajkumar, R., "Solutions for some practical problems in prioritized preemptive scheduling," *Proceedings of the 7th IEEE Real-Time Systems Symposium*, December 1986, 181-191.

[15] Sha, L., Rajkumar, R., Lehoczky, J.P. and Ramamritham, K., "Mode change protocols for priority-driven preemptive scheduling," *Journal of Real-Time Systems*, **1**, 1989, 243-264.

[16] Shih, W. K., Liu, J. W. S. and Liu, C. L., "Scheduling periodic jobs with deferred deadlines," Report No. UIUCDCS-R-90-1593, University of Illinois, 1990.

[17] Sprunt, B., Lehoczky, J. P. and Sha, L., "Exploiting unused periodic time for aperiodic service using the extended priority exchange algorithm," *Proceedings of the 9th IEEE Real-Time Systems Symposium*, December 1988, 251-258.

[18] Sprunt, B., Sha, L. and Lehoczky, J. P., "Aperiodic task scheduling for hard real-time systems," *Journal of Real-Time Systems*, **1**, 1989, 27-60.

[19] Sprunt, B., "Aperiodic task scheduling for real-time systems," Ph. D. dissertation, Department of Electrical and Computer Engineering, Carnegie Mellon University, Pittsburgh, Pa, August 1990.

[20] Strosnider, J. K., "Highly responsive real-time token rings," Ph. D. dissertation, Department of Electrical and Computer Engineering, Carnegie Mellon University, Pittsburgh, PA, August 1988.

[21] Strosnider, J.K., Marchok, T. and Lehoczky, J.P., "Advanced real-time scheduling using the IEEE 802.5 token ring," *Proceedings of the 9th Real-Time Systems Symposium,* December 1988.

[22] Strosnider, J.K. and Marchok, T., " Responsive, deterministic IEEE 802.5 token ring scheduling," *Journal of Real-Time Systems,* 1, 1989, 133-158.

[23] Tokuda, H. and Mercer, C.W., "ARTS: A distributed real-time kernel," *ACM Operating Systems Review,* **23(3)**, July 1989.

[24] Tokuda, H. and Kotera, M., "A real-time tool set for the ARTS kernel," *Proceedings of the 9th IEEE Real-Time Systems Symposium,* December 1988.

CHAPTER 2

Research in Real-Time Scheduling

Joseph Y-T. Leung
Department of Computer Science and Engineering
University of Nebraska at Lincoln
Lincoln, NE 68588-0115

Abstract

In this paper we give a survey of our recent work in real-time scheduling. This includes message routing in distributed real-time systems, minimizing mean flow time and number of late tasks in the imprecise computation model, developing efficient feasibility tests, on-line scheduling of real-time tasks, minimizing number of late tasks in the classical task system model, developing and analyzing a new model of task system that can incorporate parallel algorithms, minimizing mean flow time with release time and precedence constraints, and a host of other scheduling problems. Our work has focused on the study of complexity results, efficient algorithms, worst-case analysis of fast heuristics, and possibility and impossibility results for the existence of optimal on-line algorithms.

INTRODUCTION

In the last several years our work in real-time scheduling has extended out on several fronts. This includes message routing in distributed real-time systems, minimizing mean flow time and number of late tasks in the imprecise computation model, developing efficient feasibility tests, on-line scheduling of real-time tasks, minimizing number of late tasks in the classical task system model, developing and analyzing a new model of task system that can incorporate parallel algorithms, minimizing mean flow time with release time and precedence constraints, and a host of other scheduling problems. Our work has focused on the study of complexity results, efficient algorithms, worst-case analysis of fast heuristics, and possibility and impossibility results for the existence of optimal on-line algorithms.

In the next section we describe our work of message routing in distributed real-time systems. Our contributions consist of complexity results for the problem (polynomially solvable case versus NP-hard case) as well as possibility and impossibility results for the existence of optimal on-line routing algorithms. Section 3 is devoted to the imprecise computation model first introduced by Liu, Lin and Natarajan [36,37,40]. We extended the model to include optimization of other performance measures such as mean flow time and number of late tasks. Section 4 is devoted to efficient feasibility tests for two special classes of real-time tasks. These two classes can be solved in $O(n \log mn)$ and $O(n \log n + mn)$ times, respectively, while the general problem can be solved in $O(n^3)$ time. In Section 5 we describe our study of online scheduling of real-time tasks. The main results consist of: (i) it is impossible to have an optimal on-line scheduler for two or more processors when the tasks have two or more distinct deadlines and (ii) there is an optimal on-line scheduler for any number of processors when the tasks have one common deadline.

In Section 6 we describe results obtained for the Parallel Task System, a model introduced by us to incorporate parallel algorithms. Strong NP-hardness results and pseudo-polynomial time algorithms have been given for this model. Section 7 is devoted to the study of minimizing number of late tasks in the classical task system model. In Section 8 we describe results obtained for minimizing mean flow time with additional constraints such as release time, deadline and precedence constraints. Section 9 is devoted to results obtained for a host of other scheduling problems. Several results described in Sections 7 to 9 answer a number of long-standing open questions in scheduling theory. Finally, in the last section we indicate future directions of our research in real-time scheduling.

MESSAGE ROUTING IN DISTRIBUTED REAL-TIME SYSTEMS

In a distributed system processes residing at different nodes in the network communicate by passing messages. For a distributed real-time system, the problem of determining whether a set of messages can be sent on-time becomes an important issue. We began our study of this problem in [29,31] and the results presented here can be found in these two papers.

A network is represented by a directed graph $G = (V, E)$, where each vertex in V represents a node of the network and each directed edge in E represents a communication link. If $(u, v) \in E$, then there is a transmitter in node u and a receiver in node v dedicated to the communication link (u, v). Thus, a node can simultaneously send and receive several messages provided that they are transmitted on different communication links.

A set of n messages $M = \{M_1, M_2, \cdots, M_n\}$ needs to be routed through the network. Each message M_i is represented by the quintuple $(s_i, e_i, l_i, r_i, d_i)$, where s_i denotes the origin node of M_i (i.e., the message originates from node s_i), e_i denotes the destination node of M_i (i.e., the message is to be sent to node e_i), l_i denotes the length of M_i (i.e., the message consists of l_i packets of information), r_i denotes the release time of M_i (i.e., the message originates from node s_i at time r_i), and d_i denotes the deadline of M_i (i.e., the message must reach node e_i by time d_i).

An instance of the message routing problem consists of a network G and a set of messages M. The ordered pair $MRNS = (G, M)$ is called a message-routing network system. Given $MRNS = (G, M)$, our goal is to determine if there is a route of the messages in M such that each M_i is sent from node s_i to node e_i in the time interval $[r_i, d_i]$; $MRNS$ is said to be *feasible* if such a route exists.

In [29] the problem of determining feasibility was studied under both nonpreemptive and preemptive transmissions. In nonpreemptive transmission a message once started for transmission must continue until it is finished. In contrast, preemptive transmission allows the transmission of a message to be interrupted and resumed later. It was assumed that preemption will not incur any time loss.

There were several assumptions made in [29]. First, it was assumed that it takes one time unit to send a packet of a message on a communication link. Thus, it takes l_i time units for the message M_i to traverse any communication link. Second, we assumed that there is a central controller to construct a route for the messages and that the route pattern will be broadcast to each node. The central controller has complete information on the topology of the network and the characteristics of the messages. Third, we assumed that each message must be completely received by a node before it can be forwarded to another node.

With respect to the above model, the following theorem was proved in [29].

Theorem 2.1: Given $MRNS = (G, M)$ where G is an arbitrary network, the problem of determining if $MRNS$ is feasible with respect to preemptive (nonpreemptive) transmission is NP-complete.

Motivated by the complexity of the problem, we turned our attention to a very simple network -- an unidirectional ring, with the hope that the problem becomes tractable. We studied the message routing problem under various restrictions of the four parameters of the messages -- origin node, destination node, release time and deadline. The results obtained in [29] are summarized in Tables 1 and 2.

Table 1 shows the complexity results for nonpreemptive transmission. An entry marked "F" under one of the parameter columns denotes that the parameter is fixed (i.e., all messages have the same value for that parameter); an entry marked "V" denotes that the parameter is variable (i.e., the messages have different values for that parameter). The last column shows the complexity results. An entry marked "P" means that the problem is solvable in polynomial time and an entry marked "NP" means that the problem is NP-complete. As shown in Table 1, the message routing problem is polynomially solvable when any one of the four parameters is allowed to be arbitrary, and it becomes NP-complete when any two of the four parameters are allowed to be arbitrary. This gives a sharp boundary delineating tractable and intractable cases.

Table 1. Complexity for Nonpreemptive Transmissions

s_i	e_i	r_i	d_i	Complexity
F	V	V	V	P
V	F	V	V	P
V	V	F	V	P
V	V	V	F	P
F	F	V	V	NP
F	V	F	V	NP
F	V	V	F	NP
V	F	F	V	NP
V	F	V	F	NP
V	V	F	F	NP

Table 2 shows the complexity results for preemptive transmission. The notation in this table is the same as in Table 1. As can be seen from Table 2, the complexity results for

preemptive transmission is identical to nonpreemptive transmission, except the following two cases: (i) same origin node and
release time, and (ii) same destination node and deadline. The
complexity of these two cases remain open. While we cannot
prove it, it is likely that these two cases are also NP-complete.

Table 2. Complexity for Preemptive Transmissions

s_i	e_i	r_i	d_i	Complexity
F	V	V	V	P
V	F	V	V	P
V	V	F	V	P
V	V	V	F	P
F	F	V	V	NP
F	V	F	V	OPEN
F	V	V	F	NP
V	F	F	V	NP
V	F	V	F	OPEN
V	V	F	F	NP

The polynomial-time algorithms inferred in Tables 1 and 2
are actually on-line algorithms -- those that run with no
knowledge of future arrivals of messages and no information on
other nodes of the network. We say that an on-line algorithm is
optimal if it always produces a feasible route whenever one exists.
There are some interests to determine the possibility and

impossibility of the existence of optimal on-line algorithms. This issue was studied in [29] under various restrictions of the three parameters -- origin node, destination node and deadline; release time is assumed to be variable for this study. The following theorem was proved in [29].

Theorem 2.2: No optimal on-line preemptive (nonpreemptive) algorithm can exist unless all three parameters (origin node, destination node and deadline) are fixed.

The message routing problem was further studied in [31] under the assumption that all messages have the same length. The main focus in [31] was the study of possibility and impossibility results for the existence of optimal on-line algorithms for a variety of networks -- unidirectional ring, out-tree, in-tree, bidirectional tree and bidirectional ring. The problem was considered under various restrictions of the four parameters -- origin node, destination node, release time and deadline. The results obtained in [31] are summarized in Tables 3 to 7; the notation in these tables are the same as in Tables 1 and 2.

Table 3 gives the results for unidirectional ring. As shown in Table 3, it is possible to have an optimal on-line algorithm when any one of the four parameters is fixed, while it is impossible when all four parameters are variable. These results give a sharp boundary delineating the possible cases and the impossible cases. We note that the possibility results were obtained by demonstrating an optimal on-line algorithm for each case, while the impossibility result was obtained by adversary argument.

Table 3. Impossibility Results for Unidirectional Ring

s_i	e_i	r_i	d_i	Impossibility
F	V	V	V	Possible
V	F	V	V	Possible
V	V	F	V	Possible
V	V	V	F	Possible
V	V	V	V	Impossible

Table 4 gives the results for out-tree. As shown in Table 4, it is possible to have an optimal on-line algorithm when any one of the three parameters -- origin node, destination node and release time -- is fixed, while it is impossible when all three parameters are variable (even if deadline is fixed). Again, these results give us a sharp boundary.

Table 4. Impossibility Results for Out-tree

s_i	e_i	r_i	d_i	Impossibility
F	V	V	V	Possible
V	F	V	V	Possible
V	V	F	V	Possible
V	V	V	F	Impossible

Table 5 shows the results for in-tree. As shown in Table 5, it is possible to have an optimal on-line algorithm when any one of the three parameters -- origin node, destination node and deadline -- is fixed, while it is impossible when all three parameters are variable (even if release time is fixed). Again, these results give us a sharp boundary.

Table 5. Impossibility Results for In-tree

s_i	e_i	r_i	d_i	Impossibility
F	V	V	V	Possible
V	F	V	V	Possible
V	V	V	F	Possible
V	V	F	V	Impossible

Table 6 shows the results for bidirectional tree. As shown in Table 6, it is possible to have an optimal on-line algorithm when either the origin node or the destination node is fixed, while it is impossible when both origin node and destination node are variable (even if release time and deadline are fixed). Again, these results give us a sharp boundary.

Table 6. Impossibility Results for Bidirectional Tree

s_i	e_i	r_i	d_i	Impossibility
F	V	V	V	Possible
V	F	V	V	Possible
V	V	F	F	Impossiblie

Table 7 shows the results for bidirectional ring. As shown in Table 7, it is possible to have an optimal on-line algorithm when both the origin node and either the destination node or the release time are fixed, while it is impossible when either the origin node or both the destination node and the release time are variable. Again, these results give us a sharp boundary.

Table 7. Impossibility Results for Bidirectional Ring

s_i	e_i	r_i	d_i	Impossibility
F	F	V	V	Possible
F	V	F	V	Possible
V	F	F	F	Impossible
F	V	V	F	Impossible

IMPRECISE COMPUTATION

Meeting deadline constraint is of paramount concern in real-time systems. Sometimes it is impossible to schedule the tasks such that all deadlines are met, a situation that occurs quite often when the system is heavily loaded. To cope with this situation, one can completely give up certain less important tasks in favor of meeting the deadlines of more important ones. Another approach is to regard each task as logically composed of two subtasks, mandatory and optional. The optional part of each task begins after the end of its mandatory part. In scheduling this kind of tasks, it is required that the mandatory part of each task be completely executed, while its optional part can be partially executed by its deadline. This approach is particularly useful for iterative algorithms, where the optional part corresponds to enhancement of previously obtained results. With this approach it is possible to satisfy the deadline constraint of more tasks.

With this motivation in mind, Liu, Lin and Natarajan [36,37,40] introduced the above model of task systems, the so-called imprecise computation model. The Concord System is being developed at the University of Illinois to support imprecise computation [36]. Scheduling algorithms have been proposed to minimize average error for periodic tasks [4,5,40]. Shih, Liu, Chung and Gillies [47] studied the problem of preemptively scheduling a set of n tasks with rational ready times, deadlines and processing times on a multiprocessor system so as to minimize the average error. An $O(n^2 \log^2 n)$-time algorithm was given to solve this problem [47]. Recently, Shih, Liu and Chung [46] gave a faster algorithm for a single processor; their algorithm runs in $O(n \log n)$ time. Chong and Zhao [3] gave queueing results on task scheduling to optimally trade off between the average response time and the result quality on a single processor.

While the imprecise computation model can undoubtedly allow more real-time tasks to meet their deadlines, it is easy to envision situations in which not all tasks can meet their deadlines. In [32] we studied the problem of minimizing the number of late tasks in the imprecise computation model.

A task system $TS = (\{T_i\}, \{r(T_i)\}, \{d(T_i)\}, \{m(T_i)\}, \{o(T_i)\})$ with n independent tasks is to be scheduled on $p \geq 1$ identical processors. For each task T_i, $r(T_i)$, $d(T_i)$, $m(T_i)$ and $o(T_i)$ denote the integer ready time, deadline, execution times of the mandatory part and optional part of T_i, respectively.

Let S be a schedule for TS. If T_i has executed at least $m(T_i)$ units of time by its deadline in S, it is said to be on-time; otherwise, it is said to be late. We assume that a late task has little or no value and hence it will not be executed at all. If T_i is an on-time task, we let $\alpha(S, T_i)$ and $\sigma(S, T_i)$ denote the numbers of time units T_i and its optional part had executed by $d(T_i)$ in S, respectively. Thus, $\sigma(S, T_i) = \alpha(S, T_i) - m(T_i)$. The error incurred by T_i, denoted by $\epsilon(S, T_i)$, is defined to be $\epsilon(S, T_i) = o(T_i) - \sigma(S, T_i)$. The total error of S, denoted by $ERR(S)$, is defined to be the total error incurred by all on-time tasks. We use $\Gamma(S)$ and $\Delta(S)$ to denote the numbers of on-time and late tasks, respectively.

Our problem can be formulated as follows: Given a task system TS, $p \geq 1$ identical processors and an error threshold K, find a preemptive schedule S such that $ERR(S) \leq K$ and $\Delta(S)$ is minimized (or equivalently, $\Gamma(S)$ is maximized). Such a schedule will be called an optimal schedule. An optimal algorithm is one that always constructs an optimal schedule.

In [32] the problem of finding an optimal schedule was proved to be NP-hard even under severe restrictions on the tasks. The next theorem follows directly from [32].

Theorem 3.1: The problem of finding an optimal schedule is NP-hard for a single processor even if all tasks have the same ready time and deadline.

Motivated by the complexity of the problem, we turned our attention to simpler task systems with the hope that they can be solved efficiently. We consider the case of a single processor and a set of tasks with identical ready time. In [32] we showed that this problem can be solved in pseudo-polynomial time.

Theorem 3.2: Let TS be a task system with identical ready time. There is an $O(n^2D)$-time algorithm for finding an optimal schedule on a single processor, where n is the number of tasks in TS and $D = \max \{d(T_i) \mid 1 \leq i \leq n\}$.

In the classical task system model, minimizing the number of late tasks for tasks with identical ready time can be solved in $O(n \log n)$ time by an algorithm due to Moore [43]. In [32] we used Moore's algorithm to devise a fast heuristic for the imprecise computation model. The algorithm is given as follows.

Algorithm A

Input: A task system $TS = (\{T_i\}, \{d(T_i)\}, \{m(T_i)\}, \{o(T_i)\})$ with identical ready time, an error threshold K and a single processor. Assume that the tasks have been indexed such that $o(T_1) \leq o(T_2) \leq \cdots \leq o(T_n)$.

Output: A schedule S_a with $ERR(S_a) \leq K$.

Method:

// Part I : To obtain the schedule $\hat{S}_1$. //

(1) Define a classical task system $\ddot{TS} = (\{\ddot{T}_i\}, \{d(\ddot{T}_i)\}, \{e(\ddot{T}_i)\})$, where $d(\ddot{T}_i) = d(T_i)$ and $e(\ddot{T}_i) = m(T_i) + o(T_i)$ for each $1 \leq i \leq n$.

(2) Apply Moore's Algorithm to $\ddot{TS}$ to obtain the schedule $\hat{S}_1$.

// Part II : To obtain the schedule $\hat{S}_2$. //

(3) $k \leftarrow 1. \ l \leftarrow n.$

(4) While $k \leq l$ perform Steps (5) to (8).

(5) $j \leftarrow \lfloor (k+l)/2 \rfloor.$

(6) Let $\ddot{TS}$ be a classical task system with j tasks. $\ddot{TS} = (\{\ddot{T}_i\}, \{d(\ddot{T}_i)\}, \{e(\ddot{T}_i)\})$, where $d(\ddot{T}_i) = d(T_i)$ and $e(\ddot{T}_i) = m(T_i)$ for each $1 \leq i \leq j$.

(7) Apply Moore's Algorithm to $\ddot{TS}$ to obtain the schedule S_j.

(8) Let E be the set of on-time tasks in S_j. If $\sum_{T_i \in E} o(T_i) \leq K$ then $\{q \leftarrow j, k \leftarrow j + 1\}$ else $l \leftarrow j - 1$

(9) $\hat{S}_2 \leftarrow S_q.$

// Obtain the final schedule S_a. //

(10) If $\Gamma(\hat{S}_1) \geq \Gamma(\hat{S}_2)$ then $S_a \leftarrow \hat{S}_1$ else $S_a \leftarrow \hat{S}_2$. $\square$

Using the $O(n \log n)$ implementation of Moore's algorithm, Algorithm A can be implemented to run in $O(n \log^2 n)$ time. Furthermore, Algorithm A has a worst-case performance ratio of 3 [32].

Theorem 3.3: Let TS be a task system with identical ready time and S_o be an optimal schedule for TS on a single processor. We have $\Gamma(S_o) \leq 3\Gamma(S_a) + 1$. Furthermore, there is a task system such that $\Gamma(S_o) = 3\Gamma(S_a)$.

Suppose *TS* is a task system with identical ready time and similarly ordered mandatory and total execution times, i.e., there is a labeling of tasks $T_1, T_2, \cdots, T_n$ such that $m(T_1) \leq m(T_2) \leq \cdots \leq m(T_n)$ and $e(T_1) \leq e(T_2) \leq \cdots \leq e(T_n)$. This class of task systems can be solved in $O(n \log n)$ time, as shown in [32]. The algorithm, to be called Algorithm B, is given as follows.

Algorithm B
Input: A task system $TS = (\{T_i\}, \{d(T_i)\}, \{m(T_i)\}, \{o(T_i)\})$ with identical ready time and similarly ordered mandatory and total execution times, an error threshold K and a single processor. Assume that the tasks have been indexed such that $d(T_1) \leq d(T_2) \leq \cdots \leq d(T_n)$.
Output: An optimal schedule S_b for TS.
Method:
       // Part I : To obtain a feasible set of on-time tasks Ω. //
(1) $\Omega \leftarrow \varnothing$.
(2)   Repeat Step (3) for i from 1 to n.
       // Let $M_\Omega = \sum\limits_{T_i \in \Omega} m(T_i)$ and $O_\Omega = \sum\limits_{T_i \in \Omega} o(T_i)$. //
(3)   If $M_\Omega + m(T_i) + \max\{0, O_\Omega + o(T_i) - K\} \leq d(T_i)$ then $\Omega \leftarrow \Omega \cup \{T_i\}$ else {Let T_l be a task in $\Omega \cup \{T_i\}$ such that $m(T_l) \geq m(T_j)$ and $e(T_l) \geq e(T_j)$ for all tasks $T_j \in \Omega \cup \{T_i\}$. $\Omega \leftarrow \Omega \cup \{T_i\} - \{T_l\}$.}
       // Part II : To obtain the schedule S_b. //
(4)   Use the method described in the proof of Theorem 3.2 to construct a schedule S_b for Ω.

Using a heap, Algorithm B can be implemented to run in $O(n \log n)$ time. The next theorem was proved in [32].

Theorem 3.4: Algorithm B constructs an optimal schedule for a task system with identical ready time and similarly ordered mandatory and total execution times.

We have also considered minimizing mean flow time with respect to the imprecise computation model [28,30]. Let S be a schedule for a task system TS. The mean flow time of S, denoted by $MFT(S)$, is defined to be $MFT(S) = 1/n \sum_{i=1}^{n} f(S,T_i)$, where n is the number of tasks in TS and $f(S,T_i)$ is the finishing time of T_i in S. Given a task system TS, $p \geq 1$ identical processors and an error threshold K, our problem is to find a feasible preemptive schedule S such that $ERR(S) \leq K$ and $MFT(S)$ is minimized. Such a schedule will be called an optimal schedule.

In [30] we proved that the problem of finding an optimal schedule is NP-hard even under severe restrictions on the tasks. The next theorem follows from [30].

Theorem 3.5: The problem of finding an optimal schedule for a task system on a single processor is NP-hard even if the tasks have identical ready time and deadline.

Suppose the tasks have oppositely ordered mandatory and total execution times (i.e., there is a labeling of tasks such that $m(T_i) \leq m(T_{i+1})$ and $m(T_i) + o(T_i) \geq m(T_{i+1}) + o(T_{i+1})$ for each $1 \leq i \leq n$) in addition to identical ready time and deadline. Then, an optimal schedule can be found in pseudo-polynomial time [30].

Polynomial-time algorithms have also been found for two special classes of task systems: (i) a set of tasks with identical ready time and similarly ordered mandatory and total execution times and (ii) a set of tasks with similarly ordered ready times, deadlines, mandatory and total execution times. Both classes can be solved in $O(n \log n)$ time [30].

In [28] we proposed some heuristics for finding near-optimal solutions. A heuristic was given for a set of tasks with identical ready time on a single processor. It has a worst-case performance ratio of 2 [28]. A second heuristic was given for multiprocessors and a set of tasks with identical ready time and a very large deadline. The worst-case ratio for this heuristic lies between 5/4 and 3/2 [28].

FEASIBILITY TEST

Given a set of n independent tasks with release times and deadlines and m identical processors, the problem of deciding if there is a feasible preemptive schedule for the tasks on the processors is a fundamental problem in real-time scheduling. The general problem can be formulated as a network flow problem and hence it can be solved in $O(n^3)$ time. However, we feel that $O(n^3)$ time is still quite inefficient for most real-life situations. Thus, there is some interest in finding a more efficient algorithm for solving this problem. In this regard, Sahni [44] has given an $O(n \log mn)$-time algorithm for task systems with either one distinct release time or one distinct deadline.

Formally, we are given a set $P = \{P_1, P_2, \cdots, P_m\}$ of m identical processors and a task system $TS = (\{T_i\}, \{r(T_i)\}, \{d(T_i)\}, \{e(T_i)\})$ consisting of n independent tasks. For each task T_i, $r(T_i)$, $d(T_i)$ and $e(T_i)$ are its release time, deadline and execution time, respectively. We assume that $r(T_i) + e(T_i) \leq d(T_i)$ for each $1 \leq i \leq n$. Our problem, to be called Deadline Scheduling Problem, is to decide if there is a schedule for TS on P such that each T_i is executed within $I_i = (r(T_i), d(T_i))$. Such a schedule, if it exists, is called a feasible schedule.

In [19] we introduced the notion of monotone schedules and monotone scheduling algorithms. We showed that a particular class of monotone scheduling algorithms, the so-called Highest Level First (HLF) algorithms, can efficiently solve the Deadline Scheduling Problem for two special classes of task systems -- the nested and non-overlapping task systems [19].

A task system TS is nested if for every pair of tasks T_i and T_j, either I_i contains I_j, or I_j contains I_i. TS is a non-overlapping task system if for every pair of tasks T_i and T_j, either

I_i and I_j are disjoint, or one contains the other. From our definitions, it is clear that the class of task systems studied by Sahni [44] is properly contained in the class of nested task systems which in turn is properly contained in the class of non-overlapping task systems. The HLF algorithms can be implemented to run in $O(n \log mn)$ and $O(n \log n + mn)$ times for nested and non-overlapping task systems with at most $O(n)$ and $O(mn)$ preemptions, respectively [19].

We note that the notions of monotone schedules and monotone scheduling algorithms are important for at least two reasons. First, they give a simpler technique for proving the correctness of scheduling algorithms for the Deadline Scheduling Problem. Second, monotone scheduling algorithms are very general scheduling algorithms; they have very few restrictions on how tasks are scheduled. Thus, it is conceivable that they can be used in some other situations such as processors with down times and uniform processors. It is also conceivable that fast algorithms based on monotone scheduling algorithms can be developed for other special cases.

ON-LINE SCHEDULING

One of the most difficult problems in the design of real-time systems is the scheduling of sporadic tasks -- tasks that have hard deadlines and random arrival times. Because of the unpredictable nature of their arrivals, it is extremely difficult to design a real-time system with the guarantee that all deadlines can be met. In practice, we try to meet the deadlines of the most important tasks when the system is heavily loaded. Thus, we need an on-line scheduler that works as follows. When one or more sporadic tasks arrive at time t, their execution times and deadlines are made known to the system. The on-line scheduler is called upon to decide if the newly arrived tasks, along with the unfinished tasks at time t, could be completed by their deadlines. If it were possible to meet all deadlines, the system would execute the tasks according to the schedule constructed by the on-line scheduler. Otherwise, it would try to meet the deadlines of the most important tasks and allow the deadlines of the less important ones to be missed. The above process is repeated whenever new tasks arrive. The intention of our investigation is to study the design of such an on-line scheduler. Specifically, we want to address the issue of whether we can have an on-line scheduler that performs as well as the best off-line scheduler.

Formally, a task system $TS = (\{T_i\}, \{r(T_i)\}, \{d(T_i)\}, \{e(T_i)\})$ with n independent tasks is to be scheduled on a processor system $P = \{P_i\}$ consisting of $m \geq 1$ identical processors. For each task T_i, $r(T_i)$, $d(T_i)$ and $e(T_i)$ denote its release time, deadline and execution time, respectively. We assume the parameters of the tasks are all integers. TS is said to be feasible on $m \geq 1$ processors if there is a preemptive schedule for the tasks in TS on m processors such that each task T_i is executed within its executable interval $I_i = [r(T_i), d(T_i)]$. Such a schedule is called a feasible schedule. An off-line scheduler is one that schedules tasks with a complete knowledge of the release times of the tasks, while an on-line scheduler is one that schedules tasks without this knowledge. A scheduler (off-line or on-line) is said to be optimal for m processors if it constructs a feasible schedule for every task system that is feasible on m processors.

Horn [20] has given an optimal off-line scheduler for any $m \geq 1$, with an $O(n^3)$ time complexity. There are faster optimal off-line schedulers for special task systems; see [19,44] for examples. Since an on-line scheduler schedules tasks with less information than an off-line scheduler, it is more difficult to obtain an optimal on-line scheduler. For a single processor, it is not difficult to show that the Deadline Algorithm [7,21,38] is an optimal on-line scheduler. At each instant of time t, the Deadline Algorithm schedules that active task (one which has been released but has not yet finished execution) whose deadline is closest to t; ties can be broken arbitrarily. Sahni and Cho [45] have studied the so-called nearly on-line schedulers. A nearly on-line scheduler schedules tasks like an on-line scheduler, except that it has the additional information of when the next release time is. They gave an optimal nearly on-line scheduler for task systems with one common deadline and any $m \geq 1$. Sahni [44] has shown that for every $m > 1$, no optimal nearly on-line scheduler (and hence on-line scheduler) can exist for task systems with arbitrary deadlines.

In [18] we showed that for every $m > 1$, no optimal on-line scheduler can exist for task systems with two or more distinct deadlines. We also gave an optimal on-line scheduler for task systems with one common deadline and any $m > 1$ [18]. The next theorem is from [18].

Theorem 5.1: For any $m > 1$, no optimal on-line scheduler can exist for task systems with two or more distinct deadlines.

As a result of Theorem 5.1, we are motivated to study task systems with one common deadline. In the following we give an optimal on-line scheduler for this class of task systems. Our algorithm, to be called Algorithm C, iteratively reschedules tasks whenever new tasks arrive. The algorithm to reschedule tasks is called Algorithm Reschedule, and it is based on McNaughton's algorithm [41] that finds the shortest preemptive schedule for a set of independent tasks on m processors. The idea of McNaughton's algorithm is as follows. Let x_1 denote the length of the longest task and x_2 denote the total execution time of the tasks divided by m. Let x denote the larger of x_1 and x_2. McNaughton's algorithm schedules the tasks in the interval $[0, x]$. Tasks are sequentially scheduled on P_1, starting at time 0. When a task is encountered that finishes later than x, we reschedule that portion of the task that exceeds x on P_2, starting at time 0. The above process is iterated until all tasks have been scheduled. Algorithm Reschedule uses McNaughton's algorithm to schedule tasks as follows. If $x_1 > x_2$, then the longest tasks will be scheduled one task per processor, and the remaining tasks will be recursively scheduled on the remaining processors by Algorithm Reschedule. Otherwise, all tasks will be scheduled by McNaughton's algorithm. It was proved in [18] that Algorithm C is optimal.

Theorem 5.2: For any task system TS with one common deadline to be scheduled on $m \geq 1$ processors, Algorithm C constructs a feasible schedule for TS if and only if TS is feasible on m processors.

In [18] we also considered environments where processors can go down unexpectedly. We assumed, however, that the duration of the down time is known at the moment a processor goes down. We modeled this situation by adding urgent tasks to the task system. A task T is said to be urgent if $d(T) = r(T) + e(T)$. When a processor goes down, we treat it as if it were executing an urgent task that just arrived. Assuming that urgent tasks have arbitrary deadlines and non-urgent tasks have one common deadline, we gave an optimal on-line scheduler for this class of task systems and any $m \geq 1$ [18]. We note that our scheduler is still optimal even if the durations of processor down times are unknown. However, our scheduler might not be able to detect infeasible task systems until the common deadline is reached.

PARALLEL TASK SYSTEM

One of the assumptions made in classical scheduling theory [6] is that a task is always executed by one processor at a time. With the advances in parallel algorithms, this assumption may not be valid for future task systems. In [9] we proposed a new model of task systems, the so-called Parallel Task System, to include tasks that implement parallel algorithms. We hypothesized that a task can be executed by 1, 2, $\cdots$, m processors, each with different execution times. In scheduling a parallel task, we can assign any number of processors to it. However, once the number of processors is determined, it will remain fixed throughout its execution. This assumption is reasonable since most parallel algorithms are implemented in such a way that it is impossible to dynamically change the number of processors assigned to them. For those that can, we can model them by a chain of parallel tasks such that each task in the chain has the same processor requirement. The main purpose of our study is to examine the complexity of scheduling a Parallel Task System on $m \geq 2$ identical processors so as to minimize the schedule length. Our study includes both nonpreemptive and preemptive scheduling disciplines.

Formally, we are given a set $P = \{P_1, P_2, \cdots, P_m\}$ of $m \geq 2$ identical processors and a Parallel Task System $PTS = (TS, \tau, G)$, where $TS = \{T_1, T_2, \cdots, T_n\}$ is a set of n parallel tasks, τ is a function giving the execution times of a parallel task $(\tau(T_i,j)$ is the execution time of T_i when executed simultaneously by j processors, $1 \leq j \leq m$), and $G = (TS, E)$ is a directed acyclic graph describing the precedence constraints among the parallel tasks. Since a task takes less time to run on more processors, we assume that $\tau(T_i,j) \geq \tau(T_i,j+1)$ for each $1 \leq i \leq n$ and $1 \leq j \leq m$. Our goal is to schedule PTS on the m processors such that the length of the schedule is minimized. Such a schedule will be called an optimal schedule.

Our model is similar to the one proposed and studied in [2]. The only difference between the two models is that in their model, a task must be executed simultaneously by a specified number of processors, whereas in our model, it can be executed by any number not exceeding m. For convenience, we shall call their model the Multiprocessor Task System. We can model a Multiprocessor Task System by a Parallel Task System as follows. Let T_i be a task in a Multiprocessor Task System that requires k processors and p_i be the execution time of T_i. When transformed into a Parallel Task System, we can let $\tau(T_i,j) = \infty$ for $1 \leq j < k$, and $\tau(T_i,j) = p_i$ for $k \leq j \leq m$. Clearly, an optimal schedule for the Multiprocessor Task System has the same length as an optimal schedule for the transformed Parallel Task System. We shall denote a Multiprocessor Task System by $MTS = (TS, \tau, G)$. Since a Multiprocessor Task System can be transformed into a Parallel Task System, it is easy to see that if a special case of finding an optimal schedule for Multiprocessor Task Systems is NP-hard (or strongly NP-hard), then the corresponding case for Parallel Task Systems is also NP-hard (or strongly NP-hard). Conversely, if a special case of finding an optimal schedule for Parallel Task Systems is solvable in polynomial time (or pseudo-polynomial time), then the corresponding case for Multiprocessor Task Systems is also solvable in polynomial time (or pseudo-polynomial time). Note that the above two implications do not hold if the special case contains the condition that the tasks have equal execution times.

In [2] it was shown that finding an optimal nonpreemptive schedule for a Multiprocessor Task System with equal execution times and empty precedence constraints is strongly NP-hard for arbitrary m. However, the problem can be solved in polynomial time for each fixed m [2]. It was also shown that finding an optimal preemptive schedule for a Multiprocessor Task System with empty precedence constraints is solvable in polynomial time for each fixed m [2].

In [9] we showed that finding an optimal nonpreemptive schedule for a Parallel Task System with precedence constraints consisting of chains is strongly NP-hard for each $m \geq 2$. When the precedence constraints are empty, the problem can be solved in pseudo-polynomial time for $m = 2$ and 3, and it becomes strongly NP-hard for each $m \geq 5$ [9]. For $m = 4$, it is not known whether the problem is strongly NP-hard or solvable in pseudo-polynomial time. For preemptive scheduling, we showed that finding an optimal schedule for a Parallel Task System with empty precedence constraints is NP-hard, but solvable in pseudo-polynomial time for each $m \geq 2$ [9]. For arbitrary m, we showed that the problem is strongly NP-hard [9].

MINIMIZING NUMBER OF LATE TASKS

A fundamental problem in real-time scheduling theory is that of scheduling a set $TS = \{T_1, T_2, \cdots, T_n\}$ of n

independent tasks with release times on $m \geq 1$ identical processors so as to minimize the number of late tasks. Each task T_i has associated with it a release time $r(T_i)$, an execution time $e(T_i)$ and a deadline $d(T_i)$. A task cannot start until its release time and it is expected to be completed by its deadline. With respect to a schedule S, a task is said to be late if it is completed after its deadline; otherwise, it is said to be on-time. Our goal is to find a schedule such that the number of late tasks is minimized; or equivalently, the number of on-time tasks is maximized. This problem has received considerable interest since Moore [43] gave an $O(n \log n)$-time algorithm more than two decades ago for a special case of the problem in which $m = 1$ and the release times are identical. In [14] we considered the preemptive version of this problem for $m \geq 2$.

In nonpreemptive scheduling it is well known [17] that the problem of deciding if a given set of tasks is feasible on a single processor is strongly NP-complete; i.e., each task is scheduled between its release time and its deadline. This implies that the problem of minimizing the number of late tasks is strongly NP-hard for every fixed $m \geq 1$. However, special cases of this problem have been shown to be solvable in polynomial time. As mentioned earlier, the special case of a single processor and identical release time can be solved by an $O(n \log n)$-time algorithm due to Moore. For identical release time, the problem of minimizing the number of late tasks is NP-hard for each fixed $m \geq 2$ and it becomes strongly NP-hard for arbitrary m [17].

From the above discussions, we can see that the complexity issues for nonpreemptive scheduling have been well solved. This is not the case for preemptive scheduling. Unlike nonpreemptive scheduling, the feasibility problem for preemptive scheduling can be solved in polynomial time even for an arbitrary number of unrelated processors [26]. Thus, one would expect that more algorithmic results exist for preemptive scheduling, and indeed this is so. For example, Lawler [25] gave a dynamic programming algorithm with time complexity $O(n^5)$ for a single processor. When the release times are identical, the dynamic programming algorithms due to Lawler [23] can solve the problem for m uniform processors in $O(n^4)$ time for $m = 2$ and in $O(n^{3m-3})^3$ time for $m > 2$. Hence, for a fixed number of uniform processors and identical release time, the problem of minimizing the number of late tasks is solvable in polynomial time. Unfortunately, however, Lawler [24] also showed that the problem becomes NP-hard for an arbitrary number of identical processors.

It is somewhat unexpected that little was known about preemptive scheduling for fixed $m \geq 2$ and unequal release times. As noted in [22], the question of whether the problem can be shown to be NP-hard or shown to be solvable in polynomial time remained open. In [14] we answered this question by showing that the problem is NP-hard for every fixed $m \geq 2$.

In [11] we considered the same problem on an arbitrary number of unrelated processors. We showed that the problem is NP-hard in the strong sense, giving the first strong NP-hardness result for this problem.

MINIMIZING MEAN FLOW TIME

In the last three years we have done a fairly substantial amount of research on minimizing mean flow time in classical task systems. In this section we enumerate some of the results obtained so far.

We are given a set $P = \{P_1, P_2, \cdots, P_m\}$ of m identical processors and a task system $TS = (\{T_i\}, \{r(T_i)\}, \{d(T_i)\}, \{e(T_i)\})$ with n independent tasks. For each task T_i, $r(T_i)$, $d(T_i)$ and $e(T_i)$ denote its release time, deadline and execution time, respectively. We assume that the parameters of the tasks are all integers. TS is said to be feasible on $m \geq 1$ processors if there is a preemptive schedule for the tasks in TS on m processors such that each task T_i is executed within its interval of release time and deadline. Such a schedule is called a feasible schedule. Let S be a feasible schedule for TS on P. The mean flow time of S, denoted by $MFT(S)$, is defined to be $1/n$ $\sum_{i=1}^{n} f(T_i,S)$, where $f(T_i,S)$ is the finishing time of T_i in S. Our problem is to find a feasible schedule with the minimum mean flow time. Such a schedule will be called an optimal schedule.

For a single processor, there are two special cases of the problem that can be solved in $O(n \log n)$ time -- the case of identical release time by an algorithm of Smith [48] and the case of identical deadline by an algorithm of Baker [1]. In [12] we generalized both Baker's rule and Smith's rule to solve a much larger class of problem instances -- those which do not contain a triple of tasks (T_i, T_j, T_k) such that $\min \{r(T_i), r(T_k)\} < r(T_j) < d(T_i) < \min \{d(T_j), d(T_k)\}$ and $e(T_j) < \min \{e(T_i), e(T_k)\}$. The generalized algorithms can be implemented in $O(n^2)$ time. Finally, we showed that the problem is NP-hard for arbitrary release times and deadlines [12], answering an open question posed by Lawler [24].

For two processors, we showed in [15] that the problem is NP-hard even if all tasks have identical deadline.

If each task has an additional weight and our goal is to minimize the mean weighted flow time, then the problem becomes NP-hard for an arbitrary number of processors even if the tasks have identical execution time and deadline [34].

If the tasks have precedence constraints in the form of a chain, then the problem becomes NP-hard for two processors even if all tasks have identical release time and identical deadline [16]. This result holds for nonpreemptive scheduling as well [16].

Preemptive scheduling on open shops and flow shops are known to be NP-hard on three processors [27,38]. However, their complexity on two processors remained open [22]. In [13] we showed that they are both NP-hard.

OTHER SCHEDULING PROBLEMS

In this section we briefly mention some other scheduling problems that we have worked on. In [33] we gave an $O(n \log n)$-time algorithm for finding a minimum makespan schedule subject to the constraint that the schedule must have minimum mean flow time. In [8] we gave an $O(n^2 \log n)$-time algorithm for finding a minimum makespan schedule for a tree-structured task system with two execution times on two processors.

In [10] we showed that the problem of minimizing total tardiness on one processor is NP-hard, answering a long-standing open question. If the tasks have precedence constraints in the form of chains, then the problem becomes NP-hard even if all tasks have identical execution time [35].

CONCLUSIONS

In the last three years our work in real-time scheduling theory has focused on complexity theory. We assert that it is the right starting point, since it is important to identify those problems that can be solved efficiently and those that can not. It turns out that most of these problems are NP-hard. In the future we will devise practical and good heuristics for these NP-hard problems. Our approach will be to use randomized algorithms, neural networks and simulated annealing. We feel that these are powerful tools that could be quite useful in solving these problems. We will use mathematical analyses to guide our design of heuristics.

REFERENCES

[1]   K. R. Baker, *Introduction to Sequencing and Scheduling*, Wiley, New York, 1974.

[2]   J. Blazewicz, M. Drabowski and J. Welgarz, "Scheduling Multiprocessor Tasks to Minimize Schedule Length," *IEEE Transactions on Computers C-35*, 1986, pp. 389-393.

[3]   E. K. P. Chong and W. Zhao, "Performance Evaluation of Scheduling Algorithms for Dynamic Imprecise Soft Real-Time Computer Systems," *Australian Computer Science Communications 11*, 1989, pp. 329-340.

[4]   J-Y. Chung and J. W. S. Liu, "Algorithms for Scheduling Periodic Jobs to Minimize Average Error," *Proc. of the 9th IEEE Real-Time Systems Symposium*, 1988, pp. 142-151.

[5]   J-Y. Chung, J. W. S. Liu and K-J. Lin, "Scheduling Periodic Jobs That Allow Imprecise Results," *IEEE Transactions on Computers*, to appear.

[6]   E. G. Coffman, Jr., (Ed.) *Computer and Job-Shop Scheduling Theory*, Wiley, New York, 1976.

[7]   M. Dertouzos, "Control Robotics: The Procedural Control of Physical Processes," *Proc. of the IFIP Congress*, 1974, pp. 807-813.

[8]   J. Du and J. Y-T. Leung, "Scheduling Tree-Structured Tasks on Two Processors to Minimize Schedule Length," *SIAM J. on Disc. Math. 2*, 1989, pp. 176-196.

[9]   J. Du and J. Y-T. Leung, "Complexity of Scheduling Parallel Task Systems," *SIAM J. on Disc. Math. 2*, 1989, pp. 473-487.

[10]   J. Du and J. Y-T. Leung, "Minimizing Total Tardiness on One Machine is NP-hard," *Math. of Operations Research 15*, 1990, pp. 483-495.

[11] J. Du and J. Y-T. Leung, "Minimizing the Number of Late Jobs on Unrelated Machines," *Operations Research Letters*, to appear.

[12] J. Du and J. Y-T. Leung, "Minimizing Mean Flow Time with Release Time and Deadline Constraints," *J. of Algorithms*, to appear.

[13] J. Du and J. Y-T. Leung, "Minimizing Mean Flow Time in Two-Machine Open Shops and Flow Shops," Tech. Rept. UTDCS-12-90, Computer Science Program, University of Texas at Dallas, Richardson, TX, 1990.

[14] J. Du, J. Y-T. Leung and C. S. Wong, "Minimizing the Number of Late Jobs with Release Time Constraint," Tech. Rept. UTDCS-13-89, Computer Science Program, University of Texas at Dallas, Richardson, TX, 1989.

[15] J. Du, J. Y-T. Leung and G. H. Young, "Minimizing Mean Flow Time with Release Time Constraint," *Theoretical Computer Science 75*, 1990, pp. 347-355.

[16] J. Du, J. Y-T. Leung and G. H. Young, "Scheduling Chain-Structured Tasks to Minimize Makespan and Mean Flow Time," *Information and Computation*, to appear.

[17] M. R. Garey and D. S. Johnson, *Computers and Intractability: A Guide to the Theory of NP-Completeness*, Freeman, San Francisco, CA, 1979.

[18] K. S. Hong and J. Y-T. Leung, "On-Line Scheduling of Real-Time Tasks," *Proc. of the 9th IEEE Real-Time Systems Symposium*, 1988, pp. 244-250.

[19] K. S. Hong and J. Y-T. Leung, "Preemptive Scheduling with Release Times and Deadlines," *J. of Real-Time Systems 1*, 1989, pp. 265-281.

[20] W. Horn, "Some Simple Scheduling Algorithms," *Naval Res. Logist. Quarterly 21*, 1974, pp. 177-185.

[21] J. Labetoulle, "Some Theorems on Real-Time Scheduling," in E. Gelenbe and R. Mahls, (Eds.), *Computer Architecture and Networks*, North Holland, Amsterdam, 1974, pp. 285-293.

[22] B. J. Lageweg, E. L. Lawler, J. K. Lenstra and A. H. G. Rinnooy Kan, "Computer Aided Complexity Classification of Deterministic Scheduling Problems," Report BW 138, Mathematisch Centrum, Amsterdam, 1981.

[23] E. L. Lawler, "Preemptive Scheduling of Uniform Parallel Machines to Minimize the Weighted Number of Late Jobs," Report BW 105, Mathematisch Centrum, Amsterdam, 1979.

[24] E. L. Lawler, "Recent Results in the Theory of Scheduling," in A. Bachem, M. Grotschel and B. Korte, (Eds.), *Mathematical Programming: The State of the Art*, Springer, 1982.

[25] E. L. Lawler, "New and Improved Algorithms for Scheduling a Single Machine to Minimize the Weighted Number of Late Jobs," Preprint, Computer Science Division, University of California, Berkeley, CA ,1989.

[26] E. L. Lawler and C. U. Martel, "Scheduling Periodically Occurring Tasks on Multiple Processors," *Information Processing Letters 12*, 1981, pp. 9-12.

[27] J. K. Lenstra, unpublished results.

[28] J. Y-T. Leung, T. W. Tam and C. S. Wong, "Heuristics for Minimizing Mean Flow Time with Error Constraint," Tech. Rept. UTDCS-25-89, Computer Science Program, University of Texas at Dallas, Richardson, TX, 1989.

[29] J. Y-T. Leung, T. W. Tam, C. S. Wong and G. H. Young, "Routing Messages with Release Time and Deadline Constraints," *Proc. of Euromicro Workshop on Real Time*, Como, Italy, 1989, pp. 168-177.

[30] J. Y-T. Leung, T. W. Tam, C. S. Wong and G. H. Young, "Minimizing Mean Flow Time with Error Constraints," *Proc. of the 10th IEEE Real-Time Systems Symposium*, 1989, pp. 2-11.

[31] J. Y-T. Leung, T. W. Tam and G. H. Young, "On-Line Routing of Real-Time Messages," *Proc. of the 11th IEEE Real-Time Systems Symposium*, 1990, pp. 126-135.

[32] J. Y-T. Leung and C. S. Wong, "Minimizing the Number of Late Tasks with Error Constraint," *Proc. of the 11th IEEE Real-Time Systems Symposium*, 1990, pp. 32-40.

[33] J. Y-T. Leung and G. H. Young, "Minimizing Schedule Length Subject to Minimum Flow Time," *SIAM J. on Computing 18*, 1989, pp. 314-326.

[34] J. Y-T. Leung and G. H. Young, "Preemptive Scheduling to Minimize Mean Weighted Flow Time," *Information Processing Letters 34*, 1990, pp. 47-50.

[35] J. Y-T. Leung and G. H. Young, "Minimizing Total Tardiness on a Single Machine with Precedence Constraint," *ORSA J. on Computing 2*, 1990, pp. 346-352.

[36] K-J. Lin, S. Natarajan and J. W. S. Liu, "Concord: A Distributed System Making Use of Imprecise Results," *Proc. of COMPSAC'87*, Tokyo, Japan, 1987.

[37] K-J. Lin, S. Natarajan and J. W. S. Liu, "Imprecise Results: Utilizing Partial Computations in Real-Time Systems," *Proc of the 8th IEEE Real-Time Systems Symposium*, 1987, pp. 210-217.

[38] C. L. Liu and J. W. Layland, "Scheduling Algorithms for Multiprogramming in a Hard Real-Time Environment," *J. ACM 20*, 1973, pp. 46-61.

[39] C. Y. Liu and R. L. Bulfin, "On the Complexity of Preemptive Open-Shop Scheduling Problems," *Oper. Res. Letters 4*, 1985, pp. 71-74.

[40] J. W. S. Liu, K-J. Lin and S. Natarajan, "Scheduling Real-Time, Periodic Jobs Using Imprecise Results," *Proc. of the 8th IEEE Real-Time Systems Symposium*, 1987, pp. 252-260.

[41] R. McNaughton, "Scheduling with Deadlines and Loss Functions," *Management Science 12*, 1959, pp. 1-12.

[42] A. K. Mok, *Fundamental Design Problems of Distributed Systems for the Hard Real Time Environment*, Ph.D. Dissertation, M.I.T., 1983.

[43] J. M. Moore, "Sequencing n Jobs on One Machine to Minimize the Number of Tardy Jobs," *Management Science 15*,

1968, pp. 102-109.

[44] S. Sahni, "Preemptive Scheduling with Due Dates," *Oper. Res. 27*, 1979, pp. 925-934.

[45] S. Sahni and Y. Cho, "Nearly On-Line Scheduling of a Uniform Processor System with Release Times," *SIAM J. Computing 8*, 1979, pp. 275-285.

[46] W-K. Shih, J. W. S. Liu and J-Y. Chung, "Fast Algorithms for Scheduling Imprecise Computations," *Proc. of the 10th IEEE Real-Time Systems Symposium*, 1989, pp. 12-19.

[47] W-K. Shih, J. W. S. Liu, J-Y. Chung and D. W. Gillies, "Scheduling Tasks with Ready Times and Deadlines to Minimize Average Error," Tech. Rept. UIUCDCS-R-89-1478, Dept. of Computer Science, University of Illinois, Urbana, IL, 1989.

[48] W. E. Smith, "Various Optimizers for Single-Stage Production," *Naval Res. Logist. Quarterly 3*, 1956, pp. 59-66.

CHAPTER 3

Design and Analysis of Processor Scheduling Policies for Real-Time Systems *

J. F. Kurose[†], Don Towsley[†], and C.M. Krishna[‡]
University of Massachusetts
Amherst, MA 01003, USA

Abstract

In this paper we study the problem of scheduling jobs with real-time constraints in single and multiprocessor computer systems. We show the optimality of the minimum laxity (ML) scheduling and earliest deadline (ED) scheduling policies on multiprocessors under general workload assumptions for systems in which jobs need not be served once they miss their deadlines. We also describe a discrete-time model of these policies operating on a single processor when deadlines of all jobs are uniformly bounded. The ML and ED policies described incur an overhead that has computational complexity of $O(m)$ or $O(\log m)$ (depending on the implementation) where m is the queue length. Hence we propose and study several efficient policies (with $O(1)$ overhead) that provide most of the performance of the ML and ED policies. Last, we consider the problem of scheduling jobs with real-time constraints that provide increased reward as a function of execution time. We propose several *greedy policies* that attempt to equalize the amount of service that all jobs attain and show, through simulation and analysis, that they attain performances close to an unachievable optimistic bound.

*The work reported in this paper was supported by the Office of Naval Research under grant N00014-87-K-0796.

†Department of Computer and Information Science.

‡Department of Electrical and Computer Engineering.

INTRODUCTION

There has recently been considerable interest in developing and evaluating the performance of processor scheduling policies for real-time systems. The workloads served by these systems consist of jobs that have real-time constraints, i.e., jobs which must complete or enter service by specified deadlines. For some systems it is unacceptable for any job to miss its deadline. In such *hard* real-time systems, job service demands are usually well understood and a substantial literature has focused on the development and evaluation of scheduling policies for these workloads [11, 13]. We will not consider this workload further. In the case of *soft* real-time systems, workloads consist of jobs which are not critical to the operation of the system and thus it is not necessary that *all* jobs satisfy their timing constraints. Usually, the service requirements and the arrival patterns for these jobs are not as well understood. Although job loss is tolerable in soft real-time systems, it is nonetheless desirable that as many jobs as possible successfully meet their constraints and thus a design objective for soft real-time scheduling policies is to minimize the fraction of jobs that miss their deadlines. Recently interest has also arisen in a third type of workload in which jobs remain in the system up to their deadlines, but can receive a variable amount of service. Typically each job receives a reward that is a non-decreasing function of the amount of service that it receives and the objective is to design policies that will maximize the reward over all jobs executed.

In this paper, we will consider the last two workloads described above. For the second workload we have been able to establish the optimality of the minimum laxity (ML) and earliest deadline (ED) policies with respect to minimizing the fraction of jobs that miss their deadlines on a multiprocessor under very general workload assumptions. This work is reported in the next section. Furthermore, we have developed and analyzed a mathematical model for the ML policy operating on one processor. Briefly, the model is based on a discrete-time single server queueing system in which all laxities are less than M, but otherwise generally distributed. Service times are assumed to be geometric random variables and the resulting analysis yields an algorithm of computational complexity $O(M^4)$ for computing the fraction of jobs that miss their deadlines. This work is reported in the third section.

Although the ML and ED policies are optimal in many cases, they may not be efficient to implement. Depending on the actual implementation, they can have a computational complexity of $O(m)$ or $O(\log m)$ each time a job is added/removed to/from the queue, where m is the queue size. This may not be acceptable; hence we report on several variants of ML and ED that have computational complexity of $O(1)$ and that result in performance that is quite close to that of ML. These policies divide the queue into two portions, one of which is managed using ML scheduling and the other using the first come first serve (FCFS) discipline. We find that the ML portion need not have capacity larger than 2 or 3 in order to yield near-optimal performance. Details of this work are found in fourth section.

The next to last section is devoted to the problem of scheduling jobs which have "rewards" that are increasing concave functions of the amount of service that they receive. We develop and simulate several simple scheduling policies for the case that the deadlines are the same for all jobs. The average job reward achieved by these policies is found to be close to an unachievable optimistic bound that we provide. The last section summarizes our results.

OPTIMALITY OF THE ML AND ED POLICIES

We model a multiprocessor as an infinite capacity queue serviced by K identical servers. Let $0 \leq t_1 \leq \ldots$ denote the arrival times of the jobs to the system, i.e., the i-th job arrives at time t_i, $i = 1, \ldots$. Let $\{\sigma_i\}_1^\infty$ be a sequence of r.v.'s where σ_i is the service time of the i-th job, $i = 1, \ldots$. Last, let $\{r_i\}_1^\infty$ be a sequence of r.v.'s where r_i denotes the *relative deadline* of the i-th job, i.e., the deadline of the i-th job is given as $d_i = t_i + r_i$, $i = 1, \cdots$.

At this point we distinguish between two types of systems according to the meaning of the deadlines. In one system, the deadline is understood to be the time by which a job must commence its service. In the other system, the deadline is understood to be the time by which the job must complete service. In both systems, jobs need not be serviced once they miss their deadlines.

We are interested in the following class of policies for systems in which deadlines are until beginning of service.

- Σ_0 - The class of nonpreemptive, non-idling policies where, at time $t > 0$, each policy has available to it the past history (e.g., previous arrival, departure, deadline miss, and scheduling times) of the system. In addition, at that time each policy knows the deadlines of all jobs that arrived to the system by that time.

We are interested in the following two classes of policies for systems in which deadlines are until the end of service.

- Σ_1 - Policies in this class behave the same as the policies in Σ_0 with one modification - if a job misses its deadline while in service, it is immediately aborted and removed from the system.

- Σ_2 - Policies in this class are allowed to preempt jobs that are in service, and resume them at a later time from the point of preemption. These policies may allow processors to remain idle while there is work in the queue. They have the same information available to them as those in Σ_0. Last, if a job misses its deadline while in service, it is immediately removed from the system.

Note that none of the policies in any of these classes have available to them the service times of jobs in the system.

Let π be a policy from any one of these classes. We define $L_\pi(t)$ to be the number of jobs that miss their deadlines by time $t > 0$, under policy π. We are interested in determining the policy from each of the classes that minimizes this measure. Let $t'_1 < t'_2 < \ldots$ denote the times that a policy schedules jobs into service. At time $t > 0$, there is a set of *eligible jobs* in the system under policy π where an eligible job is one that has neither made its deadline nor missed it. Let $E_\pi(t) = \{d_1^\pi, \ldots, d_{n_\pi(t)}^\pi\}$ denote the deadlines corresponding to the eligible jobs at time t under π where $n_\pi(t)$ is the number of eligible jobs under π at time $t > 0$ and the deadlines are ordered in non-increasing order. Two policies of particular interest to us are the following:

Definition 1 *In the case of deadlines until the beginning of service, policy π is the minimum laxity policy (ML) if at time $t'_k, (k = 1, 2, \ldots)$, it always schedules the eligible job with the smallest deadline on any one of the available servers. In addition, none of the servers are allowed to be* *idle as long as eligible jobs are available which have not yet been served, i.e., as long as $E_{ML}(t'_k)$ is not empty.*

Definition 2 *In the case of deadlines until the end of service, policy π is the earliest deadline policy (ED) if at time $t'_k, (k = 1, 2, \ldots)$, it always schedules the eligible job with the smallest deadline on any one of the available servers. In addition, servers are not allowed to be idle while there are eligible jobs are available which have not yet been served, i.e., $E_{ED}(t'_k)$ has more than c entries.*

Observe that there is an ED policy within both classes of policies, Σ_1 and Σ_2.

Finally, we make the following assumptions regarding the arrival times, service times, and relative deadlines.

Assumption A_0: *The service times form an i.i.d. sequence of exponential r.v.'s that are independent of the arrival times and the deadlines.*

Note that no assumption is made regarding arrival times, relative deadlines, or their relationship to each other.

We begin by presenting our results regarding the ML policy. The basis of our results for ML and for ED is the comparison of sets of deadlines. We will show that the set of deadlines for eligible jobs under ML at time $t > 0$ *dominates* the set of deadlines under any other policy at that time. Consequently, we turn our attention to the definition of dominance and the derivation of properties that it satisfies.

Consider two sets of nonnegative real numbers $R = \{x_1, x_2, \cdots, x_n\}$ and $S = \{y_1, y_2, \cdots, y_m\}$ each ordered so that $x_i \geq x_{i+1}, i = 1, \cdots n$ and $y_i \geq y_{i+1}, i = 1, \cdots m$.

Definition 3 *We say that R dominates S $(R \succ S)$ if $n \geq m$ and $x_i \geq y_i$, $i = 1, 2, \cdots m$.*

We define the following operation

$$Shift(R, x) = \{x_i - x \mid x_i \geq x\}.$$

The following lemma gives conditions under which dominance is preserved when set operations, and the $Shift$ operation are performed on R and S.

Lemma 1 *If $R \succ S$, then:*

1. $R + \{x\} \succ S + \{x\} \succ S$, *for* $x > 0$,

2. $R - \{x_n\} \succ S$, *when* $n > m$,

3. $R \succ S - \{y\}$, *where* $y \in S$,

4. $R - \{x\} \succ S - \{y\}$, *where* $x \in R$, $y \in S$, *and* $x \leq y$,

5. $Shift(R, x) \succ Shift(S, x)$.

Proof: These properties follow directly from the definition of "$\succ$". ∎

We will use the relationship between the sets of deadlines of eligible jobs to prove stochastic ordering relationships between the number of jobs lost under different policies. Hence we introduce the notion of stochastic ordering.

Definition 4 *Let X and Y be real-valued r.v.'s. We say that Y is stochastically larger than X (written $X \leq_{st} Y$) iff*

$$\Pr[X < t] \geq \Pr[Y < t], \quad \forall t.$$

The proof of the following result on the optimality of ML is taken from [17].

Theorem 1 *The following is true under assumption A_0,*

$$L_{ML}(t) \leq_{st} L_\pi(t), \qquad \forall \pi \in \Sigma_0; \quad t > 0.$$

provided that the system is initially empty under both ML and π.

Proof: Define $T_\pi(t) = (t_\pi^{(1)}(t), \cdots, t_\pi^{(c)}(t))$ where $t_\pi^{(j)}(t) = 1$ if server j is busy under π at time t and 0 otherwise.

The proof is by forward induction on the times that the following events can occur,

- $\mathcal{E}_0$ - arrival to both systems,

- $\mathcal{E}_1$ - completion of a job in either or both systems,

- $\mathcal{E}_2$ - job missing deadline under one or both policies,

Let $(s_0, e_0), (s_1, e_1), \cdots$ be the sequence of times and events that occur at those times, i.e., event e_i occurs at time s_i where $e_i \in \{\mathcal{E}_0, \mathcal{E}_1, \mathcal{E}_2\}$.

We will demonstrate that $E_{ML}(t) \succ E_\pi(t)$ and $T_{ML}(t) \geq T_\pi(t)$ at each possible event provided that $E_{ML}(s_0) \succ E_\pi(s_0)$ and $T_{ML}(s_0) \geq T_\pi(s_0)$. According to property 5 of Lemma 1, if $E_{ML}(s_i) \succ E_\pi(s_i)$, and $s_i < s_{i+1}$, then $E_{ML}(t) \succ E_\pi(t)$ for $s_i \leq t < s_{i+1}$.

We proceed with our inductive argument.

Basis Step: The hypothesis is trivially true for $t = s_0$.

Inductive Step: Assume that $E_{ML}(s_l) \succ E_\pi(s_l)$, and $T_{ED}(s_l) \geq T_\pi(s_l))$ for $l \leq i$. We now show that it also holds for $i + 1$. There are three cases according to the type of event.

Case 1 $(e_{i+1} = \mathcal{E}_0)$: If both systems have non-empty queues, the result is assured by property 1 of Lemma 1. If $E_\pi(s_i) = \emptyset$, $E_{ML}(s_i) \neq \emptyset$, then $T_{ML}(s_i) \geq T_\pi(s_i)$ and property 1 of Lemma 1 assures that $E_{ML}(s_{i+1}) \succ E_\pi(s_{i+1})$.

Case 2 $(e_{i+1} = \mathcal{E}_1)$: Any completion under π can be coupled with a completion under ML. In this case property 2 or 3 of Lemma 1 can be invoked to show $E_{ML}(s_{i+1}) \succ E_\pi(s_{i+1})$. If there is a completion under ML only, then $T_{ML}(s_i) > T_\pi(s_i)$ and it follows that $T_{ML}(s_{i+1}) \geq T_\pi(s_{i+1})$. The relation $E_{ML}(s_{i+1}) \succ E_\pi(s_{i+1})$ follows trivially.

Case 3 $(e_{i+1} = \mathcal{E}_2)$: Again there are three subcases according to whether the job misses its deadline under π, ML, or both policies. If under π, property 3 of Lemma 1 is applicable. If under ML, then $|E_{ML}(s_i)| > |E_\pi(s_i)|$ and property 2 of Lemma 1 is applicable. Last, property 4 of Lemma 1 is applicable when the losses occur under both policies.

This completes the inductive proof. Removal of the conditioning yields the desired result. ∎

In the case of systems where the deadlines are to the end of service, we have the following result which we state without proof.

Theorem 2 *The following is true under assumption* A_o,

$$L_{ED}(t) \leq_{st} L_\pi(t), \qquad \forall \pi \in \Sigma_1; \quad t > 0,$$
$$L_{ED}(t) \leq_{st} L_\pi(t), \qquad \forall \pi \in \Sigma_2; \quad t > 0.$$

Proof. The proofs of these two statements are similar to that of the previous theorem and can be found in [17]. ∎

Similar results can also be proven for discrete-time queues under the assumption of arbitrary arrival times, deadlines and an i.i.d. sequence of geometrically distributed service times. This model is of particular use in data communications in the case that the service time is always a single time unit. It forms the basis of many models of statistical multiplexers. In the case that jobs require a single time unit of service, there is no distinction between preemptive and non-preemptive systems. Furthermore, there is no distinction between systems in which jobs must meet their deadlines either by the time service begins or by the time service completes.

Extensions of these results to systems in which servers can take vacations have been made in [17]. Such systems can be used to model systems that handle jobs with both real-time and hard real-time deadlines. Extensions have also been made to systems with finite buffers in [17].

A somewhat different set of results has been obtained for a class of parallel processing systems in which jobs are required to be serviced to completion even when they miss their deadlines. The model in this case allows an arrival stream of jobs to a set of $K \geq 1$ (possibly heterogeneous) processors. A job consists of a set of task and a partial order, described by a task graph, specifying the precedence constraints between the tasks where the task processing times are random variables with known probability distribution functions. The jobs arrive at random times, with arbitrarily distributed interarrival times and each job has a deadline associated with it.

The model further assumes that there is a predefined mapping from the set of tasks onto the set of processors, identical for all tasks, that allocates tasks to processors. In the system, each processor has a queue of tasks. When a job arrives to the system, it is immediately split into tasks which are queued up in accordance with the mapping. When a processor is free, it chooses one of the enabled tasks from its queue for processing, where a task is said to be enabled if all of its predecessors belonging to the same job are completed. Thus, each processor is multitasked and multiprogrammed.

We have been able to show the optimality of a class of earliest deadline (ED) policies and latest deadline (LD) policies for such a system. Briefly, ED policies minimize the expected value of a convex function of the *tardiness of a job* (i.e., the difference between the job completion time and the deadline) and LD policies minimize the expected value of a concave function of the job tardiness. Furthermore, we have been able to show that last come first serve (LCFS) policies maximize the fraction of jobs that complete by their deadlines out of the class of policies that do not have deadline information available to them *provided that the relative deadlines have concave cumulative distribution functions.* These results are found in [1] along with other results for non-real-time parallel processing systems.

AN ANALYSIS OF THE ML POLICY

In the previous section we proved the optimality of the ML policy for continuous (discrete) time queueing systems provided the service times are exponentially (geometrically) distributed r.v.'s. In this section we describe an exact analysis for a *discrete-time* queueing system in which the laxity associated with each job is bounded by some maximum possible value, M. We note that adopting a discrete-time model is particularly appropriate in the communication networks area, given the synchronous nature of many proposed high-speed network switches currently under design [15]. Subsequently, we also describe a method for obtaining bounds on the performance of ML for a *continuous time* queueing system in which the laxities are not bounded.

Once again, we consider the case in which jobs in the queue are scheduled according to a *minimum laxity scheduling discipline* [6, 16, 17, 2, 8], in which that job whose deadline is closest to expiring is selected for service; a job whose deadline expires is considered lost and is removed from the queue without receiving service. We consider here the case of geometrically distributed service times and a bulk arrival process in which

72

the number of jobs arriving in a slot with a deadline of i slots is also geometrically distributed (for each $i, 1 \leq i \leq M$). The main result of this section is a numerical algorithm which exactly computes job loss for this queueing system with a time complexity of $O(M^4)$. Due to space limitations, we only outline the algorithmic approach here; the reader is referred to [9] for details and extensions.

Discrete Time Model

In the basic model, we assume a single server and adopt the following assumptions about the arrival/laxity process, service time distribution, and scheduling discipline; extensions to the basic model are discussed in [9]. The unit of time is the unit slot time.

- *Arrival/Laxity Process:* We define M as the maximum possible initial laxity and model the number of jobs that arrive in a slot with an initial laxity of i slots $(i < M)$ as a geometrically distributed random variable. All arrivals are assumed to occur at the very beginning of a slot and an arrival at the beginning of a slot can potentially receive a full slot's worth of service during that slot.

  The number of arrivals in a slot with a laxity of i is also assumed to be independent from one slot to the next and also independent of the number of arrivals in a slot with a laxity of j, $j \neq i$.

- *Service Time Distribution:* The amount of service required by a job is geometrically distributed with mean $1/\mu$. We assume that a job's service time is not known when it enters service.

- *Scheduling Discipline:* The ML policy is used. In the case of ties any rule can be used to choose a job to be served.

We note that the above model permits the performance of a wide range of real-time slotted systems to be modeled, including the important case of multiple classes of jobs, each with different (fixed) deadlines.

Algorithm Overview

Figure 1 shows a sample path of the minimum laxity of all *queued* jobs (i.e., jobs waiting to enter service) as a function of time. Job arrivals are shown as asterisks and intervals of time during which there is one job in the queue (one in service, but none waiting) are indicated by bold lines along the x-axis. In the following we will define the *waiting area busy period* as an interval of time during which there is one or more queued (waiting for service) jobs during a slot. The busy period of the queue as a whole is defined in the standard manner; the queue busy period may thus contain zero, one, or two or more waiting area busy periods.

The jumps in the minimum laxity at the beginning of a slot in Figure 1 result from either job arrivals with a new minimum laxity (in which case the minimum laxity decreases) or job departures (in which case the job with the lowest laxity enters service and hence the job with the next smallest laxity becomes the minimum laxity job, thus resulting in a non-negative increase in minimum laxity). For example, the job arriving at t_1 with an initial laxity of 4 finds the server busy (with the job that entered service at t_0) and becomes the minimum laxity job. At the beginning of slot t_2 this job's laxity has decreased to 3, but another job has arrived with a laxity of 2. Note that the second job arriving at t_2 (with a laxity of 6) does not affect the minimum laxity value at t_2. At t_3 the job in service leaves the queue and the queued minimum laxity job (the one that arrived at t_2 with the smaller laxity) enters service. At this point, the new minimum laxity job is again the job that arrived at t_1; note that its laxity has decreased to 2 by the beginning of slot t_3. At t_4 the job that entered service at t_3 completes, the job that arrived at t_1 enters service, and the job that arrived with the larger laxity at t_2 becomes the minimum laxity job - with a laxity of 4 at t_4. Note that at t_{16}, the job that arrived at t_{15} is lost since its laxity becomes zero (assuming it did not enter service at t_{16}).

Given such a system evolution, we are faced with the problem of determining the fraction of jobs lost due to the fact that they do not enter service before their laxity becomes zero. We conjecture that any modeling approach based on simply tracking the minimum laxity from one slot to the next is not viable, since the future evolution of the system will be based on the individual laxities of *all* queued jobs, not just the minimum laxity job (and the laxities of all queued jobs cannot be recovered from knowing simply the laxity of the minimum laxity jobs). An exact approach based on explicitly tracking the laxity of all queued jobs has a prohibitively large state space of size M^M.

Our algorithm for computing job loss is based on the fact that the

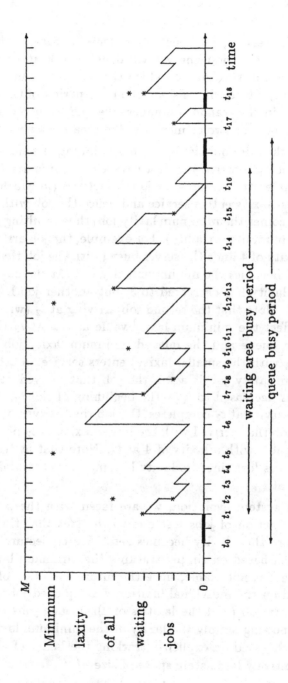

Figure 1: Minimum laxity sample path

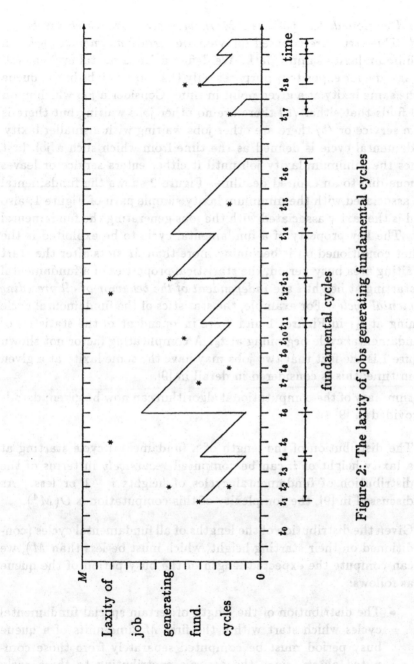

Figure 2: The laxity of jobs generating fundamental cycles

system does nonetheless possess a Markovian structure which can be exploited. This structure is based on what we term *fundamental cycles* in the minimum laxity sample path. We define a fundamental cycle as follows. Assume for expository purposes only that no two jobs in the queue have the same laxity at a given point in time. Consider a job which upon arrival finds that either *(a)* there are no other jobs waiting but there is a job in service or *(b)* there are other jobs waiting with a smaller laxity. A fundamental cycle is defined as the time from which such a job first becomes the minimum laxity job until it either enters service or leaves the queue due to an expired deadline. Figure 2 shows the fundamental cycles associated with the minimum laxity sample path of Figure 1; also plotted is the laxity associated with the jobs generating the fundamental cycles. The key property of a fundamental cycle to be exploited is the fact that conditioned on it beginning more than M slots after the start of a waiting area busy period, the statistical properties of a fundamental cycle starting at height i are *independent of the behavior of all preceding fundamental cycles.* For example, the statistics of the fundamental cycle beginning at t_{11} in Figures 1 and 2 are independent of the statistics of the fundamental cycle beginning at t_6. A complicating factor not shown in Figure 1 is the fact that two jobs may have the same laxity at a given point in time; this is considered in detail in [9].

A summary of the computational algorithm can now be given; details are provided in [9].

1. The distribution of the length of a fundamental cycle starting at a laxity height of i, can be computed *recursively* in terms of the distribution of fundamental cycles of heights $i - 1$ or less. As discussed in [9], the complexity of this computation is $O(M^4)$.

2. Given the distribution of the lengths of all fundamental cycles (conditioned on their starting height, which must be less than M), we can compute the expected length of the busy period of the queue as follows:

   • The distribution of the length of certain special fundamental cycles which start within the first M time units of a queue busy period must be computed separately from those computed above, since the arrivals contributing to these early fundamental cycles are distributed differently than those beginning more than M time units after the start of the busy period.

- The expected length of the waiting area busy period (see Figure 1) can then be computed, also with a complexity of $O(M^4)$.

- The expected length of the queue busy period can then be calculated.

3. Given the expected length of the queue busy period, the regenerative structure of the queueing system can be exploited to compute the probability that the server is busy. If $E[I]$ and $E[B]$ are the expected lengths of the idle and queue busy periods, respectively, then the probability that the server is idle, P_0, is given by

$$P_0 = \frac{E[I]}{E[I] + E[B]}.$$

4. The probability that a job is lost can now be computed using flow conservation arguments. Let λ be the mean arrival rate to the queue (including both lost and successfully served jobs) and μ be the service rate of the queue. The rate at which jobs are successfully accepted to the server is given by $\lambda(1 - P_{loss})$ and the rate at which jobs leave the queue having received service is $\mu(1 - P_0)$. Hence, by flow conservation, the probability of job loss is:

$$P_{loss} = 1 - \frac{\mu}{\lambda}(1 - P_0) \tag{1}$$

The algorithm outlined above (having a complexity of $O(M^4)$) is for the case of a single server queue with geometrically distributed service times, and a geometrically distributed number of arrivals in a slot with an initial laxity of $i, 1 \le i \le M$. In [9], we describe how the approach can be extended to handle the cases of general service times, a generally distributed number of arrivals with a laxity of i ($1 \le i \le M$) in a slot, and multiple-server queues.

A number of important related problems still remain. Two such open problems are those of computing the waiting time distribution of successfully served jobs and the laxity distribution of queued jobs.

Unbounded Laxities

We have been less successful in developing and analyzing models for systems in which the laxities can be arbitrarily large. However, in one case we have been able to develop bounds on the fraction of jobs lost. Under the assumption that arrivals are governed by a Poisson process, service times are exponentially distributed, and relative deadlines are exponentially distributed, we were able to express the system behavior as a Markov chain with a very complex state description. Beginning with this state description, we were able to develop Markov chains that provide upper and lower bounds on the fraction of lost jobs. Moreover, each chain is parameterized by an argument $n = 1, 2, \cdots$ such that the accuracy increases as a function of n, but at the cost of an increased state size, and hence, increased computational complexity. It is interesting to note that the Markov chain corresponding to the pessimistic bound on fraction of job loss is an implementable policy called $ML(n)$ where $ML(1)$ is identically FCFS and $ML(\infty)$ is identically ML. We defer our discussion of this last policy to the next section. Details of the analysis leading to bounds on the fraction of lost jobs for the M/M/K+M system may be found in [8].

APPROXIMATING THE BEHAVIOR OF THE ML AND ED POLICIES

One potential drawback of ML scheduling is that the identity of the job with the closest deadline (minimum laxity) must be determined at each scheduling point – a potentially expensive run-time cost, especially when the number of queued jobs is large. For example, if jobs are maintained in a list structure, finding the minimum laxity job in a non-laxity-ordered list or maintaining a sorted list according to laxity are both $O(m)$, when there are m jobs queued; if a dictionary-like structure is used to queue jobs, the time to maintain the data structure is $O(\log m)$.

As part of our work in developing bounds on the performance of the ML policy we developed and analyzed a policy, $ML(n)$, that attempts to approximate the behavior of the ML policy. This policy divides the overall queue into two queues, $Q1$ and $Q2$ where $Q1$ can hold at most n jobs and $Q2$ can hold an arbitrary number of jobs. If the total number of jobs waiting for service is less than or equal to n, they are all held in $Q1$. Jobs in $Q1$ are scheduled according to ML. However, if the number of jobs exceeds n, then an arriving job is placed at the *end* of $Q2$. At a service completion instant, the job with minimum laxity among all jobs queued in $Q1$ is scheduled for service. When the scheduler moves a job from $Q1$ to the server, it also moves a job from $Q2$ to $Q1$, selecting the job at the *front* of $Q2$ to enter $Q1$. In summary then, $Q1$ is an ML queue of size n, $Q2$ is of unbounded size, and $Q2$ feeds $Q1$. Note that ML(1) is same as FCFS and ML(∞) is equivalent to exact ML. The ML(n) policy can thus be viewed as an *approximate* implementation of ML, having a complexity which is independent of m, the number of queued jobs.

Our study, [8] indicated that in the case of tight deadlines, the ML(n) policy provides performance close to that of ML for values of n as small as 3. Hence we concluded that it was a promising low overhead policy that could approximate well the behavior of ML. Since then, we have studied its behavior for a wider range of workloads and have discovered that much larger values of n are required, particularly when the deadlines are loose and/or the load is high. Hence, in the remainder of this section we are thus motivated to consider four additional scheduling disciplines that approximate the behavior of ML scheduling and enjoy the advantage of having a run-time cost which is independent of the number of queued jobs. As we will see, our simulation results show that the best of the four policies provides 20–25% improvement over the ML(n) policy when $n = 5$ and performs within 5% of the ML policy over a wide range of traffic loads and laxity distributions. The run-time cost of all proposed policies is still $O(1)$.

In each of the four policies, as in the ML(n) policy described above, the overall queue is divided into two queues. At the time of a service completion, a job with minimum laxity *among the jobs in the ML queue (i.e., in $Q1$)* enters service and the job at the front of $Q2$ enters the last position in $Q1$. At the time of an arrival, if there are less than n jobs in $Q1$, the arriving job immediately enters the ML queue. If there are more than n jobs, the new arrival is handled differently by each of the four policies considered below.

Policy 1: If the number of jobs in $Q1$ (the ML queue) is equal to n (i.e., $Q1$ is full), the laxity of the new arrival is compared with the laxity of the n-th job in $Q1$. If the laxity of the new arrival is greater, it is placed at the *end* of $Q2$; otherwise, it is placed at the *end* of $Q1$ and the n-th job is placed at the *front* of $Q2$. The positional *order* of jobs in $Q1$ is maintained in an FCFS manner and thus the n-th job in $Q1$ is always that job which entered $Q1$ last. However, when the server selects a job for service, it chooses the job with minimum laxity among the jobs in $Q1$ (ignoring those jobs in $Q2$ as well as the positional order of jobs in $Q1$).

Policy 2: This policy is similar to Policy 1. If the laxity of a new arrival is greater than that of the n-th job in $Q1$, the new arrival is placed at the *end* of $Q2$; otherwise the new arrival is placed at the *end* of the ML queue but, unlike Policy 1, the n-th job is placed at the *end* of $Q2$.

Policy 3: In this policy, the laxity of the new arrival is compared with the laxity of the job with the *maximum laxity* among the n jobs in $Q1$. If the laxity of the new arrival is greater, the new arrival is placed at the *end* of $Q2$; otherwise, the new arrival is placed in the position of the job with maximum laxity among the jobs in $Q1$ and the job with maximum laxity in $Q1$ is placed at the *front* of $Q2$.

Policy 4: This policy is similar to Policy 3. If the laxity of the new arrival is smaller than that of the maximum laxity job in $Q1$, the new arrival replaces that job in $Q1$. However, unlike Policy 3, the job with maximum laxity among those jobs in $Q1$ is then placed at the *end* of $Q2$.

Some representative performance results are shown in Figure 3, which plots the fraction of jobs lost versus the job arrival rate under FCFS, ML, ML(n) and the four policies described above for the case of $n = 5$. These results were obtained via simulation, assuming exponentially distributed services times and laxities with means of 1 and 20 time units, respectively. Interarrival times were also exponentially distributed with the indicated mean arrival rate; the simulation was run until the ratio of the 90% confidence interval width to the point value was less than .1.

Figure 3 shows that Policy 4 performs the best of the four policies described above, providing a significant improvement over ML(n) and performing to within 5% of the exact ML policy. The same relative

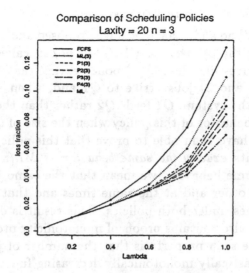

Figure 3: A Comparison of Approximate ML Policies

ordering of policy performance was found to hold over a wide range of
n, laxity values, and service time distributions; additional details can be
found in [7]. We conjecture that the superiority of Policy 4 results from
the fact that the *maximum* laxity job in $Q1$ is moved from $Q1$ to $Q2$
upon arrival of a smaller laxity job and that jobs with large laxities are
put at the *end* of $Q2$. This latter consideration avoids scenarios in which
a large laxity job is shuttled between the back of $Q1$ and the front of
$Q2$ (which would be possible under Policy 3), resulting in smaller laxity
jobs in $Q2$ eventually timing-out and leaving the system. Additional
discussion of these policies can be found in [7].

In summary, Policy 4 is an approximate implementation of minimum
laxity scheduling which is able to provide a significant performance improvement over $ML(n)$, with an additional overhead of only one additional comparison; it has also been found to perform closely to exact
ML (which is known to be optimal for a wide range of systems). The
overhead of implementing an approximate ML policy such as Policy 4
is independent of the traffic load and the number of queued jobs in the
system. This feature, together with its near-optimal performance, makes

it suitable for on-line use in real-time systems.

We note that Zhao and Stankovic have proposed and studied a policy for approximating the behavior of ML. Their policy, called the *improved FCFS* policy, behaves like the ML(n) policy except that 1) $Q1$ can hold at most two jobs and 2) jobs arrive to $Q1$ and, when there are more than two jobs in the system, $Q1$ feeds $Q2$ rather than the opposite. We have studied the behavior of this policy when the size of $Q1$ is arbitrary, $n = 1, 2, \ldots$. We have been able to prove that this policy that approximates ML exhibits *exactly the same behavior as ML(n) for the same value of n*. By same behavior, we mean that the same jobs are scheduled in the same order and at the same times and that the same jobs miss their deadlines under both policies. This result is discussed in detail in [14], which also contains proofs of monotonicity properties for the ML(n) policy; one such property is that the number of jobs lost under ML(n) is a stochastically monotonically decreasing function of n under the assumption of general arrivals, deadlines, and an i.i.d. sequence of exponentially distributed service times.

SCHEDULING JOBS WITH INCREASED-REWARD-WITH-INCREASED-SERVICE CHARACTERISTICS

In previous sections of this paper, we have been concerned with scheduling algorithms for real-time systems in which jobs are either successfully executed before their deadlines expire or are lost. In this section, we turn our attention to a different class of real-time computation in which an arriving job at time t again has some initial laxity, τ. However, rather than requiring that the job's execution begin or complete by time $t + \tau$, the job is permitted to accrue whatever amount of service it is able to receive between its arrival time and its *release time* $t + \tau$. Jobs exhibiting such behavior have been referred to in the literature as "anytime algorithms" [4, 3], "real-time approximate processing algorithms" [5], or "segmented algorithms" [12]. Informally, these real-time jobs are characterized by the fact that the longer they are able to compute (before their deadline), the higher the "quality" of their computation. Traditional iterative-refinement numerical algorithms would be an example of a class of such algorithms.

Given this new model of real-time computation, a new performance metric is also required. Specifically, rather than characterizing a job as either being successful (if it meets its deadline) or a failure (if it does not meet its deadline), we now associate a *reward function, $R(x)$*, with each job. This function specifies the *value* of the job as a function of the amount of time it has been able to execute before its release time.

Our goal is this section is to present some preliminary results regarding scheduling policies for jobs having such increased-value-with-increased-execution-time characteristics. Specifically, we present an upper bound of the performance of *any* scheduling algorithm for such an environment and show through simulation that the performance of two simple greedy scheduling algorithms is quite close to this upper bound.

The Model

As in [4, 3], we take the reward function to be a weakly concave function of a job's execution time, reflecting the decreasing *marginal* reward as a job receives more service. That is, while it is always of more value to provide a job with more service time, the incremental reward for an incremental amount of additional computation decreases as a job's accrued service time increases. As an example, [3] uses $R(x) = 1 - e^{-\delta x}$, where x is the execution time of the process and δ is a problem-specific parameter. We consider here only the case in which $R(x)$ is identical for every process. Jobs are assumed to arrive to the system according to some general arrival process, with a mean interarrival time of λ, and each job has a release time which is exactly τ units of time after its arrival. Note that no assumption is made regarding the traditional "service time" of a process; indeed none is required since it is taken as a given that the longer a process executes, the greater the value generated by its execution. Thus, no process leaves the system before its release time.

An Upper Bound on Performance

Since each job has a reward function which increases as its execution time increases, a natural system-level performance metric is the average reward per job or, equivalently, the average reward per time unit. Good scheduling algorithms will tend to achieve a high average reward per unit time while poorer scheduling policies will produce lower average reward per time unit.

Let us now consider an upper bound on the performance of *any* scheduling policy. We note that due to homogeneity assumptions and the assumptions of the concavity of the reward function, given a choice, it is preferable to balance the amount of service received by two jobs rather than allocate more service to one of the jobs (and correspondingly less to the other job); this simple observation leads immediately to the following upper bound (see [10] for details.)

Theorem 3 *The average reward is upperbounded by* 1-exp((1-exp(-$\lambda\tau$))/λ).

Two Greedy Algorithms

We now consider two greedy algorithms and compare their performance with that of the upper bound established above.

Greedy1: This algorithm is invoked on every new arrival and is based on assuming that there will be no future arrivals to the system (in which case, the jobs that are present in the system can be scheduled optimally). Suppose that a new arrival just entered the system and that prior to the arrival there were $M-1$ jobs in the system. Let us number these jobs according to increasing order of their deadlines. Thus there are jobs $J_1, J_2..J_{M-1}$ in the system with deadlines $d_1 \leq d_2 \leq d_3 \ldots \leq d_{M-1}$. The newest arrival, J_M, has a deadline d_M, where $d_M \geq d_i, 1 \leq i \leq (M-1)$.

We start at the deadline d_M and begin working backwards. The time period $[d_M, d_{M-1}]$ is allocated to job J_M for service, since it will be the only job in the system at that time (under the assumption of no new arrivals). During the interval $[d_{M-2}, d_{M-1}]$, jobs J_{M-1} and J_M are allocated service time so as to balance their total accrued service times as closely as possible. The previous service given to J_{M-1} prior to the arrival of J_M and the service time allocated by the algorithm to J_M in the interval $[d_{M-1}, d_M]$ is considered when balancing their total accrued service times. This process of balancing service times for jobs J_i through J_M to the extent possible is then is repeated for the remaining jobs.

The above scheduling process determines the *amount* of service time the jobs are allocated during each of the interdeparture intervals. However, the *order* in which jobs will receive their specified amount of service during the interdeparture interval has not yet been specified. A number of possibilities exist:

1. **Shortest Service:** In any given interval, service jobs in order of increasing service time received thus far.

2. **Closest Deadline:** In any given interval, service jobs with closest deadline first.

3. **Random Selection:** In any given interval, order the job services randomly.

4. **Round Robin:** During any interval of time within the interdeparture interval, a job receives an amount of service which is proportional to its total amount of service to be received in the interdeparture interval.

Greedy2: An even simpler greedy algorithm is to order the jobs in increasing order of service received so far and start serving the job with the least service until its accrued service time equals the accrued service time of the job with the next largest accrued service time. Then, service is allocated equally to the first two jobs until their accrued service times equal that of the third job, and so on.

Figure 4 presents simulation results showing the reward per unit time versus the arrival rate for the Greedy1 algorithm (with the four heuristics) and the Greedy2 algorithm (labelled "Really Greedy"); the theoretical upper bound is also shown. 50000 jobs were simulated and the 95% confidence intervals widths for these results found to be typically around 1 percent of the point value. An initial laxity of $\tau = 10$ was assumed and the reward curve was $R(x) = 1. - e^{-\delta x}$, with $\delta = 0.4$.

The key observation to be drawn from Figure 4 is that the performance curves of both greedy algorithms is very close to the optimum upper bound. Moreover, there is no significant difference in the performance of the two greedy algorithm themselves, and almost no difference among the four scheduling heuristics for the Greedy1 algorithm. Similar results were obtained for other values of δ, as well. It is also interesting to note that the performance of the greedy algorithms comes close to the optimum bound for very low and high values of λ, but for intermediate values of λ the difference from the optimum is slightly more. We conjecture that this is explained by the fact that for any value of δ, the reward

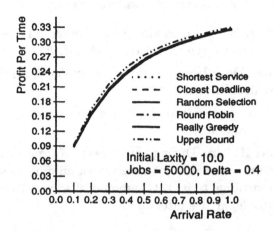

Figure 4: Reward per unit time versus arrival rate

curve can be divided roughly into three regions. In the first region (the closest to the origin), the reward curve is linear; in the third region (the farthest from the origin), the curve flattens out as it reaches its asymptotic value and thus again is linear. In the middle region, the curve is nonlinear and it is here that the decreasing marginal rewards become most significant. Note that when the arrival rate is very high, most of the jobs receive very little service, and hence almost any scheduling policy will result in jobs receiving an amount of service that falls in the first region. In this region, the reward is approximately linear, and hence the marginal reward per job is identical, regardless of the amount of accrued service. For very low arrival rates, almost all jobs receive service equal to their initial laxity, since almost all busy periods have one job. Hence the performance of any scheduling policy will be very close to the upper bound. It is only when the arrival rate is such that the received services times fall in the middle region that the difference in the performance of the greedy algorithms and the upper bound becomes noticeable; however, as evidenced in Figure 4, this difference is indeed quite small.

SUMMARY

In this paper we have considered the problem of scheduling jobs with real-time constraints to processors. Briefly, we have

- proven the optimality of the minimum laxity and earliest deadline scheduling policies for a general class of systems under the assumption of exponentially distributed service times,

- developed a mathematical model for predicting the fraction of jobs that miss their deadlines under the ML policy under the assumption of geometrically distributed service times and bounded laxities,

- developed low overhead policies that provide performance close to that of the ML policy, and

- developed simple greedy scheduling policies for jobs that receive increased reward with increased service times that yield performances close to that of an unachievable optimistic bound.

REFERENCES

[1] F. Baccelli, Z. Liu, D. Towsley, "Extremal Scheduling of Parallel Processing with and without Real-Time Constraints," to appear in *J. ACM*.

[2] P. Bhattacharya and A. Ephremides, "Optimal Scheduling with Strict Deadlines," *IEEE Trans. on Automatic Control*, Vol. 34, No. 7 (July 1989), pp. 721-728.

[3] M. Boddy and T. Dean, "Solving Time-Dependent Planning Problems," *Proc. Eleventh Int. Joint Conf. on Artificial Intelligence (IJCAI-89)*, (Aug. 1989), pp. 979-983.

[4] T. Dean and M. Boddy, "An Analysis of Time-Dependent Planning," *Proc. Seventh National Conf. on Artificial Intelligence (AAAI-88)*, (Aug. 1988), pp. 49-54.

[5] K. Decker, V. Lesser, R. Whitehair, "Extending a Blackboard Architecture for Approximate Processing," *The Journal of Real-Time Systems*, Vol. 2 (1989), pp. 47-79.

[6] H. Goldberg, "Analysis of the Earliest Due Date Scheduling Rule in Queueing Systems," *Mathematics of Operations Research*, Vol. 2, No. 2 (May 1977), pp 145-154.

[7] P. Goli, J. Kurose, and D. Towsley, "Approximate Minimum Laxity Scheduling Algorithms for Real-Time Systems," Technical Report 90-88, Department of Computer and Information Science, University of Massachusetts, Amherst, MA.

[8] J. Hong, X. Tan, D. Towsley, "A Performance Analysis of Minimum Laxity and Earliest Deadline Scheduling in a Real-Time System," *IEEE Transactions on Computers*, Vol. 38, No. 12, (December 1989), 1736–1744.

[9] J. Kurose, "An Exact Analyis of Customer Loss Under Minimum Laxity Scheduling in Discrete Time Queueing Systems," to appear in *Performance Evaluation*.

[10] J.F. Kurose, D. Towsley, C.M. Krishna, "On Scheduling Tasks with Increased-Reward-With-Increased-Service*IRIS* Characteristics," Working paper.

[11] C. Liu and J. Layland, "Scheduling Algorithms for Multi-Programming in a Hard-Real-Time Environment," *J. ACM*, Vol. 20, pp. 46-61, (1973).

[12] J. Liu, in "Report on the Embedded AI Languages Workshop, Ann Arbor, MI 1988" R. Volz, T. Mudge, G. Lindstrom (ed.), University of Michigan, Jan 27, 1990.

[13] A. Mok and M. Dertouzos, "Multiprocessor Scheduling in a Hard Real-Time Environment," *Proc. 7th Texas Conf. on Comp. Syst.*, (Nov. 1978).

[14] P. Nain, D. Towsley, "Properties of the ML(n) Policy for Scheduling Jobs with Real-Time Constraints," to appear in *Proc. 29-th IEEE Control and Decision Conf.*, Dec. 1990.

[15] Y. Oie, T. Suda, M. Murata, D. Kolson, M. Miyahara "Survey of Switching Techniques in High-speed Networks and Their Performance," *Proc. IEEE Infocom'90,* pp. 1242-1252.

[16] S. Panwar, D. Towsley and J. Wolf, "Optimal Scheduling Policies for a Class of Queues with Customer Deadlines to the Beginning of Service," *J. of the ACM,* Vol. 35, No. 4 (Oct. 1988), pp. 832-844.

[17] D. Towsley and S. Panwar, "Comparison of Service and Buffer Overflow Policies for Multiple Server Queues that Serve Customers with Deadlines," COINS Technical Report 89-72, University of Massachusetts, Amherst MA, (July, 1989).

[18] W. Zhao, J.A. Stankovic, "Performance Evaluation of FCFS and improved FCFS Scheduling for Dynamic Real-Time Computer Systems," *Proc. Real-Time Systems Symposium,* (Dec. 1989), pp. 156-165.

CHAPTER 4

Recent Results in Real–Time Scheduling

R. Bettati, D. Gillies, C. C. Han, K. J. Lin
C. L. Liu, J. W. S. Liu and W. K. Shih
Department of Computer Science
University of Illinois at Urbana–Champaign
Urbana, Illinois 61801

Abstract

This paper gives an overview of several recent results on real–time scheduling. Specifically, it presents the workload models that characterize the following types of tasks: tasks with AND/OR precedence constraints, tasks with temporal distance constraints, distributed tasks with overall deadlines, and tasks with deferrable deadlines. Suitable algorithms for scheduling tasks of each type are described.

INTRODUCTION

A (*hard*) *real–time* (*computing*) *system* is one in which some computations are time–critical. Each time–critical computation has a *deadline*; the computation must be executed to completion by the deadline so that a result can be made available in time. A result that is produced too late is of little or no use. Hence, the primary objective of real–time scheduling is to find schedules in which all deadlines are met whenever such schedules exist.

This paper gives an overview of some of our recent results on real–time scheduling. Specifically, it presents four problems: scheduling tasks with AND/OR precedence constraints, tasks with temporal distance constraints, distributed tasks with overall deadlines, and tasks with deferrable deadlines. Here, by a *task*, we mean a granule of computation that is treated by the operating system as a unit of work to be scheduled and executed.

We introduce now the notations and terms that will be used in the later sections. All the workload models described in this paper are extensions or variations of the following well–known, deterministic task model. This model characterizes the work to be scheduled and executed as a task system consisting of n tasks. We denote the task system by $\mathbf{T} = \{T_1, T_2, \cdots, T_n\}$. Each task T_i in $\mathbf{T}$ has the following parameters:

(1) *ready time* r_i after which T_i can be scheduled for execution,

(2) *deadline* d_i by which T_i must be completed, and

(3) *processing time* τ_i that is required to execute T_i to completion on a processor.

We say that a task has a deadline when its deadline is finite and has no deadline when its deadline is infinite. The time interval $[r_i, d_i]$ is called the *feasibility interval* of T_i.

The tasks in a task system $\mathbf{T}$ may be dependent on each other. Their dependencies, called *precedence constraints*, are specified by a partial order relation $<$ defined over the set $\mathbf{T}$. $T_i < T_j$ if the execution of T_j cannot begin until T_i has completed. T_i is said to be a *predecessor* of T_j, and T_j a *successor* of T_i, if $T_i < T_j$. T_i is an *immediate predecessor* of T_j if there is no other task T_k such that $T_i < T_k < T_j$; in this case T_j is an *immediate successor* of T_i. We sometimes represent a task system by a directed graph. The vertex set of this graph is the set $\mathbf{T}$, and there is an edge from T_i to T_j in the edge set of this graph if T_i is an immediate predecessor of T_j. We refer to this graph as the *dependency graph* of the task system $\mathbf{T}$.

A schedule of a task system $\mathbf{T}$ on m identical processors is an assignment of the tasks in $\mathbf{T}$ to the processors such that at any time (1) each processor is assigned at most one task and (2) each task is assigned to at most one processor. A task is said to be *scheduled* (and *executing*) in an interval if it is assigned to a processor in the interval. A time interval during which no task is assigned to a processor is an *idle interval* on the processor. The total length of all the time intervals in which a task T_i is scheduled is called the *assigned processor time* σ_i of the task. A schedule is a *valid* one if no task is scheduled before its ready time, the assigned processor time of every task is equal to its processing time, and all the precedence constraints are satisfied. Given a schedule, we call the earliest and latest time instants at which a task T_i is scheduled the *start time* s_i and the *finishing time* f_i of the task, respectively. A valid schedule is a *feasible schedule* if the finishing time of every task is at or before its deadline. A schedule is *non–preemptive* if every task is scheduled in a contiguous time interval on one processor; in other words, the execution of every task, once begun, is not interrupted. Otherwise, if the execution of some task is interrupted and resumed later, the scheduled is *preemptive*. Unless it is stated otherwise, by an *optimal scheduling algorithm* we mean one that always produces a feasible schedule of the given task system whenever feasible schedules of the task system exist.

The remainder of this paper contains five sections. Each of the following four sections discusses one of the four above mentioned scheduling problems. The last section discusses possible directions of future work.

TASKS WITH AND/OR PRECEDENCE CONSTRAINTS

This section presents an extension of the traditional deterministic workload model described in the last section; this extended model is called the *AND/OR model* [1,2]. In the traditional model, if a task has more than one immediate predecessor, then its execution cannot begin until all of its immediate predecessors have completed. In the AND/OR model, such a task is called an *AND task*. Some tasks are *OR tasks*. The execution of an OR task with more than one immediate predecessor can begin as soon as one of these predecessors has completed. Therefore, each task in the AND/OR model has an additional parameter: whether it is an AND task or an OR task. The AND/OR model has been proposed as a means of modeling distributed systems for real–time control [3]. Recently, several working systems have incorporated AND/OR precedence relations of some sort in their implementation [4,5].

There are two variants of the AND/OR model: the *unskipped* and the *skipped*. In some applications all the predecessors of an OR task must eventually be completed, that is, they are not skipped. We call this model the *AND/OR/unskipped* model. For example, in robotic assembly [6], one out of four bolts may secure an engine head well enough to allow the next step in the assembly process to proceed; the next step is modeled as an OR task. However, the remaining three bolts must eventually be installed. Therefore, these three immediate predecessors of the OR task are unskipped. The unskipped variant also models scheduling in a system with shared resources. An OR task may need a resource from one of several immediate predecessors in order to execute, and hence is ready to execute when any one of them is complete. Again, the other predecessors must eventually be completed. In other applications some immediate predecessors of an OR task may be skipped entirely. We call this variant the *AND/OR/skipped* model. One way to formulate the problem in scheduling computations with multiple versions [7,8] is to model such computations as AND/OR/skipped tasks. Corresponding to each version of a computation step, there is an immediate predecessor task of the subsequent step, and the step is modeled as an OR task. The different versions may work with different input data that are available at different times and generate different results that are needed at different times. Hence, the immediate predecessors of this OR task may have different ready times and deadlines, as well as different processing times. Only one of these tasks needs to be executed, and the others may be skipped. The AND/OR/skipped model can also be used to characterize imprecise computations that have the 0/1 constraint [8–11]. When there is insufficient time to complete a task system by its deadline, we may choose to change appropriate tasks to OR tasks, thereby enabling the task system to meet its deadline.

We are concerned with ways to schedule AND/OR precedence–constrained tasks to meet deadlines or to minimize completion time. Most of these problems are generalizations of traditional (that is, AND–only) deterministic scheduling problems, which are known to be NP–hard and, hence, are also NP–hard. However, there are polynomial–time optimal algorithms [12–14] for scheduling tasks with AND–only precedence constraints, identical processing times, and arbitrary deadlines on one or two processors. Thus, it is natural to ask whether the corresponding AND/OR scheduling problem may be solved in polynomial time. Unfortunately, this extended problem is NP–complete, even when all the deadlines are the same. This is stated in the following theorem.

Theorem 1. The problem of scheduling on a single processor an AND/OR skipped or unskipped task system in which all the OR tasks must meet a common deadline is NP–complete.

The proof of this theorem can be found in [1,2]. In the remainder of this section, we consider the two variants of the AND/OR model separately.

Scheduling AND/OR/unskipped Tasks

It is possible that there are polynomial–time, optimal scheduling algorithms for task systems whose precedence constraints are given by simple dependency graphs. In particular, two simple but meaningful types of dependency graphs are in–forests and in–trees. A dependency graph is an *in-forest* if the partial order $<$ defining the graph is such that $T_k < T_i$ and $T_k < T_j$ implies either $T_j < T_i$ or $T_i < T_j$. An in–forest is an *in-tree* if the partial order also has a unique greatest element. There exists a polynomial–time, optimal algorithm for scheduling on m identical processors any AND–only task system whose dependency graph is an in–tree [15]. Unfortunately, the corresponding AND/OR/unskipped scheduling problem is NP–complete as stated in the following theorem.

Theorem 2. The problem of AND/OR/unskipped scheduling to meet deadlines, where tasks have identical processing times, arbitrary deadlines, and a dependency graph that is an in–tree, is NP–complete.

The proof is in [1,2], where it is also shown that the problem remains NP–complete for task systems in which only the OR tasks have deadlines. We have found no simpler non–trivial combination of precedence constraints and deadlines than a third type of graph, called simple in–forests. In a simple in–forest, (1) each in–tree consists of an OR task with a deadline, no successors, and two immediate predecessors and (2) each immediate predecessor has a deadline and is the root of an in–tree of AND tasks with no deadlines. Surprisingly, even this simplified AND/OR scheduling problem is NP–complete.

Theorem 3. The problem of AND/OR/unskipped scheduling to meet deadlines, where tasks have identical processing times and simple in–forest precedence constraints, is NP–complete.

Theorems 1–3 allow us to arrive at the following conclusion. For every AND/OR/unskipped dependency graph with k OR tasks, each of which has at most l immediate predecessors, there are l^k possible AND–only dependency graphs. A feasible schedule of a task system with such an AND/OR dependency graph is a feasible schedule of a task system with one of these l^k AND–only dependency graphs. Therefore, when there are $O(\log n)$ OR tasks in the given AND/OR task system to be scheduled, it is possible to enumerate in polynomial time all the AND–only dependency graphs and apply an optimal

AND–only scheduling algorithm such as the one in [12]. On the other hand, Theorems 1–3 show that most natural problems with $O(n)$ OR tasks are NP–complete. It follows that the complexity of the AND/OR/unskipped problem is determined almost exclusively by the number of OR tasks in the task system, and the complexity of the corresponding AND–only scheduling problem.

It appears difficult to find a heuristic algorithm with good worst-case performance for scheduling AND/OR/unskipped task systems to meet arbitrary deadlines. For the simple problem stated in Theorem 3, we have produced examples that demonstrate the following fact: any algorithm that neglects to consider the individual deadlines in scheduling decisions (e.g. an algorithm that only considers slacks between deadlines and non–deadline information) may perform $\sqrt{n}$ times worse than an optimal algorithm. Some bin–packing algorithms that are known to work well have natural AND/OR generalizations of this type. Unfortunately with these generalizations, the algorithms perform poorly; the number of OR tasks meeting their deadlines may be $\sqrt{n}$, rather than n.

When all the tasks in a task system **T** to be scheduled on m processors have identical ready times and an overall, common deadline, the problem of scheduling them to meet the deadline is equivalent to that of scheduling the tasks to minimize the completion time of **T**, that is, the total amount time required to complete all the tasks in the task system. (We sometimes loosely call the completion time of the task system according to a schedule the completion time of the schedule.) This problem is known to be NP–complete even for AND–only task systems in which all tasks have identical processing times [16]. In contrast to the problems in scheduling to meet arbitrary deadlines, however, there is a good heuristic algorithm for finding suboptimal schedules. This heuristic algorithm, called the *Minimum Path Algorithm*, is *priority–driven* because it obeys the following rule: whenever a processor is available, the task with the highest priority according to a priority list among all ready tasks is scheduled on the processor.

To present the Minimum Path Algorithm, we let G denote the AND/OR dependency graph input to the algorithm. Let $\mathbf{P}_i$ be the set of all the immediate predecessors of a task T_i in G. Let $L(T_i)$ denote the length of the longest directed path that ends at T_i. $L(T_i)$ is equal to τ_i, if the task T_i has no predecessors, and is equal to $\tau_i + \max[L(T_k)|T_k \in \mathbf{P}_i]$, if T_i has predecessors. The algorithm is described in Figure 1. Any task that has no predecessors is considered to be an AND task.

The Minimum Path Algorithm can be implemented to run in time $O(n+e)$, where e is the number of edges in the dependency graph G, by reversing the directions of the arcs in G and employing depth–first search. Let W_o denote the completion time of an optimal schedule of **T**, and W_{mp} denote the completion time of a schedule of **T** produced by the Minimum Path Algorithm. The following theorem, whose proof can be found in [1,2], gives the worst–case performance of this heuristic on an m processor system.

Theorem 4. The worst–case performance of the Minimum Path Algorithm is given by the tight bound $W_{mp}/W_o \leq 2-1/m$.

The Minimum Path Algorithm

Input: The AND/OR dependency graph G and task parameters of **T**.
Output: A schedule of **T** with a small completion time.

Step 1: While there are OR tasks, for each OR task T_i all of whose predecessors are AND tasks, do the following: Let T_k be the immediate predecessor of T_i which is such that for all $T_j \in \mathbf{P}_i$, $L(T_j) \geq L(T_k)$.

  (i) Remove the edges between T_i and all of its immediate predecessors except T_k.

  (ii) Replace T_i by an AND task whose only immediate predecessor is T_k.

Step 2: The resultant task system contains only AND tasks. Schedule this task system using a priority–driven algorithm and an arbitrary priority list.

Figure 1. Minimum Path Algorithm for AND/OR/unskipped Scheduling

This bound holds for both the preemptive and the non–preemptive cases. No heuristic algorithm known to us [16] has a worst–case performance that is better than $2 - 1/m$ for AND–only task systems, and our algorithm schedules these systems as a special case. Therefore, it is not possible to get a better worst–case performance from a polynomial–time AND/OR scheduling algorithm without a better polynomial–time, AND–only scheduling algorithm. In fact, it has been a long–standing open problem to find a better polynomial–time, AND–only scheduling algorithm [16].

Scheduling AND/OR/Skipped Tasks

We have found that the complexity of any AND/OR/skipped problem is always as high as the complexity of the corresponding unskipped problem [1,2]. In particular, the problem of scheduling AND/OR/skipped tasks to meet deadlines, where tasks have identical processing times and in–tree precedence constraints, is NP–complete; so is the problem of scheduling AND/OR/skipped task systems whose dependency graphs are simple in–forests and whose tasks have arbitrary deadlines. However, there are polynomial–time optimal algorithms for scheduling, on uniprocessor systems, the following two special types of AND/OR/skipped task systems: (1) where all tasks are OR/skipped tasks and the partial order defining the precedence constraints has a unique least element and a unique greatest element, and (2) where all tasks have identical processing times, only the OR tasks have deadlines, and the dependency graph is a simple in–forest.

In case (1) where all tasks in a task system **T** are OR tasks, the *BFS (Breadth–First–Search) Algorithm* shown in Figure 2 can be used to feasibly schedule **T** if feasible schedules of **T** exist. Without loss of generality, we assume that the given deadlines of the tasks are consistent with their precedence constraints [17]. According to the BSF Algorithm, each task T_i is first labeled with three labels: α_i, β_i, and γ_i, starting from the task T_1 that has no predecessor. α_i and β_i are the possible start time and possible finishing time of T_i, respectively. γ_i is a pointer to the immediate predecessor of T_i that has the smallest possible finishing time. After all the tasks are labeled, we then examine the tasks in turn, starting from the last task T_n that has no successors, and generate a feasible schedule if such a schedule exists. Figure 2 describes the operations of this algorithm; its complexity is $O(n^2)$

The BFS Algorithm

Input: An OR dependency graph G, in which there are only one task without predecessors and one task without successors, and the parameters of **T**.

Output: A feasible schedule of **T** or the conclusion "**T** is infeasible."

Step 1: For the task T_1 that has no predecessor, label the task by $\alpha_1 = r_1$, $\beta_1 = r_1 + \tau_1$, and $\gamma_i = \phi$. If $\beta_1 > d_1$, the task system cannot be feasibly scheduled; stop.

Step 2: For each unlabeled task T_i whose immediate predecessors are all labeled, let $T_k \in \mathbf{P}_i$ be the immediate predecessor of T_i that has the least possible finishing time, that is, $\beta_k \leq \beta_j$ for all $T_j \in \mathbf{P}_i$. Label T_i by $\alpha_i = \max(r_i, \beta_k)$, $\beta_i = \alpha_i + \tau_i$, and $\gamma_i = k$.

Step 3: Construct a feasible schedule from the end of the schedule, or conclude no feasible schedule exists, as follows:

(i) Start from the task T_n that has no successor, if its feasibility interval $[r_i, d_i]$ does not contain $[\alpha_n, \beta_n]$, the task set **T** cannot be feasibly scheduled; stop. Otherwise, schedule T_n in the interval $[\alpha_n, \beta_n]$.

(ii) Starting from γ_n and following the pointers $\{\gamma_k\}$ that give the chain of tasks to be scheduled, examine each task on the chain in turn until T_1 is examined. When a task T_i is examined, check whether its feasibility interval $[r_i, d_i]$ contains $[\alpha_i, \beta_i]$. If not, **T** cannot be feasibly scheduled; stop. Otherwise, schedule T_i in $[\alpha_i, \beta_i]$. The index of the next task on the chain to be examined is given by γ_i.

Figure 2. The BFS Algorithm for Scheduling OR–only Tasks

In case (2), the dependency graph consists of a number of in–trees each of which has only one OR task at the root of the tree. This OR task has a deadline and AND–only predecessors whose precedence constraints are given by two subtrees. We note that for every one of these in–trees, an algorithm to find a feasible schedule should pick the AND–only predecessor subtree that contains the fewest number of AND tasks. This method always produces a feasible schedule if the task system can be feasibly scheduled. When the given task system is infeasible, it is possible to produce a schedule that maximizes the number of OR tasks meeting their deadlines. To see how, we note that an OR task together with one predecessor subtree consisting of k_i AND tasks may be thought of as one large task with processing time k_i+1. Then the algorithm of [18], which minimizes the number of late tasks scheduled on a single processor, may be used to schedule the large tasks with processing times k_i+1, to meet the deadlines of OR tasks.

There is a reasonably good heuristic algorithm for scheduling a system **T** of AND/OR/skipped tasks that have identical ready times and an in–tree dependency graph G to minimize the completion time of the task system. This algorithm is called the *Path Balancing Algorithm*. To present this algorithm, we let $E(G, T_i)$ be the total processing time of all the predecessors of T_i. Let $L^*(G)$ denote the sum of the processing times of all the tasks on the longest chain in G, and let $E^*(G) = \sum_i \tau_i - L^*(G)$ in an AND–only graph. Finally, let

$$f(G) = E^*(G)/m + L^*(G).$$ $f(G)$ is an estimate of the worst–case completion time of a priority–driven schedule of a task system with dependency graph G. The Path Balancing Algorithm, described in Figure 3, first converts an AND/OR in–tree into an AND–only in–tree that minimizes this function. Step 1 of the Path Balancing Algorithm minimizes the worst–case completion time of the priority–driven schedule produced in Step 2. The complexity of this algorithm is $O(n^2)$. Given a task system **T** whose dependency graph is an in–tree, let W_{pb} denote the completion time of a schedule of **T** produced by the Path Balancing Algorithm and W_o be the completion time of an optimal schedule of **T**. The worst–case performance of the Path Balancing Algorithm is given by the following theorem.

Theorem 5. The completion time of the Path Balancing Algorithm is bounded by the ratio $W_{pb}/W_o \leq 2 - 1/m$.

Path–Balancing Algorithm

Input: The in–tree AND/OR dependency graph G and the task parameters of **T**.

Output: A schedule of **T** with a small completion time.

Step 1: Convert the OR tasks in G into AND tasks to obtain an AND–only graph G' that minimizes $f(G')$ as follows: For each path C_i in G in order of non–increasing length, do (i) — (iv)

(i) Copy G to G_t.

(ii) Examine each path C_j in G_t, starting from the longest path and in order of non–increasing length. If $C_j = C_i$, go to (iii). Otherwise, if $C_j - (C_j \cap C_i)$ contains no OR tasks, go to (iii). Otherwise, let T_k be the least OR task on C_j. For each $T_l \in \mathbf{P}_k$ on a path no longer than C_i, remove the edge between T_k and T_l from G_t until T_k has only one immediate predecessor, that is T_k becomes an AND task.

(iii) Until no OR tasks remain in G_t, convert each OR task T_k with 2 or more immediate predecessors into an AND task as follows: Let T_l be the task in the set $\mathbf{P}_k$ of immediate predecessors of T_k; T_l is such that for all $l' \neq l$ $E(G_t, T_{l'}) \geq E(G_t, T_l)$. Choose T_l as the sole immediate predecessor of T_k.

(iv) If the resulting AND–only graph yields an improved value of $f(G_t)$, record $f(G_t)$ and the choice of the immediate predecessor of each OR task. Modify G' according to the recorded choices.

Step 2: Schedule the resultant AND–only task system with dependency graph G' using a priority–driven algorithm according to an arbitrary priority list.

Figure 3. The Path Balancing Algorithm

Again, this bound holds for both the preemptive and non–preemptive cases. The proof of this algorithm can be found in [1,2].

TASKS WITH TEMPORAL DISTANCE CONSTRAINTS

In the traditional task model, deadlines of tasks are static, independent of the way tasks are scheduled and executed. A natural extension is to let tasks have dynamic deadlines as well as the given, static deadlines. Specifically, in the *temporal distance model* [19,20] each task has a fourth parameter, called its *temporal distance*, or simply *distance*, in addition to the three parameters r_i, d_i and τ_i defined in Section I. The distance c_i of a task T_i that has no predecessors is infinite. To define the distance of a task T_i that has predecessors, let f denote the finishing time of the immediate predecessor of T_i that completes execution last among all of its immediate predecessors in a schedule. If T_i has distance c_i, then T_i is required to complete by $f + c_i$ in the schedule. In other words, in addition to its static deadline d_i, the task also has a *dynamic deadline* $f + c_i$. In a *feasible schedule* of **T**, every task is scheduled in its feasibility interval and is complete by its dynamic deadline. The traditional model is a special case of the temporal distance model in which the . distances of all tasks are infinite. A task with infinite distance is said to have no distance constraint.

An example of an application that requires the temporal distance model is a database used to store monitoring data in a real–time monitor/controller. When a data integrity constraint (e.g. surface temperature < 1000) is violated as data changes, the system recovers from this fault condition by executing a corrective transaction (e.g. activate coolant pump). The execution of this transaction may in turn lead to the violation of other integrity constraints (e.g. number of running pumps < 3) and the executions of the required corrective transactions. The transactions can be modeled as a system of dependent tasks with temporal distances. The distance between a task and its immediate predecessor is equal to the maximum length of time the fault condition is allowed to exist. Another example is scheduling acknowledgement transmissions; an acknowledgement of a reliable message must be delivered within a given timeout period after the receipt of the message. In this case, the acknowledgement transmission task does not have a static deadline, but has a temporal distance. Other applications where it is more natural to use the distance constraint model include process control and intelligent manufacturing systems.

The problems in scheduling tasks with temporal distances are generalizations of the corresponding problems in scheduling tasks without temporal distances. Therefore, it is not surprising that we have the following theorem.

Theorem 6. The problem of non–preemptive scheduling, on one processor, a system T of tasks with arbitrary processing times, deadlines and distance constraints to meet deadlines and distance constraints is NP–complete.

We now confine our attention to the special case studied in [19,20]. In this special case, the dependency graph consists solely of chains which are independent from each other but have a common least element. Figure 4 shows a general dependency graph with this property. We refer to each chain of tasks as a job. Hence the task system T shown in Figure 4 contains $n+1$ jobs. The job that is the least element in the dependency graph is T_0, containing only one task. The i th job, denoted by T_i, contains k_i tasks, and they are denoted by $T_{i,1}, T_{i,2}, \cdots, T_{i,k_i}$. For the sake of convenience, we sometimes refer to the first task $T_{i,1}$ in each job T_i as the *head task* and the other tasks as the *tail tasks* of T_i. The distance of the head task of T_i is c_i, while the distances of all the tail tasks are $c_i{}'$. We note that because all the head tasks have a common predecessor, the distance of each head task effectively also specifies the deadline $(d_{i,1} = \tau_0 + c_i)$ of the task. When all the tasks in a task system T have (1) unit processing times, (2) no deadlines, (3) identical ready times, and (4) integer–valued distances given by a dependency graph of the type shown in Figure 4, the problem of non–preemptive scheduling the task system T to meet the distance constraints is called the *general Multi–Level, Unit–Time JSD*, or *general MUJSD*, problem. Unfortunately, it is not likely for this problem to have a polynomial–time, optimal solution, as stated in the following theorem [19,20].

Theorem 7. The general MUJSD problem is NP–complete in the strong sense.

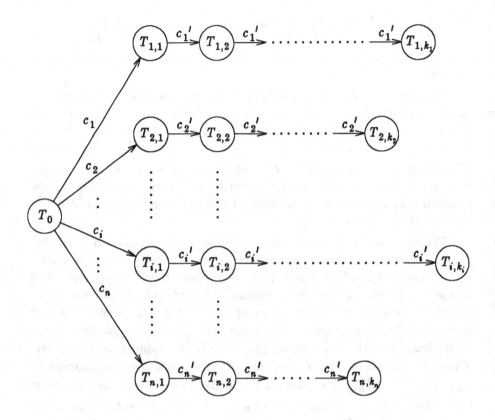

Figure 4. The Dependency Graph of the MUJSD problem

A special case of the general MUJSD problem, called the *simple MUJSD problem*, or the MUJSD problem for short, is one in which the distances of all the tail tasks c_i' are equal to a constant c. The problem of scheduling timed, reliable message exchanges is an example of the simple MUJSD problem. The head task in each job models the transmission of the first message in a conversation, and the tail tasks model the subsequent acknowledgements and replies. There is an optimal algorithm, with complexity $O(n^2)$, for scheduling MUJSD task systems non–preemptively on a single processor. The description of this algorithm can be found in [19,20].

DISTRIBUTED TASKS WITH OVERALL DEADLINES

In a multiprocessor or distributed system, tasks may need to be executed on more than one processor. When all the tasks execute on different processors in turn, the problem of end–to–end scheduling on the processors is either a *job–shop* problem, if the orders in which tasks execute on different processors are arbitrary, or a *flow–shop* problem, if the orders are the same. Our attention has been focused on the latter [21,22]. A flow shop models a multiprocessor or distributed system in which processors and devices (also modeled as processors) are functionally dedicated. For example, in a real–time control system, there is an input processor, a computation processor, and an output processor. The input processor reads all sensors; the computation processor processes the sensor inputs and generates commands; the output processor delivers the commands to the actuators controlled by the system. This system can be modeled as a flow shop in which there are three processors. Each task, modeling a closed–loop tracker and controller, must be executed first on the input processor, then on the computation processor, and finally on the output processor. In this section, we describe a polynomial–time optimal algorithm for scheduling homogeneous tasks with identical processing times. This algorithm is then used as the basis of a heuristic algorithm for scheduling tasks with arbitrary processing times.

We also consider here two variations of the traditional flow–shop model, called *flow shop with recurrence* and *periodic flow shop*. In a flow shop with recurrence, each task executes more than once on one or more processors. A system that has limited resources, and hence does not have a dedicated processor for every function, can often be modeled as a flow shop with recurrence. As an example, suppose that the three processors in the control system mentioned earlier are connected by a bus. We can model the bus as a processor and the system as a flow shop with recurrence. Each task executes first on the input processor, then on the bus, on the computation processor, on the bus again, and finally on the output processor. In a periodic flow shop, each task is a periodic sequence of requests for the same computation. It can be viewed as a special case of the flow shop with recurrence, as well as a generalization of the traditional periodic–job model.

Most of the past efforts in flow–shop scheduling have focused on minimization of completion time and on the two–processor flow–shop problem [16,23–26]. Almost every flow–shop problem that goes beyond the two–processor flow–shop problem is NP–complete. Consequently, many studies of flow–shop problems were concerned with finding restrictions of the problem that make it tractable. Other efforts focused on enumerative methods and heuristic algorithms that yield optimal and suboptimal schedules in reasonable amounts of time. The end–to–end scheduling problem addressed in [27] can be formulated as one of meeting deadlines in flow shops. Flow–shop scheduling is similar to pipeline scheduling in pipelined multiprocessors, where the objective of scheduling is to maximize throughput [28–30].

Scheduling in Traditional Flow–Shops

The *flow shop model* is a well–known variant of the traditional identical–processor model presented in the introduction. In this variant, the m processors, denoted by $\Pi_1, \Pi_2, \cdots, \Pi_m$, on which tasks are scheduled are different. Each task T_i in the given task system **T** consists of m subtasks $T_{i,1}, T_{i,2}, \cdots, T_{i,m}$. These subtasks have to be executed in order; first $T_{i,1}$ on processor Π_1, then $T_{i,2}$ on processor Π_2, and so on. The given ready times and deadlines of the subtasks $T_{i,j}$ are the same as the ready time and deadline of the task T_i, respectively. Let $\tau_{i,j}$ denote the processing time of $T_{i,j}$, that is the time required for the subtask to complete its execution on processor Π_j. The processing time requirements of a task in a flow shop are given by the m parameters $\tau_{i,j}$.

When the task parameters are arbitrary, the flow–shop problem on $m > 2$ processors is NP–complete, for both the preemptive and non-preemptive cases [21–24]. We examine now two special cases of the flow–shop problem that have polynomial–time solutions. Our algorithms make use of the *effective deadlines* of subtasks. The effective deadline $d_{i,j}$ of the subtask $T_{i,j}$ is the point in time by which the execution of the subtask $T_{i,j}$ must be completed to allow the later subtasks, and the task T_i, to complete by the given deadline d_i. $d_{i,j}$ is computed as $d_{i,j} = d_i - \sum_{k=j+1}^{m} \tau_{i,k}$, for $j < m$, and $d_{i,m} = d_i$. Similarly, we define the *effective ready time* $r_{i,j}$ of a subtask $T_{i,j}$ to be the earliest point in time at which the subtask can be scheduled. Since $T_{i,j}$ cannot be scheduled until earlier subtasks are completed, $r_{i,j}$ is given by $r_{i,j} = r_i + \sum_{k=1}^{j-1} \tau_{i,k}$, for $j > 1$, and $r_{i,1} = r_i$.

The simplest flow shop is one in which the processing times $\tau_{i,j}$ of all tasks on all processors are identical, that is, $\tau_{i,j} = \tau$ for all i and j. If the ready times and deadlines are multiples of τ, we can simply use the classical *earliest–effective–deadline–first* (EEDF) algorithm to optimally schedule all tasks [12]. According to the EEDF algorithm, the subtasks $T_{i,1}$ on the first processor Π_1 are scheduled non–preemptively in a *priority–driven* manner, and priorities are assigned to subtasks according to their effective deadlines: the earlier the effective deadline, the higher the priority. The scheduling decision is then propagated on to the subsequent processors; whenever the subtask $T_{i,j}$ completes on Π_j, $T_{i(j+1)}$ starts on Π_{j+1}. The scheduling decision on the first processor is slightly more complicated if ready times and deadlines are arbitrary rational numbers, that is, not multiples of τ. Garey et al. [13] introduces the concept of forbidden regions, where tasks are not allowed to start execution. Their algorithm postpones the ready times of selected tasks. This is done to adequately insert the necessary idle times to make an EEDF schedule optimal. We call the ready times generated from the given effective ready times by the algorithm in [13] the *modified ready times*. In our subsequent discussion, by ready times, we mean modified ready times. By the earliest–effective–deadline–first algorithm, we mean the earliest–effective–deadline–first algorithm using the modified ready times as input parameters rather than the given effective ready times. It is easy to show that for non–preemptive flow–shop scheduling of tasks whose subtasks have identical processing times, the EEDF algorithm is optimal [21,22]. When the ready times of all tasks are identical, the schedules of all the subtasks on Π_1 produced by the preemptive and nonpreemptive EEDF algorithms are the same. Hence the non–preemptive EEDF algorithm is optimal among all algorithms.

We now consider a more general case of homogeneous task systems. In a homogeneous task system, the subtasks $T_{i,j}$ on each processor Π_j have identical processing times, that is $\tau_{i,j} = \tau_j$ for all i, but subtasks on different processors may have different processing

---

Algorithm A

Input: Parameters $r_{i,j}$, $d_{i,j}$ and τ_j of a homogeneous task system **T**.

Output: A feasible schedule S of **T** or "**T** has no feasible schedules".

Step 1:   Determine the processor Π_b where $\tau_b \geq \tau_j$ for all $j = 1, 2, \cdots, m$. Π_b is the *bottleneck processor*.

Step 2:   Schedule the subtasks on the bottleneck processor Π_b according to the EEDF algorithm. If the resultant schedule S_b is not a feasible schedule, stop; no feasible schedule exists. Otherwise, if S_b is a feasible schedule of $\{T_{i,b}\}$, let $s_{i,b}$ be the start time of $T_{i,b}$.

Step 3:   Propagate the schedule S_b onto the remaining processors as follows:

(i)   Schedule $T_{i,(b+1)}$ on Π_{b+1} immediately after $T_{i,b}$ completes, $T_{i,(b+2)}$ on Π_{b+2} immediately after $T_{i,(b+1)}$ completes, and so on until $T_{i,m}$ is scheduled.

(ii) For any processor Π_r, where $r < b$, schedule $T_{i,r}$ on Π_r to start at time $s_{i,b} - \sum_{s=r}^{b-1} \tau_s$, for $r = 1, 2, \cdots b-1$.

Figure 5. Algorithm A for Scheduling Homogeneous Task Systems

times. We use *Algorithm A*, described in Figure 5, to schedule such a task system. The fact that this algorithm is optimal is shown in [21,22].

In real-world applications, the task system **T** to be scheduled may contain heterogeneous tasks whose subtasks have arbitrary processing times. We can use the heuristic algorithm described in Figure 6, called *Algorithm H*, in this case. This algorithm uses a schedule S_b on the bottleneck processor Π_b as the starting point for the construction of an overall schedule S for the tasks in **T**. Algorithm H is relatively simple, with complexity $O(n \log n)$ or $O(n \log n + nm)$, depending on whether compaction is done. It provides us with a way to find a feasible schedule of task systems whose parameters are arbitrary rational

Algorithm H

Input: Parameters r_i, d_i and $\tau_{i,j}$ of **T**.

Output: A feasible schedule of **T**, or "the algorithm fails".

Step 1: Determine the effective ready times $r_{i,j}$ and effective deadlines $d_{i,j}$ of all subtasks.

Step 2: Find the indices l and b such that $\tau_{l,b} \geq \tau_{i,j}$ for all i and j. Π_b is the *bottleneck processor*: on this processor the subtask $T_{l,b}$ has the largest processing time among all subtasks in all tasks. Call the maximal processing time of this subtask $\tau_{\max}$.

Step 3: Inflate all the subtasks in $\{T_{i,b}\}$ on the bottleneck processor by making their processing times equal to $\tau_{\max}$. Each inflated subtask $T_{i,b}$ consists of a busy segment with processing time $\tau_{i,b}$ and an idle segment with processing time $\tau_{\max} - \tau_{i,b}$. All inflated subtasks on Π_b have identical processing times.

Step 4: Schedule the inflated subtasks in $\{T_{i,b}\}$ on Π_b using the EEDF algorithm. Specifically, the resultant schedule is S_b.

Step 5: Let $s_{i,b}$ be the start of $T_{i,b}$ in S_b on Π_b. Propagate the schedule S_b onto the remaining processors as follows: For any task T_i,

   (i) schedule $T_{i,(b+1)}$ to start at time $s_{i,b} + \tau_{\max}$ on processor Π_{b+1}, $T_{i,(b+2)}$ to start at at time $s_{i,b} + 2\tau_{\max}$ on Π_{b+2}, and so on until $T_{i,m}$ is scheduled at time $s_{i,b} + (m-b)\tau_{\max}$ on Π_m; and

   (ii) schedule $T_{i,(b-1)}$ to start at time $s_{i,b} - \tau_{i,(b-1)}$ on processor Π_{b-1}, $T_{i,(b-2)}$ to start at time $s_{i,b} - \tau_{\max} - \tau_{i,(b-2)}$ on Π_{b-2}, and so on, until $T_{i,1}$ is scheduled to start at time $s_{i,b} - (b-1)\tau_{\max} - \tau_{i,1}$ on Π_1.

Step 6: Compact the schedule by reducing as much as possible the lengths of the idle intervals on Π_b that were introduced in Step 3 and Step 5. Return the resultant schedule of **T** if it is feasible or report the failure of the algorithm if it is not. Stop.

Figure 6. Algorithm H for Scheduling Arbitrary Tasks in Flow Shops

numbers. The example in Figure 7 illustrates this algorithm. The task parameters are listed in Figure 7a. Since $\tau_{4,3}$ is the largest among the processing times of all subtasks, $\tau_{max} = \tau_{4,3}$, and Π_3 is the bottleneck processor. Figure 7b shows the schedule produced in the first five steps in Algorithm H. After compaction in Step 6, the final schedule is shown in Figure 7c. We note that two tasks, namely T_1 and T_5 miss their deadlines in the schedule of Figure 7b. Moreover, T_1 and T_4 are forced to start before their ready times. All tasks meet their ready times and deadlines after Step 6 has compacted the infeasible schedule to produce the feasible schedule of Figure 7c.

We note that Algorithm H is not optimal for three reasons. First, Step 4 defines the order in which the tasks are executed on the processors. This step is not optimal for scheduling the original set of subtasks $T_{i,b}$ on Π_b. Second, Step 5 propagates the schedule on Π_b to the remaining processors by reserving τ_{max} time units for the execution of each subtask. This step may lead to an infeasible schedule of **T** even when the schedule S_b of $\{T_{i,b}\}$ on Π_b is feasible. The resultant schedule S is a *permutation schedule*, that is, a schedule according to which all tasks are scheduled in the same sequence on all processors. The fact that in flow shops with more than three processors there may be no feasible permutation schedules for some feasible task systems has been demonstrated by examples. In other words, the order of execution of the subtasks may vary from processor to processor in all feasible schedules of such task systems. By generating only permutation schedules, Algorithm H fails to find a feasible schedule for such cases. Third, both Step 3 and Step 5 add intentional idle times on all the processors and therefore generate schedules that can be improved. The compaction in Step 6 is a way to improve the chance for Algorithm H to find a feasible schedule when such a schedule exists. The compaction process work with the schedule S that has been constructed in Step 5. Let $s_{i,j}$ be the start time of $T_{i,j}$ on Π_j in this schedule. Let the tasks be indexed so that $s_{i,j} < s_{h,j}$ whenever $i < h$. The subtask $T_{i,j}$ starts execution on processor Π_j at time $s_{i,j} = s_{i,b} + (j-b)\tau_{max}$ for $j > b$ and at $s_{i,j} = s_{i,b} - (b-j+1)\tau_{max} - \tau_{i,j}$ for $j < b$. However, we can start the execution of the subtask $T_{i,j}$ as soon as $T_{(i-1),j}$ terminates and frees the processor Π_j as long as we

Task	r_i	d_i	$\tau_{i,1}$	$\tau_{i,2}$	$\tau_{i,3}$	$\tau_{i,4}$
T_1	1	10	1	2	3	2
T_2	1	16	2	3	4	1
T_3	1	22	3	2	3	3
T_4	14	28	2	1	5	3
T_5	14	29	1	1	4	1

(a) Task Parameters

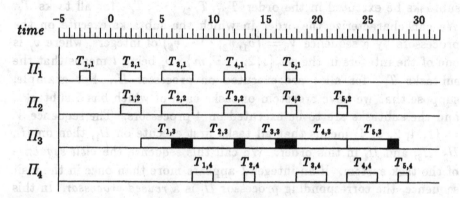

(b) Before Compaction
(■ indicates an idle interval due to inflation.)

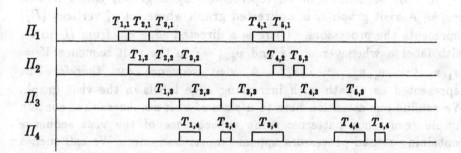

(c) After Compaction

Figure 7. An Example Illustrating Algorithm H

take care not to begin the execution of $T_{i,j}$ before its effective ready time $r_{i,j}$. The $O(nm)$ algorithm described in [21,22] for compacting the schedule S takes these considerations into account in the process of reducing the idle times on the different processors.

Scheduling in Flow Shops with Recurrence

In the more general flow–shop–with–recurrence model, each task T_i has k subtasks, and $k > m$. Without loss of generality, we let the subtasks be executed in the order $T_{i,1}, T_{i,2}, \cdots, T_{i,k}$ for all tasks T_i. We can characterize the order in which the subtasks execute on the processors by a sequence $V = (v_1, v_2, \cdots, v_k)$ of integers, where v_j is one of the integers in the set $\{1, 2, \cdots, m\}$. v_j being l means that the subtasks $T_{i,j}$ for all i are executed on processor Π_l. For example, suppose that we have a system of tasks each of which has 5 subtasks, and the subtasks are to be executed on 4 processors. The sequence $V = (1, 4, 2, 3, 4)$ means that all tasks first execute on Π_1, then on Π_4, Π_2, Π_3, and Π_4 in this order. We call this sequence the *visit sequence* of the task system. If an integer l appears more than once in the visit sequence, the corresponding processor Π_l is a *reused processor*. In this example Π_4 is reused, and each task visits it twice. The flow–shop model described earlier is therefore a special case of the flow–shop–with–recurrence model in which the visit sequence is $(1, 2, \cdots, m)$, and all processors are visited only once.

A visit sequence can be represented by a graph, called a *visit graph*. A visit graph G is a directed graph whose set of vertices $\{\Pi_i\}$ represents the processors. There is a directed edge $e_{i,j}$ from Π_i to Π_j with label a whenever $v_a = i$ and $v_{a+1} = j$ in the visit sequence $V = (v_1, v_2, \cdots, v_a, v_{a+1}, \cdots, v_k)$. A visit sequence can therefore be represented as a path with increasing edge labels in the visit graph. We confine our attention here to a class of visit sequences that contain simple recurrence patterns: some subsequence of the visit sequence containing reused processors appears more than once. We call such a recurrence pattern a *loop* in the visit sequence. The notion of loops becomes intuitively clear when we look at the representation of a loop in the visit graph. In the example shown in Figure 8, the reused processors are Π_3 and Π_4. The sub–sequence $(3, 4)$ occurs twice and, therefore, makes the sequence $(2, 3, 4)$ following the first occurrence of

$(3,4)$ into a loop. This loop is *simple* because it contains no subloop. The *length* of a loop is the number of vertices on the loop. The loop in Figure 8 therefore has length 3.

In the simple case where (1) all tasks have identical ready times, arbitrary deadlines, and the same processing time τ on all processors, and (2) the visit sequence contains a single simple loop, there is an optimal, polynomial–time algorithm, called *Algorithm R*, for scheduling tasks to meet deadlines. Algorithm R is essentially a modified version of the EEDF algorithm. We observe that if a loop in the visit graph has length q, the second visit of every task to a reused processor cannot be scheduled before $(q-1)\tau$ time units after the termination of its first visit to the processor. Let Π_{v_l} be the first processor in the loop of length q. Let $\{T_{i,l}\}$ and $\{T_{i,(l+q)}\}$ be the sets of subtasks that are executed on Π_{v_l}. $T_{i,l}$ is the subtask at the first visit of T_i to Π_{v_l}, and $T_{i,(l+q)}$ is the subtask at the second visit of T_i to the processor. $T_{i,(l+q)}$ is dependent on $T_{i,l}$ and, hence, cannot begin until $T_{i,l}$ is completed. The key strategy used in Algorithm R is based on this observation. This algorithm is described in Figure 9.

Step 1 in Algorithm R differs from the EEDF algorithm because the effective ready times of the second visits are postponed whenever necessary as the first visits are scheduled. Therefore, the optimality of

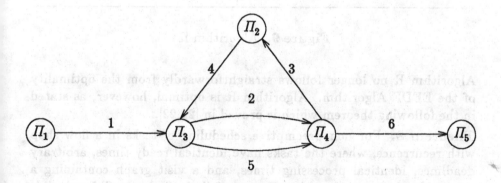

Figure 8. Visit Graph for Visit Sequence $V = (1, 3, 4, 2, 3, 4, 5)$.

Algorithm R

Input: Parameters $r_{i,j}$, $d_{i,j}$, τ, and the visit graph G.

Π_{v_l} is the first processor in the single loop of length q in G.

Output: A feasible schedule S or "**T** has no feasible schedules."

Step 1: Schedule the subtasks in $\{T_{i,l}\} \bigcup \{T_{i,(l+q)}\}$ on the processor Π_{v_l} using the modified EEDF algorithm described below: the following actions are taken whenever Π_{v_l} becomes idle

  (i) If no subtask is ready, leave the processor idle.

  (ii) If one or more subtasks are ready, schedule the one with the earliest effective deadline. When a subtask $T_{i,l}$ (that is, the first visit of T_i to the processor) is scheduled to start at time $s_{i,l}$, set the effective ready time of its second visit $T_{i,(l+q)}$ to $s_{i,l} + q\,\tau$.

Step 2: Let $s_{i,l}$ and $s_{i,(l+q)}$ to be the start times of $T_{i,l}$ and $T_{i,(l+q)}$ in the partial schedule S_R produced in Step 1. Propagate the schedule to the other processors according to the following rules:

  (i)   If $j < l$, schedule $T_{i,j}$ at time $s_{i,l} - (l-j)\tau$.

  (ii) If $l < j \leq l+q$, schedule $T_{i,j}$ at time $s_{i,l} + (j-l)\tau$.

  (iii) If $l+q < j < m$, schedule $T_{i,j}$ at time $s_{i,(l+q)} + (j-l-q)\tau$.

Figure 9. Algorithm R

Algorithm R no longer follows straightforwardly from the optimality of the EEDF Algorithm. Algorithm R is optimal, however, as stated in the following theorem which is proved in [21,22].

Theorem 8. For non–preemptive scheduling of tasks in a flow shop with recurrence, where the tasks have identical ready times, arbitrary deadlines, identical processing times, and a visit graph containing a single, simple loop, Algorithm R never fails to find a feasible schedule whenever such schedules exist.

Scheduling in Periodic Flow Shops

The periodic flow–shop model is a generalization of both the traditional flow–shop model and the traditional periodic–job model [31–34]. As in the traditional periodic–job model, the periodic *job system* **J** (previously referred to as a task system) to be scheduled in a flow shop consists of n independent periodic jobs; each job consists of a periodic sequence of requests for the same computation. In our previous terms, each request is a *task*. The *period* p_i of a job J_i in **J** is the time interval between the ready times of two consecutive tasks in the job. The deadline of the task in each period is the ready time of the task in the next period. In an m–processor flow shop, each task consists of m subtasks that are to be executed on the m processors in turn following the same order. The processing time of the subtask on processor Π_j of each task in the job J_i is $\tau_{i,j}$.

To explain a simple method that can be used to schedule periodic jobs in flow shops, we note that each job J_i in a periodic flow–shop job system can be logically divided into m subjobs $J_{i,j}$. The period of $J_{i,j}$ is p_i. The subtasks in all periods of $J_{i,j}$ are executed on processor Π_j and have processing time $\tau_{i,j}$. In other words, each of these m subjobs can be characterized by the 2–tuple $(p_i, \tau_{i,j})$. The set of n periodic subjobs $\mathbf{J}_j = \{J_{i,j}\}$ is scheduled on the processor Π_j. The *total utilization factor* of all the subjobs in $\mathbf{J}_j$ is $u_j = \sum_{i=1}^{n} \tau_{i,j}/p_i$. When it is necessary to distinguish the individual subtasks, we call the subtask in the k th period of subjob $J_{i,j}$ $T_{i,j}(k)$. For a given j, the subjobs $J_{i,j}$ of different jobs J_i are independent, since the jobs are independent. On the other hand, for a given i, the subjobs $J_{i,j}$ of J_i on the different processors are not independent since the subtask $T_{i,j}(k)$ cannot begin until $T_{i,(j-1)}(k)$ is completed. Unfortunately, there are no known polynomial–time optimal algorithms that can be used to schedule dependent periodic jobs to meet deadlines, and there is no known schedulability criteria that can be used to determine when such jobs can be feasibly scheduled. Therefore, it is not fruitful to view the subjobs of each job J_i on different processors as dependent subjobs. We consider all subjobs to be scheduled on all processors as independent periodic subjobs and schedule the subjobs on each processor independently from the subjobs on the other processors. We effectively take into account the actual dependencies between subjobs of each job in the manner described below.

For the sake of concreteness, let us for the moment give the periodic jobs in our model the following specific interpretation: the consecutive tasks in each job are dependent, that is, the subtask $T_{i,1}(k)$ cannot begin until the subtask $T_{i,m}(k-1)$ is completed. Let λ_i denote the time at which the first task $T_{i,1}(1)$ in the job J_i becomes ready. λ_i is called the *phase* of J_i; it is also the phase $\lambda_{i,1}$ of the subjob $J_{i,1}$ of J_i on the first processor. Hence the k th period of the subjob $J_{i,1}$ begins at $\lambda_{i,1}+(k-1)p_i$. Without loss of generality, suppose that the set $\mathbf{J}_1$ is scheduled on the first processor Π_1 according to the well–known rate–monotone algorithm. This algorithm is priority–driven; it assigns priorities statically to jobs (and, hence, to individual tasks in them) on the basis of their periods; the shorter the period of a job, the higher its priority. Suppose that the total utilization factor u_1 of all the subjobs on Π_1 is such that we can be sure that every subtask $T_{i,1}(k)$ is completed by the time $\delta_1 p_i$ units after its ready time $\lambda_i+(k-1)p_i$ for some $\delta_1<1$. Now, we let the phase of every subjob $J_{i,2}$ of J_i on processor Π_2 be $\lambda_{i,2}=\lambda_{i,1}+\delta_1 p_i$. By postponing the ready time of every subtask $T_{i,2}(k)$ in every subjob $J_{i,2}$ on processor Π_2 until its predecessor subtask $T_{i,1}(k)$ is surely completed on processor Π_1, we can ignore the precedence constraints between subjobs on the two processors. Any schedule produced by scheduling the subjobs on Π_1 and Π_2 independently in this manner is a schedule that satisfies the precedence constraints between the subjobs $J_{i,1}$ and $J_{i,2}$. Similarly, if the total utilization factor u_2 of all the subjobs on Π_2 is such that every task in $J_{i,2}$ is guaranteed to complete by the time instant $\delta_2 p_i$ units after its ready time, for some $\delta_2<1-\delta_1$, we postpone the phase $\lambda_{i,3}$ of $J_{i,3}$ by this amount, and so on.

Suppose that the total utilization factors u_j for all $j=1,2,\cdots,m$ are such that when the subjobs on each of the m processors are scheduled independently from the subjobs on the other processors according to the rate–monotone algorithm, all subtasks in $J_{i,j}$ complete by $\delta_j p_i$ units of time after their respectively ready times, for all i and j. Moreover, suppose that each δ_j is a positive fraction, and

$\sum_{j=1}^{m} \delta_j \leq 1$. We can postpone the phase of each subjob $J_{i,j}$ on Π_j by $\delta_j p_i$ units. The resultant schedule is a feasible schedule where all deadlines are met. Given the parameters of **J**, we can compute the set $\{u_j\}$ and use the existing schedulability bounds given in [32,33] to determine whether there is a set of $\{\delta_j\}$ where $\delta_j > 0$ and $\sum_{j=1}^{m} \delta_j \leq 1$. The job system **J** can be feasibly scheduled in the manner described above if such a set of δ_j's exists. It is easy to see that with a small modification of the required values of δ_j, this method of scheduling periodic jobs in flow shops can handle the case where the deadline of each task in a job with period p_i is equal to or less than $m\, p_i$ units from its ready time. Similarly, this method can be used when the subjobs are scheduled according to other algorithms, or even different algorithms on different processors, so long as schedulability criteria of the algorithms are known.

TASKS WITH DEFERRED DEADLINES

In the traditional periodic–job model, the deadline of every task in every job is either at or before the end of the period. Periodic jobs are typically scheduled on uniprocessor systems preemptively using some priority–driven algorithms [31–36]. A well–known example is the *rate–monotone algorithm* described in the last section. It has been shown [31] that as long as the total utilization factor U of a set **J** of n jobs is less than or equal to $n(2^{1/n} - 1)$ (that is, 0.82 for $n = 2$ and $\ln 2$ for large n), no deadline will be missed if the jobs in **J** are scheduled according to this algorithm. Because of its simplicity, it is more frequently used in practice than the *earliest–deadline–first algorithm*, which assigns priorities to tasks in jobs dynamically on the basis of their deadlines; the earlier the deadline of a task, the higher its priority. The earliest–deadline–first algorithm is optimal. Here, by an optimal algorithm, we mean one which always finds a feasibly schedule of a periodic job system **J** as long as the total utilization factor of **J** is less than or equal to 1.

We now consider a modified periodic–job model in which jobs have deferred deadlines [37,38]. Again, the workload on a single processor is a system **J** of n periodic jobs. Each job J_i consists of a periodic sequence of tasks each of which has a processing time τ_i. The utilization factor of the job J_i is $u_i = \tau_i / p_i$. The total utilization factor $U = \sum_{i=1}^{n} u_i$ of the job system **J** is the fraction of time all the jobs in **J** keep the processor busy. We refer to the task in the j th period of job J_i as $T_i(j)$. Let λ_i denote the phase of J_i. λ_i is the ready time of the first task $T_i(1)$ of J_i. The *ready time* $r_i(j)$ of the jth task in J_i is $\lambda_i + (j-1) p_i$ for $j = 1, 2, \cdots$. In the modified periodic–job model, the deadline of every task in the job J_i is deferred by an amount Δ_i beyond the end of it period. In other words, the deadline of the task $T_i(j)$ in the jth period of J_i is $d_i(j) = \lambda_i + j p_i + \Delta_i$ for some $\Delta_i > 0$. We refer to the parameters Δ_i as the *amounts of (deadline) deference*. This modified model allows us to characterize applications where the tasks in each job arrive and become ready for execution at a higher rate than the rate at which individual tasks must be completed. For example in [39], the task in one period does not need to be completed until the end of the following period. Other examples include statistical jobs [40] in which the execution of any task, if not completed in its period, is allowed to continue until completion in some subsequent period. Allowing the execution of any incompleted task to continue beyond the end of its period is a way to handle a transient overload condition. When it is not possible to complete every task by the end of the current period, it is often acceptable if the task is guaranteed to complete soon enough afterwards.

An algorithm for scheduling periodic jobs with deferred deadlines is the *modified rate–monotone algorithm*; it is based on the rate–monotone algorithm. To describe this algorithm, let us suppose that the jobs are indexed so that $p_1 \leq p_2 \leq \cdots \leq p_n$. At any time t after λ_i, there is exactly one period in each job J_i which begins before t and ends at or after t. We refer to the task whose ready time is the beginning of this period as the *current task* of J_i at t. The *old tasks* of J_i refer to those yet to be completed tasks in J_i whose periods ended before t. The modified rate–monotone algorithm is a preemptive, priority–driven algorithm which assigns two sets of priorities to the current and the old tasks on a rate–monotone basis. Specifically, priorities of all tasks are assigned according to the following rules:

(1) All the current tasks have lower priorities than all the old tasks.

(2) The priorities of all current tasks relative to each other are assigned on a rate–monotone basis. Hence, the current task of a job with a shorter period has a higher priority than the current task of a job with a longer period.

(3) The priorities of all old tasks relative to each other are assigned on a rate–monotone basis. Hence, the old task of a job with a shorter period has a higher priority than the old task of a job with a longer period. The priorities of old tasks of any job are assigned on the first–in–first–out basis.

In other words, if the execution of a task is not completed at the end of its period of arrival, its priority is raised to be higher than the current tasks of all jobs regardless of their periods.

The schedule segment in Figure 10 illustrates this algorithm. The job system **J** contains two jobs: J_1 of period 1 and J_2 of period 1.5, both with zero phase. Their processing times are 0.9 and 0.15, respectively. Therefore, the total utilization factor of this job system is one. We note that **J** cannot be feasibly scheduled using the rate–monotone algorithm if the deadlines of all tasks are at the end of their periods of arrival. However, if Δ_1 is zero and Δ_2 is 0.15, the modified rate–monotone algorithm can feasibly schedule **J** as shown by the

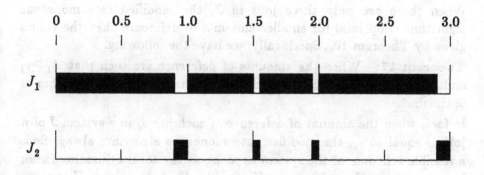

Figure 10. An Illustrating Example

segment in Figure 10. In the time interval $(0,1.5)$, this schedule is the same as a rate–monotone schedule, since there are no old tasks in this interval. At $t = 1.5$, the end of the first period of J_2, the task $T_{2,1}$ is still not completed. It becomes an old task and is, therefore, assigned a higher priority than the current tasks $T_{1,2}$ and $T_{2,2}$. It preempts the task $T_{1,2}$ and executes from $t = 1.5$ until completion at $t = 1.55$. The execution of $T_{1,2}$ resumes, and the segment from this point until $t = 3$ is again similar to a rate–monotone schedule. The optimality of the modified rate–monotone algorithm in the case of 2–job job systems is stated in the following theorem [38].

Theorem 9: Given a job system **J** containing two jobs, if the amounts of deference Δ_i are equal to or larger than τ_i for $i = 1$ and 2, the modified rate–monotone algorithm always finds a feasible schedule if the total utilization factor of **J** is less than or equal to 1. In other words, the modified rate–monotone algorithm is optimal for scheduling such two jobs.

When there are three or more jobs to be scheduled, the modified rate–monotone algorithm is no longer optimal when $\Delta_i \geq \tau_i$. It becomes optimal, however, when the amount of deference is sufficiently large. In particular, we have the following theorem [38].

Theorem 10: When the amounts of deference are such that $\Delta_1 \geq \tau_1$ and $\Delta_i \geq p_n$ for $i = 2, 3, \cdots, n$, the modified rate–monotone algorithm is optimal.

When there are only three jobs in **J**, the modified rate–monotone algorithm is optimal for smaller amounts of deference than the values given by Theorem 10. Specifically, we have the following.

Theorem 11: When the amounts of deference are such that $\Delta_1 \geq \tau_1$ and $\Delta_i \geq p_{i-1}$ for $i = 2, 3$, the modified rate–monotone algorithm is optimal.

In fact, when the amount of deference of each job J_i in a system **J** of n jobs is equal to p_i, the modified rate–monotone algorithm always finds a feasible schedule of the system as along as the total utilization factor is not greater than $U_{\max} = U_{rm}(n)(2 - U_{rm}(n))$, where $U_{rm}(n) = n(2^{1/n} - 1)$. $U_{\max}$ is equal to 0.968 for n equal to 2 and equal to 0.89 for large n.

SUMMARY

We have presented two variants of the AND/OR model and analyzed the complexity of the AND/OR scheduling problems which are not known to be NP–hard. Our analysis have shown that the complexity of a problem in scheduling AND/OR/unskipped tasks to meet deadlines is determined almost exclusively by the number of OR tasks to be scheduled and the complexity of the corresponding AND–only scheduling problem. In the problem of scheduling to meet deadlines, we have found that the problem remains NP–complete even when only OR tasks have deadlines, or when OR tasks have a fixed number of immediate predecessors, or when the dependency graphs are in–trees or in–forests. The AND/OR/skipped scheduling problems we considered were generally of higher complexity than the corresponding unskipped problems. We have shown that there are polynomial–time algorithms for scheduling two special cases of AND/OR/skipped task systems: (1) where all tasks have identical processing times, only the OR tasks have deadlines, and the dependency graph is a simple in–forest; and (2) where all tasks are OR tasks and the partial order defining the precedence constraints has a unique least element and a unique greatest element. The problem of scheduling to minimize completion time is also NP–complete for both the skipped and unskipped variants of AND/OR task systems. We have presented two heuristic algorithms that can be used to produce schedules with small completion times. One algorithm is for AND/OR/unskipped tasks that have general precedence constraints, and the other is for AND/OR/skipped tasks whose precedence–constraint graphs are in–trees. These algorithms have small running time and bounded worst–case performance. With minor modification, they can be used to schedule AND/OR task systems in which each OR task becomes ready when any number of its immediate predecessors are complete. A future direction is in scheduling AND/OR task systems that contain probabilistic OR tasks; when executed in parallel, the immediate predecessors of each probabilistic OR task have different probabilities of completing first. This variant models applications such as a parallel hueristic search where disjoint search spaces are examined concurrently and the subsequent step, the OR task, can begin execution as soon as the search in anyone of the spaces is successful.

The traditional workload model also does not adequately characterize some applications in which tasks do not have static deadlines but must be executed close in time to each other. In other words, the executions of the tasks must meet their (temporal) distance constraints. The temporal distance model presented earlier extends the traditional model by letting tasks have temporal distances which account for this type of constraint. We have been concerned with ways to schedule distance–constrained tasks non–preemptively on a single processor. The problems of scheduling distance–constrained tasks generalize the corresponding traditional scheduling problems, most of which are known to be NP–hard. Our attention has been confined to a special type of task system, known as Multi–level, Unit–time JSD task systems. An $O(n^2)$ algorithm is currently available for optimal scheduling of multi–level, unit–time JSD task systems. Natural extensions of this work include finding faster optimal and heuristic algorithms for more general types of task systems. Preemption is often allowed for tasks with distance constraints. Optimal algorithms and good heuristics are needed in the preemptive case.

We have described ways to schedule tasks with hard deadlines in three variants of the flow shop model: the traditional flow shop, flow shop with recurrence and periodic flow shop. The general problems of scheduling tasks in flow shops and flow shops with recurrence to meet deadlines are NP–complete. We have described two optimal algorithms for the special cases that are tractable: (1) scheduling homogeneous tasks with identical processing times on each of the processors but different processing times on different processors in traditional flow shops, and (2) scheduling tasks with identical ready times and processing times in flow shops with recurrence where the visit graph contains only one simple loop. We have also described a heuristic algorithm for scheduling tasks with arbitrary processing times in traditional flow shops. As a natural extension of this work, we are evaluating this heuristic algorithm. Another question that needs to be answered is whether our optimal algorithm for scheduling tasks with identical ready times in flow shops with recurrence can be generalized to handle the case when the ready times are arbitrary. We have also described a method for preemptive scheduling of periodic jobs in traditional flow shops as well as a way to determine whether a set of periodic jobs can be scheduled in a flow shop. Since there are many examples illustrating that preemptive scheduling in flow shops is usually not optimal, our preemptive method is definitely not optimal. However, since very little is known about non–preemptive scheduling of periodic jobs on a single processor, we do not expect to find a way to do non–preemptive scheduling in flow shops. Consequently, we do not expect to find a more effective method than the one described here.

Finally, we have described the modified rate–monotone algorithm for scheduling periodic jobs that have deferred deadlines. This algorithm is a static priority–driven algorithm. It is based on the traditional rate–monotone algorithm and is equally simple to implement. When the amounts of deference are sufficiently long, jobs can be feasibly scheduled on a single processor using this algorithm as long as their total utilization is equal to or less than one, that is, the algorithm is optimal. We have determined the sufficient conditions under which this algorithm is optimal.

ACKNOWLEDGEMENT

The authors wish to thank Susan Vrbsky for her comments and suggestions. This work was partially supported by the U. S. Navy ONR contracts No. NVY N00014 87–K–0827 and No. NVY N00014 89–J–1181.

REFERENCES

[1] D. W. Gillies and J. W. S. Liu, "Scheduling Tasks with AND/OR Precedence Constraints," *Proceeding of the 2nd IEEE Conference on Parallel and Distributed Processing*, Dallas, Texas, December 1990.

[2] D. W. Gillies and J. W. S. Liu, "Scheduling Tasks with AND/OR Precedence Constraints," Technical Report No. UIUCDCS–R–90–1627, Department of Computer Science, University of Illinois, September 1990.

[3] D. Peng and K. G. Shin, "Modeling of Concurrent Task Execution in a Distributed System for Real–Time Control," *IEEE Transactions on Computers*, vol. 36, no. 5, pp. 500–516, April 1987.

[4]   M. C. McElvany, "Guaranteeing Deadlines in MAFT," *Proceedings of the IEEE Real–Time Systems Symposium*, vol. 9, pp. 130–139, December 1988.

[5]   V. Saletore and L. V. Kale, "Obtaining First Solution Faster in AND and OR Parallel Execution of Logic Programs," *North American Conference on Logic Programming* vol. 1, pp. 390–406, October 1989.

[6]   P. R. Chang, "Parallel Algorithms and VLSI Architectures for Robotics and Assembly Scheduling," Ph.D. Thesis, Purdue University, West Lafayette, Indiana, December 1988

[7]   K. Kenny and K. J. Lin, "Structuring Real–Time Systems with Performance Polymorphism," *Proceedings of the 11th IEEE Real–Time Systems Symposium*, Orlando, Florida, December 1990.

[8]   P. Gopinath and R. Gupta, "Applying Compiler Techniques to Scheduling in Real–Time Systems," *Proceedings of the 11th IEEE Real–Time Systems Symposium*, Orlando, Florida, December 1990.

[9]   W. K. Shih, J. W. S. Liu, and J. Y. Chung, "Fast Algorithms for Scheduling Tasks with Ready Times and Deadlines to Minimize Total Error," *Proceedings of the 10th IEEE Real–Time Systems Symposium*, December 1989.

[10] W. K. Shih, J. W. S. Liu, and J. Y. Chung, "Algorithms for Scheduling Imprecise Computations with Timing Constraints," to appear in *SIAM Journal of Computing*.

[11] J. W. S. Liu, K. J. Lin, W. K. Shih, A. C. Yu, J. Y. Chung, and W. Zhao, "Algorithms for Scheduling Imprecise Computations," Technical Report No. UIUCDCS–90–R–1628, Department of Computer Science, University of Illinois, September 1990.

[12] M. R. Garey and D. S. Johnson, "Two–Processor Scheduling with Start–Times and Deadlines," *SIAM Journal on Computing*, vol 6, pp 416–428, 1977.

[13] M. R. Garey, D. S. Johnson, B. B. Simons and R. E. Tarjan, "Scheduling Unit–Time Tasks with Arbitrary Release Times and Deadlines," *SIAM J. Computing*, vol. 10, no. 2, pp. 256–269, May 1981

[14] M. R. Garey and D. S. Johnson, "Scheduling Tasks with Nonuniform Deadlines on Two Processors", *J. Assoc. Comput. Mach.*, vol. 23, pp. 461–467, 1976.

[15] T. C. Hu, "Parallel Sequencing and Assembly Line Problems," *Operations Research*, vol. 9, pp. 841–848, 1961.

[16] E. L. Lawler, J. K. Lenstra, A. H. G. Rinnooy Kan and D. B. Shmoys, "Sequencing and Scheduling: Algorithms and Complexity," Technical Report, Centre for Mathematics and Computer Science, Amsterdam, 1989.

[17] E. L. Lawler and J. M. Moore, "A Functional Equation and Its Application to Resource Allocation and Scheduling Problem," *Management Science*, Vol. 16, pp. 77–84, 1969.

[18] J. M. Moore, "An n Job, One Machine Sequencing Algorithm for Minimizing the Number of Late Jobs," *Management Science*, vol. 15, pp. 102–109, 1968.

[19] C.-C. Han, and K. J. Lin, "Scheduling Jobs with Temporal Consistency Constraints," *Proc. 6th IEEE Workshop on Real-Time Operating Systems and Software*, Pittsburgh, PA, May 1989. Also Technical Report No. UIUCDCS-90-1630, Department of Computer Science, University of Illinois, September 1990.

[20] Han, C., K. J. Lin and J. W. S. Liu, "A Polynomial-Time Scheduling Algorithm for Jobs with Temporal Distance Constraint," submitted for publication.

[21] R. Bettati and J. W. S. Liu, "Algorithms for End-to-End Scheduling to Meet Deadlines," *Proceedings of the 2nd IEEE Conference on Parallel and Distributed Systems, Dallas, Texas December 1990*.

[22] R. Bettati and J. W. S. Liu, "Algorithms for End-to-End Scheduling to Meet Deadlines," Technical Report No. UIUCDCS-R-1594, Department of Computer Science, University of Illinois, 1990.

[23] M. R. Garey and D. S. Johnson, *Computers and Intractability: A Guide to the Theory of NP-Completeness*, W. H. Freeman and Company, New York, 1979.

[24] M. R. Garey, D. S. Johnson, and R. Sethi, "The Complexity of Flowshop and Jobshop scheduling," *Math. Oper. Res.* vol. 1, pp. 117–129, 1976.

[25] J. Blazewicz, W. Kubiak and J. Szwarcfiter, "Scheduling Unit–Time Tasks on Flow Shops under Resource Constraints," *Annals of Operations Research*, 16, 255–266, 1988.

[26] C. M. Woodside and D. W. Graig, "Local Non–Preemptive Scheduling Policies for Hard Real–Time Distributed Systems," *Proceeding of Real–Time Systems Symposium*, December 1987.

[27] L. Sha, J. P. Lehoczky, and R. Rajkumar, "Solutions for Some Practical Problems in Prioritized Preemptive Scheduling," *Proceeding of Real–Time Systems Symposium*, December 1986.

[28] E. Lawler, J. K. Lenstra, C. Martel, B. Simons, and L. Stockmeyer, "Pipeline Scheduling: A Survey," Technical Report, RJ 5738, IBM Research Division, San Jose, CA., 1987.

[29] K. V. Palem and B. Simons, "Scheduling Time–Critical Instructions on RISC Machines," to appear in Sigplan '90.

[30] T. Gonzalez and S. Sahni, "Flowshop and Jobshop Schedule: Complexity and Approximation," *Operation Research* (1978) vol. 26–1, pp. 37–52.

[31] C. L. Liu and J. W. Layland, "Scheduling Algorithms for Multiprogramming in a Hard Real–Time Environment," *J. Assoc. Comput. Mach.*, vol. 20, pp. 46–61, 1973.

[32] J. P. Lehoczky and L. Sha, "Performance of Real–Time Bus Scheduling Algorithms," *ACM Performance Evaluation Review*, 14, 1986

[33] D. T. Peng and K. G. Shin, 'A New Performance Measure for Scheduling Independent Real–Time Tasks," Technical Report, Department of Electrical Engineering and Computer Science, University of Michigan, 1989.

[34] S. K. Dhall and C. L. Liu, "On A Real–Time Scheduling Problem," *Operations Research*, Vol. 26, No. 1, pp. 127–140, 1978.

[35] A. K. Mok and M. L. Dertouzos, "Multiprocessor Scheduling in A Hard Real–Time Environment," *IEEE Proceedings Seventh Texas Conf. Comput. Symp.*, pp. 5–1,5–12, November 1978.

[36] J. Y.-T. Leung and M. L. Merrill, "A Note on Preemptive Scheduling of Periodic, Real–Time Tasks," *Information Processing Letters*, Vol. 11, No. 3, pp. 115–118, November 1980.

[37] J. Lehoczky, "Fixed Priority Scheduling of Jobs with Variable Deadlines," *Proceedings of the 11th IEEE Real–Time Systems Symposium, December 1990.*

[38] W. K., Shih, J. W. S. Liu, and C. L. Liu, "Scheduling Periodic Jobs with Deferred Deadlines," Technical Report No. UIUCDCS–R–90–1593, Department of Computer Science, University of Illinois, April 1990.

[39] J. W. Stoughton and R. R. Mielke, "Strategies for Concurrent Processing of Complex Algorithms in Data–Driven Architectures," NASA Contractor Report No. 181657, Nasa Langley Research Center, February 1988.

[40] J. R. Ellis, "A New Approach to Ensuring Deterministic Processing in an Integrated Avionics Software System," *Proceedings of the IEEE NAECON*, pp. 756–764, 1985.

CHAPTER 5

Rate Monotonic Analysis for Real-Time Systems

Lui Sha, Mark H. Klein, and John B. Goodenough

Software Engineering Institute

Carnegie Mellon University

As a mathematical discipline travels far from its empirical source, or still more, if it is a second and third generation only indirectly inspired by the ideas coming from 'reality,' it is beset with very grave dangers. It becomes more and more pure aestheticizing, more and more purely *l' art pour l' art....*

There is grave danger that the subject will develop along the line of least resistance, that the stream, so far from its source, will separate into a multitude of insignificant branches, and that the discipline will become a disorganized mass of details and complexities. In other words, at a great distance from its empirical source, or after much "abstract" breeding, a mathematical subject is in danger of degeneration." — John Von Neumann, "The Mathematician," an essay in *The Works of Mind*, Editor E. B. Heywood, University of Chicago Press, 1957.

1. Introduction

The essential goal of the Rate Monotonic Analysis for Real-Time Systems[1] (RMARTS) Project at the Software Engineering Institute (SEI) is to catalyze an improvement in the state of the practice for real-time systems engineering. Our core strategy for accomplishing this is to provide a solid analytical foundation for real-time resource management based on the principles of rate monotonic theory. However, influencing the state of the practice requires more than research advances; it requires an ongoing interplay between theory and practice. We have encouraged this interplay between theory and practice through cooperative efforts among academia, industry, and government. These efforts include:

---

[1]This is a follow-on to the Real-Time Scheduling in Ada (RTSIA) Project.

- Conducting proof of concept experiments to explore the use of the theory on test case problems and to understand issues related to algorithm implementation in commercially available runtime systems.

- Working with major development projects to explore the practical applicability of the theory and to identify the fundamental issues related to its use.

- Conducting tutorials and developing instructional materials for use by other organizations.

- Publishing important findings to communicate results to practitioners and to stimulate the research community.

- Working to obtain support from major national standards.

The interplay between research and application has resulted in our extending rate monotonic theory from its original form of scheduling independent periodic tasks [11] to scheduling both periodic and aperiodic tasks [24] with synchronization requirements [15, 16, 19] and mode change requirements [18]. In addition, we have addressed the associated hardware scheduling support [10] [22], implications for Ada scheduling rules [5], algorithm implementation in an Ada runtime system [1], and schedulability analysis of input/output paradigms [7]. Finally, we also have performed a number of design and analysis experiments to test the viability of the theory [2, 13]. Together, these results constitute a reasonably comprehensive set of analytical methods for real-time system engineering. As a result, real-time system engineering based on rate monotonic theory has been:

- Recommended by both the 1st and 2nd International Workshop on Real-Time Ada Issues for real-time applications using Ada tasking. The rate monotonic approach has been supported by a growing number of Ada vendors, e.g, DDC-I and Verdix, and is influencing the Ada 9X process.

- Provides the theoretical foundation in the design of the real-time scheduling support for IEEE Futurebus+, which has been widely endorsed by industry, including both VME and MultiBUS communities. It is also the standard adopted by the US Navy. The rate monotonic approach is the recommended approach in the *Futurebus+ System Configuration Manual (IEEE 896.3)*.

- Recommended by IBM Federal Sector Division (FSD) for its real-time projects. Indeed, IBM FSD has been conducting workshops in rate monotonic scheduling for its engineers since April 1990.

- Successfully applied to both the active and passive sonar of a major submarine system of the US Navy.

- Selected by the European Space Agency as the baseline theory for its Hard Real-Time Operating System Project.

- Adopted in 1990 by NASA and its Space Station contractors for development of real-time software for the Space Station data management subsystem and associated avionics applications.

Many of the important results of the rate monotonic approach have been reviewed elsewhere [20, 21]. In this paper, we would like to illustrate the interplay between rate monotonic theory and practice by drawing on three examples. The first example, which is discussed in the next section, describes how this interplay influenced the developmental history of the theory itself. The second example, discussed in Section 3, outlines several issues arising from the use of the theory to understand the timing behavior of real-time input/output paradigms. Section 4 discusses the importance of considering standard hardware architectures.

2. The Development of Rate Monotonic Theory

The development of rate monotonic theory after the initial work of Liu and Layland [11] has been closely related to practical applications from its very beginning. Many of the significant results are the product of the close cooperation between Carnegie Mellon University, the Software Engineering Institute, IBM's Federal Sector Division, and other industry partners. The interplay between research and practice has guided us to develop analytical methods that are not only theoretically sound but also have wide applicability.

2.1. Selection of Rate Monotonic Theory

The notion of rate monotonic scheduling was first introduced by Liu and Layland in 1973 [11]. The term *rate monotonic* (RM) derives from a method of assigning priorities to a set of processes: assigning priorities as a monotonic function of the rate of a (periodic) process. Given this simple rule for assigning priorities, rate monotonic scheduling theory provides the following simple inequality—comparing total processor utilization to a theoretically determined bound—that serves as a sufficient condition to ensure that all processes will complete their work by the end of their periods.

$$\frac{C_1}{T_1} + \cdots + \frac{C_n}{T_n} \leq U(n) = n(2^{1/n}-1)$$

C_i and T_i represent the execution time and period respectively associated with periodic task τ_i. As the number of tasks increases, the scheduling bound converges to *ln 2* (69%). We will refer to this as the basic rate monotonic *schedulability* test.

In the same paper, Liu and Layland also showed that the earliest deadline scheduling algorithm is superior since the scheduling bound is always 1:

$$\frac{C_1}{T_1} + \cdots + \frac{C_n}{T_n} \leq U(n) = 1$$

The 31% theoretical difference in performance is large. At first blush, there seemed to be little justification to further develop the rate monotonic approach. Indeed, most publications on the subject after [11] were based on the earliest deadline approach. However, we found that our industrial partners at the time had a strong preference for a static priority scheduling approach for hard real-time applications. This appeared to be puzzling at first, but we quickly learned that the preference is based on important practical considerations:

1. The performance difference is small in practice. Experience indicates that an approach based on rate monotonic theory can often achieve as high as 90% utilization. Additionally, most hard real-time systems also have soft real-time components, such as certain non-critical displays and built-in self tests that can execute at lower priority levels to absorb the cycles that cannot be used by the hard real-time applications under the rate monotonic scheduling approach.

2. Stability is an important problem. Transient system overload due to exceptions or hardware error recovery actions, such as bus retries, are inevitable. When a system is overloaded and cannot meet all the deadlines, the deadlines of essential tasks still need to be guaranteed provided that this subset of tasks is schedulable. In a static priority assignment approach, one only needs to ensure that essential tasks have relatively high priorities. Ensuring that essential tasks meet their deadlines becomes a much more difficult problem when earliest deadline scheduling algorithms are used, since under them a periodic task's priority changes from one period to another.

These observations led members of the Advanced Real-Time Technology (ART) Project at Carnegie Mellon University to investigate the following two problems:

1. What is the average scheduling bound of the rate monotonic scheduling algorithm and how can we determine whether a set of tasks using the rate monotonic scheduling algorithm can meet its deadlines when the Liu & Layland bound is exceeded? This problem was addressed in Lehoczky et al. [9], which provides an exact formula to determine if a given set of periodic tasks can meet their deadlines when the rate monotonic algorithm is used. In addition, the bound for tasks with harmonic frequencies is 100%, while the average bound for randomly generated task sets is 88%.

2. If an essential task has a low rate monotonic priority (because its period is relatively long), how can its deadline be guaranteed without directly raising its priority and, consequently, lowering the system's schedulability? This problem led to the discovery of the period transformation method [17], which allows a critical task's priority to be raised in a way that is consistent with rate monotonic priority assignment. In addition, the period transformation method can be used to increase a task set's scheduling bound should a particular set of periods result in poor schedulability.

While these results were encouraging, the ART Project still faced the problem of scheduling both aperiodic and periodic tasks, as well as the handling of task synchronization in a unified framework.

2.2. Scheduling Aperiodic Tasks

The basic strategy for handling aperiodic processing is to cast such processing into a periodic framework. Polling is an example of this. A polling task will check to see if an aperiodic event has occurred, perform the associated processing if it has, or if no event has occurred, do nothing until the beginning of the next polling period. The virtue of this approach is that the periodic polling task can be analyzed as a periodic task. The execution time of the task is the time associated with processing an event and the period of the task is its polling period. There are two problems with this model:

- If many events occur during a polling period, the amount of execution time associated with the periodic poller may vary widely and on occasion cause lower priority periodic tasks to miss deadlines.

- If an event occurs immediately after the polling task checks for events, the associated processing must wait an entire polling period before it commences.

A central concept introduced to solve these problems is the notion of an aperiodic server [8, 24]. An aperiodic server is a conceptual task[2] that is endowed with an execution budget and a replenishment period. An aperiodic server will handle randomly arriving requests at its assigned priority (determined by the RM algorithm based on its replenishment period) as long as the budget is available. When the server's computation budget has been depleted, requests will be executed at a background priority (i.e., a priority below any other tasks with real-time response requirements) until the server's budget has been replenished. The execution budget bounds the execution time, thus preventing the first problem with the polling server. The aperiodic server provides on-demand service as long as it has execution time left in its budget, thus preventing the second problem.

The first algorithm using this concept to handle aperiodic tasks was known as the *priority exchange algorithm* [8, 23]. This algorithm was shown to have very good theoretical performance and to be fully compatible with the rate

---

[2]It is conceptual in the sense that it may manifest itself as an application-level task or as part of the runtime system scheduler. Nevertheless, it can be thought of as a task.

monotonic scheduling algorithm. However, our industry partners were not pleased with the runtime overhead incurred by this algorithm.

This led to the design of the second algorithm known as the *deferrable server algorithm* [8]. This algorithm has a very simple computation budget replenishment policy. At the beginning of every server period, the budget will be reset to the designated amount. While this algorithm is simple to implement, it turns out to be very difficult to analyze when there are multiple servers at different priority levels due to a subtle violation of a rate monotonic scheduling assumption known as the *deferred execution effect* [8, 15]. It is interesting to note that the deferred execution effect appears in other contexts. This effect is further discussed in Section 3.

This problem led to a third revision of an aperiodic server algorithm known as the *sporadic server algorithm* [24]. The sporadic server differs from the deferrable server algorithm in a small, but theoretically important, way: the budget is no longer replenished periodically. Rather, the allocated budget is replenished only if it is consumed. In its simplest form, a server with a budget of 10 msec and a replenishment period of 100 msec will replenish its 10 msec budget 100 msec after the budget is completely consumed. Although more sophisticated replenishment algorithms provide better performance, the important lesson is that with relatively little additional implementation complexity, the deferred execution effect was eliminated, making the sporadic server equivalent to a regular periodic task from a theoretical point of view and thus fully compatible with RMS algorithm.

The sporadic server algorithm represents a proper balance between the conflicting needs of implementation difficulty and analyzability. Such balance is possible only with the proper interaction between theory and practice.

2.3. Handling Task Synchronization

To provide a reasonably comprehensive theoretical framework, task synchronization had to be treated. However, the problem of determining necessary and sufficient schedulability conditions in the presence of synchronization appeared to be rather formidable [14]. The ART project team realized that for practical purposes all that is needed is a set of sufficient conditions coupled with an effective synchronization protocol that allows a high degree of schedulability. This led to an investigation of the cause of poor schedulability when tasks synchronize and use semaphores; this investigation, in turn, led to the discovery of unbounded priority inversion [3].

Consider the following three-task example that illustrates unbounded priority inversion. The three tasks are "High," "Medium," and "Low." High and Low share a resource that is protected by a classical semaphore. Low locks the semaphore; later High preempts Low's critical section and then attempts to lock the semaphore and, of course, is prevented from locking it. While High is waiting for Low to complete, Medium preempts Low's critical section and executes. Consequently, High must wait for both Medium to finish executing and for Low to finish its critical section. The duration of blocking that is experienced by High can be arbitrarily long if there are other Medium priority tasks that also preempt Low's critical section. As a result, the duration of priority inversion is not bounded by the duration of critical sections associated with resource sharing. Together with our industry partners, we initially modified a commercial Ada runtime to investigate the effectiveness of the basic priority inheritance protocol at CMU, and later, at the SEI, the priority ceiling protocol as solutions to the unbounded priority inversion problem [12].

Although the basic priority inheritance protocol solved the problem of unbounded priority inversion, the problems of multiple blocking and mutual deadlocks persisted. Further research resulted in the *priority ceiling protocol*, which is a real-time synchronization protocol with two important properties: 1) freedom from mutual deadlock and 2) bounded priority inversion, namely, at most one lower priority task can block a higher priority task during each task period [5, 19].

Two central ideas are behind the design of this protocol. First is the concept of priority inheritance: when a task τ blocks the execution of higher priority tasks, task τ executes at the highest priority level of all the tasks blocked by τ. Second, we must guarantee that a critical section is allowed to be entered only if the critical section will always execute at a priority level that is higher than the (inherited) priority levels of any preempted critical sections. It was shown [19] that following this rule for entering critical sections leads to the two desired properties. To achieve this, we define the *priority ceiling* of a binary semaphore S to be the highest priority of all tasks that may lock S. When a task τ attempts to execute one of its critical sections, it will be suspended unless its priority is higher than the priority ceilings of all semaphores currently locked by tasks other than τ. If task τ is unable to enter its critical section for this reason, the task that holds the lock on the semaphore with the highest priority ceiling is said to be blocking τ and hence inherits the priority of τ. As long as a task τ is not attempting to enter one of its critical sections, it will preempt any task that has a lower priority.

Associated with these results is a new schedulability test (also referred to as the *extended rate monotonic schedulability test*) that accounts for the blocking that may be experienced by each task. Let B_i be the worst-case total amount of blocking that task τ_i can incur during any period. The set of tasks will be schedulable if the following set of inequalities are satisfied:

$$\frac{C_1}{T_1} + \frac{B_1}{T_1} \le 1(2^{1/1}-1) \ and$$

$$\frac{C_1}{T_1} + \frac{C_2}{T_2} + \frac{B_2}{T_2} \le 2(2^{1/2}-1) \ and$$

$$\cdots$$

$$\frac{C_1}{T_1} + \frac{C_2}{T_2} + \cdots + \frac{C_k}{T_k} + \frac{B_k}{T_k} + \ \le k(2^{1/k}-1) \ and$$

$$\cdots$$

$$\frac{C_1}{T_1} + \frac{C_2}{T_2} + \cdots + \frac{C_n}{T_n} + \ \le n(2^{1/n}-1)$$

This set of schedulability inequalities can also be viewed as a mathematical model that predicts the schedulability of a set of tasks. Each task is modeled with its own inequality and there are terms in the inequality that account for all factors that impact that task's schedulability. This idea is discussed further in Section 3. The priority ceiling protocol was also extended to address the multi-processor issues [15, 16, 21].

2.4. The Requirements of the Mode Change Protocol

Potential users of the rate monotonic algorithm were uncomfortable with the notion of a fixed task set with static priorities. Their point was that in certain real-time applications, the set of tasks in the system, as well as the characteristics of the tasks, change during system execution. Specifically, the system moves from one mode of execution to another as its mission progresses. A change in mode can be thought of as a deletion of some tasks and the addition of new tasks, or changes in the parameters of certain tasks (e.g., increasing the sampling rate to obtain a more accurate result). Our dialogue with practitioners made it clear that the existing body of rate monotonic theory needed to be expanded to include this requirement. This precipitated the development of the mode change protocol.

At first sight, it appeared that the major design goal was to achieve near optimal performance in terms of minimal mode change delay.[3] However, having surveyed the complaints about the difficulties associated with maintaining the software of a cyclical executive with embedded mode change operations, we realized that performance was only part of the requirement. To be useful, rate monotonic theory must address software engineering issues as well. The requirements include:

- *Compatibility:* The addition of the mode change protocol must be compatible with existing RM scheduling algorithms, e.g., the preservation of the two important properties of the priority ceiling protocol: the freedom from mutual deadlocks and the blocked-at-most-once (by lower priority tasks) property.

- *Maintainability:* To facilitate system maintenance, the mode change protocol must allow the addition of new tasks without adversely affecting tasks that are written to execute in more than one mode. Tasks must be able to meet deadlines, before, during, and after the mode change. In addition, a task cannot be deleted until it completes its current transaction and leaves the system in a consistent state.

---

[3]The elapsed time between the initiation time of a mode change command to the starting time of a new mode.

- *Performance:* The mode change protocol for rate monotonic scheduling should perform at least as fast as mode changes in cyclical executives.

Once the mode change requirements were clear, designing the protocol was straightforward.

1. *Compatibility:* The addition and/or the deletion of tasks in a mode change may lead to the modification of the priority ceilings of some semaphores across the mode change. Upon the initiation of a mode change:

   - For each unlocked semaphore S whose priority ceiling needs to be raised, S's ceiling is raised immediately and indivisibly.

   - For each locked semaphore S whose priority ceiling needs to be raised, S's priority ceiling is raised immediately and indivisibly after S is unlocked.

   - For each semaphore S whose priority ceiling needs to be lowered, S's priority ceiling is lowered when all the tasks which may lock S, and which have priorities greater than the new priority ceiling of S, are deleted.

   - If task τ's priority is higher than the priority ceilings of locked semaphores $S_1, ..., S_k$, which it may lock, the priority ceilings of $S_1, ... S_k$ must be first raised before adding task τ.

2. *Maintainability and Performance:* A task τ, which needs to be deleted, can be deleted immediately upon the initiation of a mode change if τ has not yet started its execution in its current period. In addition, the spare processor capacity due τ's deletion may be reclaimed immediately by new tasks. On the other hand, if τ has started execution, τ can be deleted after the end of its execution and before its next initiation time. In this case, the spare processor capacity due to τ's deletion cannot become effective until the deleted task's next initiation time. In both cases, a task can be added into the system only if sufficient spare processor capacity exists.

Sha et al. [18] showed that the mode change protocol described above is compatible with the priority ceiling protocol in the sense that it preserves the properties of freedom from mutual deadlock and blocked-at-most-once. In addition, under this protocol tasks that execute in more than one mode can always meet their deadlines as long as all the modes are schedulable [18]. Since a task is not deleted until it completes its current transaction, the consistency of the system state will not be adversely affected. Finally, Sha et al. [18] showed that the mode change delay is bounded by the larger of two numbers: the longest period of all the tasks to be deleted and the shortest period associated with the semaphore that has the lowest priority ceiling and needs to be modified. This is generally much shorter and will never be longer than the least common multiple (LCM) of all the periods. In the cyclical executive approach, the major cycle is the LCM of all the periods and a mode change will not be initiated until the current major cycle completes. In addition, the mode change protocol also provides the flexibility of adding and executing the most urgent task in the new mode before the mode change is completed.

The development of the mode change protocol illustrates how the interaction between the real-time systems development and research communities guided the extension of rate monotonic theory.

3. Analysis of Real-Time Paradigms

An important goal of the RMARTS Project is to ensure that the principles of rate monotonic theory as a whole provide a foundation for a solid engineering method that is applicable to a wide range of realistic real-time problems. One mechanism for ensuring the robustness of the theory is to perform case studies. In this vein, the concurrency architecture of a generic avionics system [13] was designed using the principles of rate monotonic theory. Additionally, an inertial navigation system simulator written at the SEI [1] is an example of an existing system that was subjected to rate monotonic analysis and improved as a consequence.

Another mechanism for ensuring the robustness of the theory is to apply it to common design paradigms that are pervasive in real-time systems. Klein and Ralya examined various input/output (I/O) paradigms to explore how the principles of rate monotonic scheduling can be applied to I/O interfaces to predict the timing behavior of various design alternatives [7]. Two main topics they explored [7] will be reviewed here:

- Reasoning about time when the system design does not appear to conform to the premises of rate monotonic scheduling.

- Developing mathematical models of schedulability.

3.1. Reasoning About Time

On the surface, it appears that many important problems do not conform to the premises of rate monotonic theory. The basic theory [11] gives us a rule for assigning priorities to periodic processes and a formula for determining whether a set of periodic processes will meet all of their deadlines. This result is theoretically interesting but its basic assumptions are much too restrictive. The set of assumptions that are prerequisites for this result are (see [1]):

- Task switching is instantaneous.

- Tasks account for all execution time (i.e., the operating system does not usurp the CPU to perform functions such as time management, memory management, or I/O).

- Task interactions are not allowed.

- Tasks become ready to execute precisely at the beginning of their periods and relinquish the CPU only when execution is complete.

- Task deadlines are always at the start of the next period.

- Tasks with shorter periods are assigned higher priorities; the criticality of tasks is not considered.

- Task execution is always consistent with its rate monotonic priority: a lower priority task never executes when a higher priority task is ready to execute.

Notice that under these assumptions, only higher priority tasks can affect the schedulability of a particular task. Higher priority tasks delay a lower priority task's completion time by preempting it. Yet we know there are many circumstances, especially when considering I/O services, where these assumptions are violated. For example:

- Interrupts (periodic or aperiodic) generally interrupt task execution, independent of the period of the interrupt or the importance of the event that caused the interrupt. Interrupts are also used to signal the completion of I/O for direct memory access (DMA) devices.

- Moreover, when a DMA device is used, tasks may relinquish the CPU for the duration of the data movement, allowing lower priority tasks to execute. This will, of course, result in a task switch to the lower priority task, which requires saving the current task's state and restoring the state of the task that will be executing.

- It is not uncommon that portions of operating system execution are non-preemptable. In particular, it may be the case that portions of an I/O service may be non-preemptable.

It appears that the above mentioned aspects of performing I/O do not conform to the fundamental assumptions of rate monotonic scheduling and thus are not amenable to rate monotonic analysis. To show how rate monotonic analysis can be used to model the aforementioned seemingly non-conforming aspects of I/O, we will examine:

- Non-zero task switching time.

- Task suspension during I/O.

- Tasks executing at non-rate monotonic priorities.

From [7] we know that task switching can be modeled by adding extra execution to tasks. More specifically, let C_i represent the execution time of task τ_i and the worst-case context switching time between tasks is denoted by C_s. Then C' is the new execution time that accounts for context switching, where $C_i' = C_i + 2C_s$. Thus, context switching time is easily included in the basic rate monotonic schedulability test.

Task I/O time refers to the time interval when a task relinquishes the CPU to lower priority tasks. Clearly, this I/O time (or interval of suspension time) must be accounted for when considering a task's schedulability. A task's completion time is postponed by the duration of the I/O suspension. Notice, however, that this period of suspension is not execution time for the suspending task and thus is not preemption time for lower priority tasks.

On the surface, it appears as if lower priority tasks will benefit only from I/O-related suspension of higher priority tasks. This is not totally true. A subtle effect of task suspension is the *jitter penalty* (also known as the *deferred execution effect*), which is discussed in [7, 15, 21]. This is an effect that I/O suspension time for task τ_i has on lower priority tasks. Intuitively, I/O suspension has the potential to cause a "bunching of execution time."

Imagine the case where the highest priority task has no suspension time. It commences execution at the beginning of every period and there is always an interval of time between the end of one interval of execution and the beginning of the next. This pattern of execution is built into the derivation of the basic rate-monotonic inequality. Now imagine if this same task is allowed to suspend and spend most of its execution time at the end of one period, followed by a period in which it spends all of its execution at the beginning of the period. In this case, there is a contiguous "bunch" of execution time. Lower priority tasks will see an atypical amount of preemption time during this "bunching." Also, this "bunching" is not built into the basic rate monotonic inequality. However, this situation can be accommodated by adding an extra term in the inequalities associated with lower priority tasks. Alternatively, Sha et al. discuss a technique for eliminating the jitter penalty completely by eliminating the variability in a task's execution [21].

Another factor that affects the schedulability of a task is priority inversion. Priority inversion was first discussed in [3] in the context of task synchronization, where the classic example of so called unbounded priority inversion was described. This synchronization-induced priority inversion motivated the creation of a class of priority inheritance protocols that allows us to bound and predict the effects of synchronization-induced priority inversion (briefly discussed in Section 2).

However, there are other sources of priority inversion. This becomes more apparent when we consider the definition of priority inversion: delay in the execution of higher priority tasks caused by the execution of lower priority tasks. Actually, we are concerned with priority inversion relative to a *rate monotonic priority assignment*. Intervals of non-preemptability and interrupts are sources of priority inversion. When a higher priority task is prevented from preempting a lower priority task, the higher priority task's execution is delayed due to the execution of a lower priority task. Interrupts in general preempt task processing independent of event arrival rate and thus clearly have an impact on the ability of other tasks to meet their deadlines. Once again, additional terms can be added to the schedulability inequalities to account for priority inversion.

3.2. Schedulability Models

The preceding discussion merely offers a sample of how rate monotonic analysis allows us to reason about the timing behavior of a system. In fact, we have found that the principles of rate monotonic scheduling theory provide analytical mechanisms for understanding and predicting the execution timing behavior of many real-time requirements and designs. However, when various input/output paradigms are viewed in the context of a larger system, it becomes apparent that timing complexity grows quickly. It is not hard to imagine a system comprised of many tasks that share data and devices, where the characteristics of the devices vary. The question is, how do we build a model of a system's schedulability in a realistically complex context?

We refer to a mathematical model that describes the schedulability of a system as a *schedulability model*. A schedulability model is basically a set of rate monotonic inequalities (i.e., the extended schedulability test) that captures the schedulability-related characteristics of a set of tasks. As described in [1], there is generally one inequality for each task. Each inequality has terms that describe or model various factors that affect the ability of a task to meet its deadline. For example, there are terms that account for preemption effects due to higher priority tasks; a term is needed that accounts for the execution time of the task itself; there may be terms to account for blocking due to resource sharing or priority inversion due to interrupts; and terms may be needed to account for schedulability penalties due to the jitter effect.

An incremental approach for constructing schedulability models is suggested by [7] . The approach basically involves striving to answer two fundamental questions for each task τ_i:

1. How do other tasks affect the schedulability of τ_i?

2. How does task τ_i affect the schedulability of other tasks?

In effect, answering these two questions is like specifying a schedulability interface for process τ_i: importing the information needed to determine its schedulability and exporting the information needed to determine the schedulability of other processes. This approach facilitates a separation of concerns, allowing us to focus our attention on a single task as different aspects of its execution are explored. It is not hard to imagine extending this idea of a schedulability interface to collections of task that represent common design paradigms.[4] The person responsible for implementing the paradigm would need to determine how other tasks in the system affect the schedulability of the paradigm, and it would be incumbent upon this person to offer the same information to others. These ideas were illustrated in [7], where schedulability models were constructed for several variations of synchronous and asynchronous input/output paradigms. The analysis at times confirmed intuition and common practice, and at times offered unexpected insights for reasoning about schedulability in this context.

4. Systems Issues

The successful use of RMS theory in a large scale system is an engineering endeavor that is constrained by many logistical issues in system development. One constraint is the use of standards. For reasons of economy, it is important to use open standards. An open standard is, however, often a compromise between many conflicting needs, and provides a number of primitive operations which usually allow a system configuration to be optimized for certain applications while maintaining inter-operability. The RMARTS Project has been heavily involved with an emerging set of standards including IEEE Futurebus+, POSIX real-time extension and Ada 9x.

The RMS theory belongs to the class of priority scheduling theory. Hence, it is important to ensure that primitives for priority scheduling are properly embedded in the standards. In this section, we will review some the design considerations in the context of IEEE 896 (Futurebus+).

---

[4] For example, the client-server model for sharing data between tasks [1].

4.1. Overview of Futurebus+

The Futurebus+ is a specification for a scalable backplane bus architecture that can be configured to be 32, 64, 128 or 256 bits wide. The Futurebus+ specification is a part of the IEEE 896 family of standards. The Futurebus+ specification has become a US Navy standard and has also gained the support of the VMEbus International Trade Association and other major industry concerns. This government and industry backing promises to make the Futurebus+ a popular candidate for high-performance and embedded real-time systems of the 1990s. The important features of Futurebus+ include:

- A true open standard in the sense that it is independent of any proprietary technology or processor architecture.

- A technology-independent asynchronous bus transfer protocol whose speed will be limited only by physical laws and not by existing technology. Transmission line analysis [4] indicates that Futurebus+ can realize 100M transfers of 32, 64, 128, or 256 bits of data per second.

- Fully distributed connection, split transaction protocols and a distributed arbiter option that avoid single point failures. Parity is used on both the data and control signals. Support is available for dual bus configuration for fault tolerant applications. In addition, Futurebus+ supports on-line maintenance involving live insertion/removal of modules without turning off the system.

- Direct support for shared memory systems based on snoopy cache. Both strong and weak sequential consistency are supported.

- Support for real-time mission critical computation by providing a sufficiently large number of priorities for arbitration. In addition, there is a consistent treatment of priorities throughout the arbitration, message passing and DMA protocols. Support is available for implementing distributed clock synchronization protocols.

From the viewpoint of real-time computing, the Futurebus+ is perhaps the first major national standard that provides extensive support for priority-driven preemptive real-time scheduling. In addition, the support for distributed clock synchronization protocols provides users with accurate and reliable timing information. In summary, Futurebus+ provides strong support for the use of priority scheduling algorithms that can provide analytical performance evaluation such as the rate monotonic theory [11, 10, 15, 20]. As a result, the Futurebus+ architecture facilitates the development of real-time systems whose timing behavior can be analyzed and predicted.

In the following, we provide an overview on the design considerations. Readers interested in a more comprehensive overview of this subject may refer to [22]. Those who are interested in the details of Futurebus+ are referred to the three volumes of Futurebus+ documents. IEEE 896.1 defines the logical layer that is the common denominator of Futurebus+ systems. IEEE 896.2 defines the physical layer which covers materials such as live insertion, node management, and profiles. IEEE 896.3 is the system configuration manual which provides guidelines (not requirements) for the use of Futurebus+ for real-time systems, fault-tolerant systems, or secure computing environments.

4.2. The Design Space for Real-Time Computing Support
It is important to realize that the design space is highly constrained not only by technical considerations but also by cost and management considerations. The final specification is determined by a consensus process among representatives from many industrial concerns. The constraints include:

- *Pin count*: The pin count for the bus must be tightly controlled. Each additional pin increases power requirements in addition to increasing weight and imposing connector constraints. Many of these costs are recurring.

- *Arbitration logic complexity*: The complexity of bus arbitration driver logic is low in the context of modern VLSI technology. The addition of simple logic such as multiplexing arbitration lines for dual or multiple functions is not a recurring cost once it has been designed. The major constraint here is managerial. The development process must converge to a standard that would meet the manufacturers' expected schedules. This implies that a good idea that comes too late is of little value.

- *Arbitration speed*: Priority levels can be increased by multiplexing the same priority pins over two or more cycles. While such straightforward multiplexing of the arbitration lines will increase the priority levels without adding pins, it will also double the arbitration time for even the highest priority request.

- *Bus transaction complexity*: While specialized bus transaction protocols can be introduced for functions useful for real-time systems (such as clock synchronization), each additional transaction type can add to the size and complexity of the bus interface chips. In other words, whenever possible, existing transaction types should be used to achieve real-time functions like clock synchronization.

To summarize, support mechanisms for real-time systems must not add non-negligible overhead to either the performance or the manufacturing cost of a bus that is designed primarily for general data processing applications. However, these constraints do not have an equal impact on different support features for real-time computing. For example, while they heavily constrain the design space of arbitration protocols, they are essentially independent of the design of real-time cache schemes.[5]

4.3. The Number of Priority Levels Required

Ideally, there should be as many priority levels as are required by the scheduling algorithm, and a module must use the assigned priority of the given bus transaction to contend for the bus. For example, under the rate-monotonic algorithm [11], if there are 10 periodic tasks each with a different period, each of these tasks should be assigned a priority based on its period. The bus transactions executed by each of these tasks should reflect the task priority. From the viewpoint of backplane design, only a small number of pins should be devoted to arbitration and the degree of multiplexing for arbitration speed should be limited.

As a result, we need to find a way that can use a smaller number of priority levels than the ideal number for the rate monotonic algorithm. When there is a smaller number of priority levels available compared with the number needed by the priority scheduling algorithm, the schedulability of a resource is lowered [10]. For example, suppose that we have two tasks τ_1 and τ_2. Task τ_1 has 1 msec execution and a period 100 msec while task τ_2 has 100 msec execution time and a period of 200 msec. If we have only a single priority to be shared by these two tasks, it is possible that task τ_2 may take

---

[5]Readers who are interested in using cache for real-time applications are referred of [6].

precedence over task τ_1 since ties are broken arbitrarily. As a result, task τ_1 will miss its deadline even though the total processor utilization is only 51%.

Fortunately, the loss of schedulability due to a lack of sufficient number of priority levels can be reduced by employing a *constant ratio* priority grid for priority assignments. Consider a range of the task periods such as 1 msec to 100 seconds. A constant-ratio grid divides this range into segments such that the ratio between every pair of adjacent points is the same. An example of a constant ration priority grid is $\{L_1 = 1$ msec, $L_2 = 2$ msec, $L_3 = 4$ msec, ...$\}$ where there is a constant ratio of 2 between pairs of adjacent points in the grid.

With a constant ratio grid, a distinct priority is assigned to each interval in the grid. For example, all tasks with periods between 1 to 2 msec will be assigned the highest priority, all tasks with periods between 2 to 4 msec will have the second highest priority and so on when using the rate-monotonic algorithm. It has been shown [10] that a constant ratio priority grid is effective only if the grid ratio is kept smaller than 2. For the rate-monotonic algorithm, the percentage loss in worstcase schedulability due to the imperfect priority representation can be computed by the following formula [10]:

$$\text{Loss} = 1 - (\ln(2/r) + 1 - 1/r)/\ln 2$$

where r is the grid ratio.

For example, suppose that the shortest and longest periods in the system are 1 msec and 100,000 msec respectively. In addition, we have 256 priority levels. Let $L_0 = 1$ msec and $L_{256} = 100,000$ msec respectively. We have $(L_1/L_0) = (L_2/L_1) = ... = (L_{256}/L_{255}) = r$. That is, $r = (L_{256}/L_0)^{1/256} = 1.046$. The resulting schedulability loss is $(1 - (\ln(2/r) + 1 - 1/r)/\ln 2) = 0.0014$, which is small.

Figure 1 plots the schedulability loss as a function of priority bits under the assumption that the ratio of the longest period to the shortest period in the system is 100,000. As can be seen, the schedulability loss is negligible with 8 priority bits. In other words, the worst case obtained with 8 priority bits is

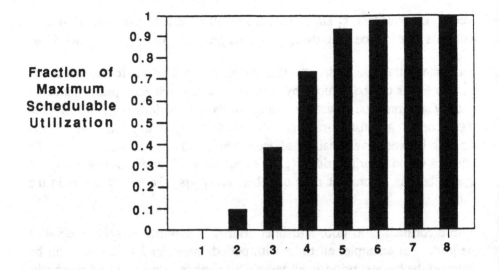

Fraction of Maximum Schedulable Utilization

Figure 1: Schedulability Loss vs. The Number of Priority Bits

close to that obtained with an unlimited number of priority levels.[6] As a result, Futurebus+ arbiters have real-time options that support 8 priority bits for arbitration.

4.4. Overview of Futurebus+ Arbitration

The Futurebus+ supports up to 31 modules. Each module with a request contends during an arbitration cycle, and the winner of an arbitration becomes bus master for one transaction. Futurebus+ designers can choose between one of two possible arbiters:

- A distributed arbiter scheme: As the name implies, the arbitration of multiple requests happens in a distributed fashion in this model. Its chief advantage is that its distributed nature tends to

---

[6]The ratio of 100,000 was chosen here for illustration purposes only. The equation for schedulability loss indicates that 8 priority bits (256 priority levels) are effective for a wide range of ratios.

make it fault-tolerant. However, the arbitration procedure is relatively slow, because the request and grant process has to be resolved over the backplane wired-or logic bit by bit.

- A central arbiter scheme: In this scheme, all requests for bus access are transmitted to the central arbiter, which resolves the contention and grants the bus to one module at a time. The obvious disadvantage is that the central arbiter could cause single point failure unless a redundant arbiter is employed. On the other hand, fault tolerance is not a major concern in workstation applications, and a central arbiter operates faster since there is no contention over the dedicated request and grant lines for each module.

The difference between the two is performance vs reliability. One can, however, combine the two schemes to achieve both performance and reliability. For example, Texas Instrument's Futurebus+ Arbitration Controller chip set, TFB2010, allows one to first operate in centralized arbitration mode after initialization for performance. If the central arbiter fails, the system can switch into the slower but more robust distributed arbitration mode.

5. Summary

The essential goal of the Real-Time Scheduling in Ada Project at the Software Engineering Institute (SEI) is to catalyze an improvement in the state of the practice for real-time systems engineering. Our goals naturally include contributing to the advancement of the state-of-the-art, but we are equally concerned with advancing the state-of-the-practice. While research is central to changing the state-of-the-practice, research alone is not sufficient. We have tried to illustrate through several examples the importance of the interplay between research and practice, which at times forces tradeoffs between solving theoretically interesting problems versus producing practicable results.

The first example illustrated this interplay by examining the rationale for selecting a research agenda. The second example illustrated several issues concerning the use of the theory in a potentially complex but realistic setting. The third example exposed the problem of having to consider the current and future technology infrastructure when attempting to push a technology from research to practice.

References

1. Borger, M. W., Klein, M. H., and Veltre, R. A. "Real-Time Software Engineering in Ada: Observations and Guidelines". *Software Engineering Institute Technical Review* (1988).

2. Borger, M.W., and Rajkumar, R. Implementing Priority Inheritance Algorithms in an Ada Runtime System. Tech. Rept. CMU/SEI-89-TR-15, ADA20967, Software Engineering Institute, April 1989.

3. Cornhill, D. "Tasking Session Summary". *Proceedings of ACM International Workshop on Real-Time Ada Issues, Ada Newsletter VII Vol. 6* (1987), pp. 29-32.

4. *Futurebus P896.1 Specification, Draft 1.0.* IEEE, 345 East 47th St., New York, NY 10017, 1990. Prepared by the P896.2 Working Group of the Microprocessor Standards Committee.

5. Goodenough, J. B., and Sha, L. "The Priority Ceiling Protocol: A Method for Minimizing the Blocking of High Priority Ada Tasks". *Proceedings of the 2nd International Workshop on Real-Time Ada Issues* (June 1988).

6. Kirk, D., and Strosnider, J. K. "SMART (Strategic Memory Allocation for Real-Time) Cache Design Using MIPS R3000". *Proceedings of the IEEE Real-Time Systems Symposium* (1990).

7. Klein, M. H., and Ralya, T. An Analysis of Input/Output Paradigms for Real-Time Systems. Tech. Rept. CMU/SEI-90-TR-19, ADA226724, Software Engineering Institute, July 1990.

8. Lehoczky, J.P., Sha, L., and Strosnider, J.K. "Enhanced Aperiodic Scheduling In Hard Real-Time Environments". *Proceedings of the IEEE Real-Time Systems Symposium* (December 1987), 261-270.

9. Lehoczky, J.P., Sha, L., and Ding, Y. "The Rate Monotonic Scheduling Algorithm: Exact Characterization and Average Case Behavior". *Proceedings of IEEE Real-Time System Symposium* (1989).

10. Lehoczky, J. P., and Sha, L. "Performance of Real-Time Bus Scheduling Algorithms". *ACM Performance Evaluation Review, Special Issue 14*, 1 (May 1986).

11. Liu, C.L., and Layland, J.W. "Scheduling Algorithms for Multi-Programming in a Hard Real-Time". *Journal of the Association for Computing Machinery Vol. 20*, 1 (January 1973), pp. 46-61.

154

12. Locke, D., Sha, L., Rajkumar, R., Lehoczky, J. P., and Burns, G. "Priority Inversion and Its Control: An Experimental Investigation". *Proceedings of the 2nd ACM International Workshop on Real-Time Ada Issues* (1988).

13. Locke, C. D., Vogel, D. R., Lucas, L., and Goodenough, J. B. Generic Avionics Software Specification. Tech. Rept. CMU/SEI-90-TR-08, Software Engineering Institute, Carnegie Mellon University, November 1990.

14. Mok, A. K. *Fundamental Design Problems of Distributed Systems for The Hard Real Time Environment*. Ph.D. Th., Massachusetts Institute of Technology, 1983. Ph. D. Thesis.

15. Rajkumar, R., Sha, L., and Lehoczky, J.P. "Real-Time Synchronization Protocols for Multiprocessors". *Proceedings of the IEEE Real-Time Systems Symposium* (December 1988).

16. Rajkumar, R. "Real-Time Synchronization Protocols for Shared Memory Multi-Processors". *Proceedings of The 10th International Conference on Distributed Computing* (1990).

17. Sha, L., Lehoczky, J.P., and Rajkumar, R. "Solutions for Some Practical Problems in Prioritized Preemptive Scheduling". *Proceedings of the IEEE Real-Time Systems Symposium* (December 1986), 181-191.

18. Sha, L., Rajkumar, R., Lehoczky, J., and Ramamritham K. "Mode Change Protocols for Priority-Driven Preemptive Scheduling". *The Journal of Real-Time Systems Vol. 1* (1989), pp. 243-264.

19. Sha, L., Rajkumar, R. and Lehoczky, J. P. "Priority Inheritance Protocols: An Approach to Real-Time Synchronization". *IEEE Transactions on Computers* (September 1990).

20. Sha, L. and Goodenough, J. B. "Real-Time Scheduling Theory and Ada". *IEEE Computer* (April, 1990).

21. Sha, L., Rajkumar, R., and Locke, D. Real-Time Applications Using Multiprocessors: Scheduling Algorithms and System Support. Tech. Rept. in preparation, Software Engineering Institution, Carnegie Mellon, Pgh., PA, 1990.

22. Sha, L., Rajkumar, R., and Lehoczky, J. "Real-Time Computing Using Futurebus+". *IEEE Micro* (To appear in 1991).

23. Sprunt, B., Lehoczky, J. P., and Sha, L. "Exploiting Unused Periodic Time For Aperiodic Service Using The Extended Priority Exchange Algorithm". *Proceedings of the IEEE Real-Time Systems Symposium* (December 1988).

24. Sprunt, B., Sha, L., and Lehoczky, J.P. "Aperiodic Task Scheduling for Hard Real-Time Systems". *The Journal of Real-Time Systems* , 1 (1989), pp. 27-60.

CHAPTER 6

Scheduling In Real-Time Transaction Systems*

John A. Stankovic, Krithi Ramamritham, and Don Towsley

Dept. of Computer and Information Science
University of Massachusetts
Amherst, Mass. 01003

Abstract

In many application areas database management systems may have to operate under real-time constraints. We have taken an integrated approach to developing algorithms for cpu scheduling, concurrency control (based both on locking and on optimistic concurrency control), conflict resolution, transaction restart, transaction wakeup, deadlock, buffer management, and disk I/O scheduling. In all cases the algorithms directly address real-time constraints. We have developed new algorithms, implemented them on an experimental testbed called RT-CARAT, and evaluated their performance. We have paid particular note to how the algorithms interact with each other and to actual implementation costs and their impact on performance. The experimental results are numerous and constitute the first such results on an actual real-time database testbed. The main algorithms and conclusions reached are presented in this Chapter.

*This work was supported by ONR under contracts NOOO14-85-K-0389 and N00014-87-K-796, and NSF under grants IRI-8908693 and DCR-8500332.

INTRODUCTION

Real-time transaction systems are becoming increasingly important in a wide range of applications. One example of a real-time transaction system is a computer integrated manufacturing system where the system keeps track of the state of physical machines, manages various processes in the production line, and collects statistical data from manufacturing operations. Transactions executing on the database may have deadlines in order to reflect, in a timely manner, the state of manufacturing operations or to respond to the control messages from operators. For instance, the information describing the current state of an object may need to be updated before a team of robots can work on the object. The update transaction is considered successful only if the data (the information) is changed consistently (in the view of all the robots) and the update operation is done within the specified time period so that all the robots can begin working with a consistent view of the situation. Other applications of real-time database systems can be found in program trading in the stock market, radar tracking systems, command and control systems, and air traffic control systems.

Real-time transaction processing is complex because it requires an integrated set of protocols that must not only satisfy database consistency requirements but also operate under timing constraints. In our work we have developed, implemented, and evaluated integrated suites of algorithms that support real-time transaction processing. In total, the algorithms that we have developed deal with the following issues: cpu scheduling, concurrency control (based on locking and on optimistic concurrency control), conflict resolution, transaction restart, transaction wakeup, deadlock, buffer management, and disk I/O scheduling. In all cases the algorithms directly address real-time constraints. The implementation was performed on a single node testbed called Real-Time Concurrency And Recovery Algorithm Testbed (RT-CARAT). This testbed contains all the major features of a transaction processing system.

As an example of the evaluation of one suite of algorithms, based on two-phase locking, we have implemented and evaluated 4 cpu scheduling algorithms, 5 conflict resolution policies, 3 policies for transaction wakeup, 4 deadlock resolution policies, and 3 transaction restart policies, all tailored to real-time constraints. We compared various combinations of these algorithms to each other and to a baseline system where timing constraints are ignored. In addition, we have studied other suites of algorithms to investigate real-time buffering, using priority inheritance in a real-time database setting, real-time optimistic concurrency control, and real-time disk scheduling. We also studied (1) the relationship between transaction timing constraints and criticality, and their combined effects on system performance, (2) the behavior of a CPU bound system vs. an I/O bound system, and (3) the impact of deadline distributions on the conducted experiments. The major observations from these experiments are presented in this Chapter. For detailed performance data the reader is referred to the referenced material.

The Chapter is organized in the following manner. We first describe our database and transaction model. We then describe the suite of algorithms we have developed to study real-time transaction processing based on two-phase locking. Extensions to the basic work that include real-time buffer management, the impact of applying priority inheritance to real-time transaction systems, and a comparison of two-phase locking with optimistic concurrency control are then presented. The main performance results are presented throughout. All of the evaluations to this point in the Chapter were conducted on the RT-CARAT testbed. In the last part of the Chapter we present two new real-time disk scheduling algorithms and their performance results. The evaluation of the disk scheduling algorithms was performed via simulation since it was impossible for us to modify the physical disk controllers on our testbed. We conclude with a summary of the results and present several open questions.

A REAL-TIME DATABASE MODEL

In our work to date we have investigated a centralized, secondary storage real-time database. As is usually required in traditional database systems, we also require that all the real-time transaction operations maintain data consistency as defined by serializability. Serializability may be relaxed in some real-time database systems, depending on the application environment and data properties [27, 29, 23], but this is not considered here. Serializability is enforced either by using the two-phase locking protocol or via optimistic concurrency control.

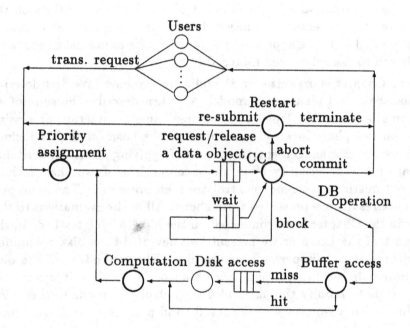

Figure 1: Real-Time Database Model

Figure 1 depicts our system model from the perspective of transaction flow. This model is an extended version of the model used in [4]. The system contains a fixed number of users that submit transaction requests separated by a think time. This model captures many applications in the real world, although certainly not all applications (e.g., an open system model is more appropriate for a process control system). For example, in an airline reservation system, there is a fixed number of computer terminals. The airline clerk at each terminal may check a flight, reserve a seat, or cancel a reservation for customers. After submitting a request to the system, the clerk waits for a result. He may submit another request after getting a response from the previous one.

In the system, any new or re-submitted transaction is assigned a priority that orders it relative to other concurrent transactions. Before a transaction performs an operation on a data object, it must go through the *concurrency control* component (CC), e.g., to obtain a lock on that object. If the request is denied, the transaction will be placed into a wait queue. The waiting transaction will be awakened when the requested lock is released. If the request is granted, the transaction will perform the operation which consists of *global buffer access*, *disk access* (if there is a buffer miss) and *computation*. A transaction may continue this "request-operation cycle" many times until it commits. At its commit stage, the transaction releases all the locks it has been holding. The concurrency control algorithm may abort a transaction for any number of reasons (to be discussed later). In that case, the *restart* component will decide, according to its current policy, whether the aborted transaction should be re-submitted or terminated.

Note that this model only reflects the logical operations involved in transaction processing and it shows neither the interaction of the processing components with physical resources nor the CPU scheduling algorithm. In practice, all of the processing components depicted by a double circle in Figure 1 compete for the CPU.

A real-time transaction is characterized by its length and a value function.[1] The transaction length is dependent on the number of data objects to be accessed and the amount of computation to be performed, which may not always be known. In this study, some of the protocols

---

[1]Note that there are no standard workloads for real-time transactions, but a value function has been used in other real-time system work [24, 1].

assume that the transaction length is known when the transaction is submitted to the system. This assumption is justified by the fact that in many application environments like banking and inventory management, the transaction length, i.e., the number of records to be accessed and the number of computation steps, is likely be known in advance.

In a real-time database, each transaction imparts a value to the system, which is related to its criticalness and to when it completes execution (relative to its deadline). In general, the selection of a value function depends on the application [24]. In this work, we model the value of a transaction as a function of its criticalness, start time, deadline, and the current system time. Here criticalness represents the importance of transactions, while deadlines constitute the time constraints of real-time transactions. Criticalness and deadline are two characteristics of real-time transactions and they are not necessarily related. A transaction which has a short deadline does not imply that it has high criticalness. Transactions with the same criticalness may have different deadlines and transactions with the same deadline may have different criticalness values. Basically, the higher the criticalness of a transaction, the larger its value to the system. On the other hand, the value of a transaction is time-variant. A transaction which has missed its deadline will not be as valuable to the system as it would be if it had completed before its deadline. We use the following formula to express the value of transaction T:

$$V_T(t) = \begin{cases} c_T, & s_T \leq t < d_T \\ c_T \times (z_T - t)/(z_T - d_T), & d_T \leq t < z_T \\ 0, & \text{otherwise} \end{cases} \qquad (1)$$

where t - current time;
s_T - start time of transaction T;
d_T - deadline of transaction T;
c_T - criticalness of transaction T,
$1 \leq c_T \leq c_{Tmax}$;
c_{Tmax} - the maximum value of criticalness.

In this model, a transaction has a constant value, i.e., its criticalness value, before its deadline. The value starts decaying when the transaction

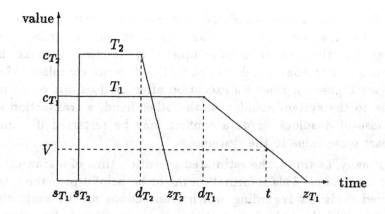

Figure 2: Value functions for transaction T_1 and T_2

passes its deadline and decreases to zero at time z_T. We call z_T the *zero-value point*. As an example, Figure 2 shows the value functions of two transactions T_1 and T_2. Note that when a transaction passes its zero-value point it is not immediately aborted because this may negatively affect the currently executing transaction. Rather, the transaction is aborted the next time the cpu scheduling algorithm attempts to execute it.

The decay rate, i.e., the rate at which the value of a transaction drops after its deadline, is dependent on the characteristics of the real-time transaction. To simplify the performance study, we model the decay rate as a linear function of deadline and criticalness. We have studied two models with z_T expressed by the following two formulas.

$$z_T = d_T + (d_T - s_T)/c_T \qquad (2)$$

$$z_T = d_T + (d_T - s_T)/(c_{Tmax} - c_T + 1). \qquad (3)$$

For a given c_{Tmax}, when c_T increases, under Eq. (2), z_T decreases, whereas under Eq. (3), z_T increases. With Eq. (2), if a transaction is extremely critical ($c_T \to \infty$), its value drops to zero immediately after its deadline. This is typical of many hard real-time systems. In this work, we use Eq. (1) and Eq. (2) as the base model, and we consider Eq. (3) as an alternative to Eq. (2).

The transactions considered here are solely soft real-time. Given the value function, real-time transactions should be processed in such a way that the total value of completed transactions is maximized. In particular, a transaction should abort if it does not complete before time z_T (see Figure 2), since its execution after z_T does not contribute any value to the system at all. On the other hand, a transaction aborted because of deadlock or data conflict may be restarted if it may still impart some value to the system.

Finally, at times, the estimated execution time of a transaction, r_T, may be known. This information might be helpful in making more informed decisions regarding which transactions are to wait, abort, or restart. This hypothesis is tested in our experiments by using certain algorithms that make use of r_T.

REAL-TIME TRANSACTION PROCESSING

Given the above system model and the characteristics of real-time transactions, one objective of our work is to develop and evaluate policies that provide the necessary support for real-time transactions. In this section, we explicitly address the problems of CPU scheduling, conflict resolution, and deadlock resolution. The algorithms for transaction wakeup and transaction restart are not presented here due to space limitations and due to the fact that these algorithms do not significantly impact performance. See [15] for a full description of all these algorithms and their performance evaluation.

CPU Scheduling

There is a wide variety of algorithms for scheduling the CPU in traditional database systems. Such algorithms usually emphasize fairness and attempt to balance CPU and I/O bound transactions. These scheduling algorithms are not adequate for real-time transactions. In real-time environments, transactions should get access to the CPU based on criticalness and deadline, not fairness. If the complete data access requirements and timing constraints are known in advance, then scheduling can be done through transaction preanalysis [5]. On the other hand, in many cases complete knowledge may not be available. Then a priority based scheduling algorithm may be used, where the priority is set based on deadline, criticalness, length of the transaction, or some combination of these factors.

We consider three simple CPU scheduling algorithms. The first two algorithms are commonly found in real-time systems, and the third is an attempt to combine the first two so as to achieve the benefits of both.

- **Scheduling the most critical transaction first (MCF)**

- **Scheduling by transaction with the earliest deadline first (EDF)**

- **Scheduling by criticalness and deadline (CDF)**: In this algorithm, when a transaction arrives, it is assigned a priority based on the formula $(d_T - s_T)/c_T$. The smaller the calculated value, the higher the priority.

Under all of these cpu scheduling algorithms, when a transaction begins its commit phase, its priority is raised to the highest value among all the active transactions. This enables a transaction in its final stage of processing to complete as quickly as possible so that it will not be blocked by other transactions. This policy also reduces the chance for the committing transaction to block other transactions. Under all three algorithms, the transactions are preemptable, i.e., an executing transaction (not in its commit phase) can be preempted by a transaction with higher priority.

Conflict Resolution Protocols (CRP)

Two or more transactions have a data conflict when they require the same data in incompatible lock modes (i.e. *write-write* and *write-read*). The conflict should be resolved according to the characteristics of the conflicting transactions. Here we present five protocols for conflict resolution.

In the following descriptions, T_R denotes the transaction which is requesting a data item D, and T_H is another transaction that is holding a lock on D. The five protocols have the following common algorithmic structure:

T_R requests a lock on the data item D
if no conflict with T_H
   then T_R accesses D
   else call CRPi $(i = 1,2,3,4,5)$
end if

We start with the simple protocols in terms of complexity and the amount of information required.

Protocol 1 (CRP1): Based on criticalness only.

This simple protocol only takes criticalness into account.

if $c_{T_R} < c_{T_H}$ for all T_H
   thenT_R waits
   else
       if $c_{T_R} > c_{T_H}$ for all T_H
        then T_R aborts all T_H
        else T_R aborts itself
       end if
end if

Note that protocol 1 is a deadlock-free protocol, since waiting transactions are always considered in order of criticalness. In addition, this protocol implements an *always-abort* policy in a system where all the transactions have the same criticalness.

Protocol 2 (CRP2): Based on deadline-first-then-criticalness.

We anticipate that criticalness and deadlines are the most important factors for real-time transactions. Protocol 2 only takes these two factors into account. Here we separate deadline and criticalness by checking the two parameters sequentially. The algorithm for this protocol is:

if $d_{T_R} > d_{T_H}$ for any T_H
   then T_R waits
   else
       if $c_{T_R} \leq c_{T_H}$ for any T_H

```
            then T_R waits
            else T_R aborts all T_H
        end if
    end if
```

Protocol 3 (CRP3): Based on deadline, criticalness and estimation of remaining execution time.

CRP3 is an extension of CRP2. This protocol takes the remaining execution time of the transaction into account in addition to deadline and criticalness. Here we assume that the computation time and I/O operations of a transaction are known and that they are proportional to each other. Then the remaining execution time of transaction T can be estimated by the following formula:

$$time\_needed_T(t) = (t-s_T) \times (R\_total_T - R\_accessed_T(t))/R\_accessed_T(t)$$

where R_total_T is the total number of records to be accessed by T; $R\_accessed_T(t)$ is the number of records that have been accessed as of time t. The protocol is as follows:

```
    if d_{T_R} > d_{T_H} for any T_H
        then T_R waits
    else
            if c_{T_R} < c_{T_H} for any T_H
                then T_R waits
            else
                    if c_{T_R} = c_{T_H} for any T_H
                    then
                            if (time_needed_{T_R}(t) + t) > d_{T_R}
                                then T_R waits
                                else T_R aborts all T_H
                            end if
                    else  T_R aborts all T_H
                    end if
            end if
    end if
```

Protocol 4 (CRP4): Based on a virtual clock.

Each transaction, T, has a virtual clock associated with it. The virtual clock value, $VT_T(t)$, for transaction T is calculated by the following formula.

$$VT_T(t) = s_T + \beta_T * (t - s_T), \quad t \geq s_T$$

where β_T is the clock running rate which is proportional to transaction T's criticalness. The higher the c_T, the larger the value β_T. The protocol controls the setting and running of the virtual clocks. When transaction T starts, $VT_T(t)$ is set to the current real time s_T. Then, the virtual clock runs at rate β_T. That is, the more critical a transaction is, the faster its virtual clock runs. In this work, $\beta_T = c_T$. The protocol is given by the following pseudo code.

```
if dT_R > dT_H for any T_H
   then T_R waits
   else
        if any VT_T_H(t) ≥ dT_H
           then T_R waits
           else T_R aborts all T_H
        end if
end if
```

In this protocol, transaction T_R may abort T_H based on their relative deadlines, and on the criticalness and elapsed time of transaction T_H. When the virtual clock of an executing transaction has surpassed its deadline, it cannot be aborted. Intuitively, this means that for the transaction T_H to make its deadline, we are predicting that it should not be aborted. For further details about this protocol, the reader is referred to [29].

Protocol 5 (CRP5): Based on combining transaction parameters.

This protocol takes into account a variety of different information about the involved transactions. It uses a function $CP_T(t)$ to make decisions.

$$CP_T(t) = c_T * (w_1 * (t - s_T) - w_2 * d_T + w_3 * p_T(t) + w_4 * io_T(t) - w_5 * l_T(t))$$

where $p_T(t)$ and $io_T(t)$ are the CPU time and I/O time consumed by the transaction, $l_T(t)$ is the approximate laxity[2] (if known), and the w_k's are non-negative weights. The protocol is described by the following pseudo code.

> **if** $CP_{T_R}(t) \leq CP_{T_H}(t)$ for any T_H
> **then** T_R waits
> **else** T_R aborts all T_H
> **end if**

By appropriately setting weights to zero it is easy to create various outcomes, e.g., where a smaller deadline transaction always aborts a larger deadline transaction. Again, the reader is referred to [29] for further discussion of this protocol.

In a disk resident database system, it is difficult to determine the computation time and I/O time of a transaction. In our experiments, we simplify the above formula for CP calculation as follows:

$$CP_T(t) = c_T * [w1 * (t - s_T) - w2 * d_T + w3 * (R\_accessed_T(t) / R\_total_T)]$$

where R_total_T and $R\_accessed_T(t)$ are the same as defined in CRP3.

In summary, the five protocols resolve data conflict by either forcing the lock-requesting transaction to wait or aborting the lock holder(s), depending on various parameters of the conflicting transactions.

Deadlock Resolution

The use of a locking scheme may cause deadlock. This problem can be resolved by using deadlock detection, deadlock prevention, or deadlock avoidance. For example, CRP1 presented in the previous section prevents deadlock. In this study, we focus on the problem of deadlock

---

[2]Laxity is the maximum amount of time that a transaction can afford to wait but still make its deadline.

detection as it is required by the remaining concurrency control algorithms.

Under the deadlock detection approach, a deadlock detection routine is invoked every time a transaction is queued for a locked data object. If a deadlock cycle is detected, one of the transactions involved in the cycle must be aborted in order to break the cycle. Choosing a transaction to abort is a policy decision. For real-time transactions, we want to choose a victim so that the timing constraints of the remaining transactions can be met as much as possible, and at the same time the abort operation will incur the minimum cost. Here we present five deadlock resolution policies which take into account the timing properties of the transactions, the cost of abort operations, and the complexity of the protocols.

Deadlock resolution policy 1 (DRP1): *Always abort the transaction which invokes deadlock detection.* This policy is simple and efficient since it does not need any information from the transactions in the deadlock cycle.

Deadlock resolution policy 2 (DRP2): *Trace the deadlock cycle. Abort the first transaction T with $t > z_T$; otherwise abort the transaction with the longest deadline.*

Recall that a transaction which has passed its zero-value point, z_T, may not have been aborted yet because it may not have executed since passing z_T, and because preempting another transaction execution to perform the abort may not be advantageous. Consequently, in this and the following deadlock protocols we first abort any waiting transaction that has passed its zero-value point.

Deadlock resolution policy 3 (DRP3): *Trace the deadlock cycle. Abort the first transaction T with $t > z_T$; otherwise abort the transaction with the earliest deadline.*

Deadlock resolution policy 4 (DRP4): *Trace the deadlock cycle. Abort the first transaction T with $t > z_T$; otherwise abort the transaction with the least criticalness.*

Deadlock resolution policy 5 (DRP5): Here we use $time\_needed_T(t)$ as defined in CRP3. A transaction T is *feasible* if $(time\_needed_T(t)+t) < d_T$ and *tardy* otherwise. This policy aborts a tardy transaction with the least criticalness if one exists, otherwise it aborts a feasible transaction with the least criticalness. The following algorithm describes this policy.

Step 1: set tardy_set to empty
       set feasible_set to empty

Step 2: trace deadlock cycle
       for each T in the cycle do
       if $t > z_T$
          then abort T
             return
          else
             if T is tardy
                then add T to tardy_set
                else add T to feasible_set
             end if
       end if

Step 3: **if** tardy_set is not empty
       then search tardy_set for T with the least criticalness
       else search feasible_set for T with the least criticalness
       end if
       abort T
       return

In general, the experimental results from the testbed indicate the following:

- In a CPU-bound system, the CPU scheduling algorithm has a significant impact on the performance of real-time transactions, and dominates all of the other types of protocols. In order to obtain good performance, both criticalness and deadline of a transaction should be used for CPU scheduling;

- Various conflict resolution protocols which directly address deadlines and criticalness produce better performance than protocols that ignore such information. In terms of transaction's criticalness, regardless of whether the system bottleneck is the CPU or the I/O, criticalness-based conflict resolution protocols always improve performance; performance improvement due to cpu scheduling predominates that due to conflict resolution;

- Both criticalness and deadline distributions strongly affect transaction performance. Under our value weighting scheme, criticalness is a more important factor than the deadline with respect to the performance goal of maximizing the deadline guarantee ratio for high critical transactions and maximizing the value imparted by real-time transactions;

- Overheads such as locking and message communication are shown to be non-negligible and cannot be ignored in real-time transaction analysis.

Real-Time Buffer Management

Data buffering plays an important role in database systems where part of the database is retained in a main memory space so as to reduce disk I/O and, in turn, to reduce the transaction response time. The principle of buffer management is based on transaction reference behaviors [20]. In terms of *locality*, there are basically three kinds of reference strings in database systems:

1. *intra-transaction locality*, where each transaction has its own reference locality, i.e., the probability of reference for recently referenced pages is higher than the average reference probability.

2. *inter-transaction locality*, where concurrent transactions access a set of shared pages.

3. *restart-transaction locality*, where restarted transactions repeat their previous reference behavior.

Buffer management policies should capitalize on one or more of these three types of locality.

Buffer allocation and buffer replacement are considered to be two basic components of database buffer management [11]. Buffer allocation strategies attempt to distribute the available buffer frames among concurrent database transactions, while buffer replacement strategies attempt to minimize the buffer fault rate for a given buffer size and allocation. The two schemes are closely related to each other and are usually integrated as a buffer management component in database systems.

In this work, we consider buffer management in real-time database systems where transactions have timing constraints, such as deadlines.

In a real-time environment, the goal of data buffering is not merely to reduce transaction response time, but more importantly, to increase the number of transactions satisfying their timing constraints. To achieve this goal, buffer management should consider not only transaction reference behaviors, but also the timing requirements of the referencing transactions.

We investigated several real-time buffer organizations based on the system structure of RT-CARAT which includes a workspace buffer for each transaction [16]. On RT-CARAT, we then implemented a global buffer in connection with a transaction recovery scheme using after-image journaling. Based on the overall system structure, we studied both real-time buffer allocation and real-time buffer replacement for the management of this global buffer which captures inter-transaction locality and restart-transaction locality.

Our basic idea for real-time buffer allocation is to distribute the available (global) buffer frames to the transactions with shorter deadlines. Let $T_i (i = 1, 2, ...n)$ be the total of n concurrent transactions in the system. The allocation scheme is described by the following algorithm.

1. sort T_i by $T_i.dl$ in *ascending* order, for $i = 1, 2, ...n$;

2. allocate the global buffer to the first m T_j's such that the following condition holds.

$$\sum_{j=1}^{m} T_j.ws \leq G\_buffer\_size < \sum_{j=1}^{m+1} T_j.ws \qquad (4)$$

The replacement policy comes into play when there are no free global buffer frames for newly fetched pages. In a real-time database environment, the replacement scheme should aim not only at minimizing the buffer fault rate, but also at maximizing the number of transactions in meeting their timing constraints. The replacement scheme considered in this study is a modification of the LRU policy. Under the real-time replacement scheme a deadline and a count of active transactions using the page, is associated with each page. The deadline represents the largest deadline value of the transactions that have accessed that page. We also define a search window which is the maximum distance from the bottom of the LRU stack which the new algorithm will traverse. The algorithm then searches the LRU stack backwards checking either if no active transaction is using the page or if all transactions using the page have now passed their deadlines. If so the page is removed. If we do not find any such page in the window, then simply remove the last page in the window.

The experimental results obtained from the testbed indicate that under two-phase locking, the real-time oriented buffer management schemes do not significantly improve system performance. With regard to global buffer allocation, we have shown that data contention is a constraint on the performance improvement of buffer management. Under data contention, conflict resolution becomes a key factor in real-time transaction processing. In addition, CPU scheduling is more important than buffer allocation, even if the system is not CPU bound. Concerning buffer replacement, we have seen that the modified LRU algorithm which deals with dealines performs no better than the simple LRU policy. Again, under data contention, it is the conflict resolution that significantly improves transaction performance. This study suggests that, given an architecture with both local and global buffers, rather than developing sophisticated real-time buffer management schemes, it is more important to improve the performance of other processing components, such as conflict resolution, CPU scheduling and I/O scheduling.

Priority Inheritance Applied to Real-Time Transactions

Priority Inheritance is a technique for dealing with soft real-time tasks that access shared resources. In this approach, a task blocked by a lower priority task imparts its priority value to the task holding its needed resource. The idea is to allow the lower priority task to finish and release its resources quickly so that the higher priority task can continue. It has been shown that this approach is effective in real-time operating systems.

The goal of this work is to investigate Priority Inheritance in real-time transaction systems. By implementing and evaluating Priority Inheritance in our testbed [17], we found that for short transactions the performance of the system using Priority Inheritance is better than using simple two-phase locking. However, when compared to a priority abort scheme (where priority inversions are avoided by simply aborting the lower priority transaction), and to a combined abort and priority inheritance scheme which we call conditional priority inheritance, the basic Priority Inheritance protocol performed poorly. The reasons that the abort policy works well are that the higher priority transaction is never blocked, and an abort occurs as early as possible, not wasting system resources. Conditional priority inheritance works well because it aborts a low priority transaction when that transaction has not executed for very long (thereby wasting few resources), but raises the priority of low priority transactions when they are near completing (again, wasting few resources and also permitting more low priority transactions to complete). Further, we found that the performance for basic Priority Inheritance is even worse than simple two-phase locking for long transactions. This occurs because Priority Inheritance increases the deadlock rate and the transactions which get an increased priority execute for too long a time for the strategy to be effective (i.e., they significantly increase the blocking time for higher priority transactions). The main conclusion is that basic Priority Inheritance is inappropriate for conflict resolution under two-phase locking, and that both simple priority abortion (best under low data contention or loose deadlines) and conditional priority inheritance (best under high data and resource contention) work very well.

Optimistic Concurrency Control

While two-phase locking is widely used for concurrency control in non real-time database systems, this approach has some inherent disadvantages for real-time systems, such as the possibility of deadlocks and long and unpredictable blocking times. In seeking alternatives of two-phase locking, we investigate the optimistic approach [22] which ideally has the properties of non-blocking and deadlock freedom. Owing to its potential for a high degree of parallelism, optimistic concurrency control is expected to perform better than two-phase locking when integrated with priority-driven CPU scheduling in real-time database systems.

In this study [18, 19], we examine the overall effects and the impact of the overheads involved in implementing real-time optimistic concurrency control. Using a locking mechanism to ensure the correctness of the OCC implementation, we develop a set of optimistic concurrency control protocols. The protocols possess the property of deadlock freedom and have the potential for a high degree of parallelism. Integrated with priority-driven preemptive scheduling, the blocking time under the proposed protocol is limited and is predictable compared with 2PL.

Our performance studies conducted on RT-CARAT show that the blocking effect caused by the locking mechanism adopted in the implementation scheme has a major impact on the performance of the optimistic concurrency control protocol. In particular, the protocols are sensitive to priority inversion, but not to resource contention (as measured by I/O utilization). Furthermore, in contrast to the simulation results from [12, 13], our experimental results show that OCC may not always outperform a 2PL protocol which aborts the lower priority transaction when conflict occurs. The optimistic scheme performs better than the two-phase locking scheme when data contention is low, and vice versa when data contention is high. The "degraded" performance of the optimistic approach becomes apparent only because we considered the implementation details and since ours is a testbed, the overheads of the implementation manifest themselves in the performance figures. The experimental results indicate that the physical implementation schemes have a significant impact on the performance of real-time optimistic concurrency control.

We also investigate optimistic concurrency control in the context of the starvation problem. Because of their higher probability to conflict with other transactions, long transactions are likely to be repeatedly restarted and thus have less chance to meet their deadline than short transactions. Instead of limiting the number of transaction restarts, as is often proposed for traditional database systems, we use length and deadline sensitive priority assignment to address the problem. We show that integrated with the proposed weighted priority scheduling policy the optimistic concurrency control approach is more flexible in coping with the starvation problem than the two-phase locking scheme.

REAL-TIME I/O (DISK) SCHEDULING

In this section, we present two new disk scheduling algorithms for real-time systems and discuss their performance. The two algorithms, called SSEDO(for *Shortest Seek and Earliest Deadline by Ordering*) and

SSEDV(for *Shortest Seek and Earliest Deadline by Value*), combine *deadline* information and *disk service time* information in different ways. While the algorithms were evaluated as part of an integrated collection of protocols for real-time transaction processing, we believe that the results can be applied to any soft real-time system that requires real-time disk scheduling.

Before describing the algorithms we make some preliminary remarks and define a few symbols. Both algorithms maintain a queue of I/O requests sorted according to the (absolute) deadline of each request. A window of size m is defined as the first m requests in the queue. Hence, we may also refer to these two algorithms, SSEDO and SSEDV, as window algorithms. Let

r_i : be the I/O request with the i-th smallest deadline at a scheduling instance;

$dist_i$: be the distance between the current arm position and request r_i's position;

L_i : be the absolute deadline of r_i.

The SSEDO Algorithm

At each scheduling instance, the I/O scheduler selects one of the disk I/O requests from the window of size m for service. The scheduling rule is to assign each request r_i, a weight, say w_i where $w_1 = 1 \leq w_2 \leq ... \leq w_m$ and m is the window size, and to choose the one with the minimum value of $w_i * dist_i$. We shall refer to this quantity $w_i * dist_i$ as p_i, the *priority value* associated with request r_i. If there is more than one request with the same priority value, the one with the earliest deadline is selected. It should be clear that for any specific request, its priority value varies at each scheduling instance, since $dist_i$, r_i's position with respect to the disk arm position, is changing as the disk arm moves.

The idea behind the above algorithm is that we want to give requests with smaller deadlines higher priorities so that they can be serviced earlier. This can be accomplished by assigning smaller values to their weights. On the other hand, when a request with large deadline is "very" close to the current arm position (which means less service time), it should get higher priority. This is especially true when a request is to access the cylinder where the arm is currently positioned. Since there is no seek time in this case and we are assuming the seek time dominates the service time, the service time can be ignored. Therefore these requests should be given the highest priority. There are various ways to assign these weights w_i. In our experiments, the weights are simply set to

$$w_i = \beta^{i-1} \quad (\beta \geq 1) \qquad i = 1, 2, ..., n.$$

where β is an adjustable scheduling parameter. Note that w_i assigns priority only on the basis of the *ordering* of deadlines, not on their absolute or relative *values*. In addition, when all weights are equal ($\beta = 1$), we obtain an approximate Shortest Seek Time First (SSTF) algorithm which converges to pure SSTF as the window size becomes large. When the window size is equal to one, the algorithm is the same as the ED algorithm. Experimentally, we have shown that the performance of the system improves dramatically over ED when a window size of three or four is chosen even when the average queue length is as high as 15.

The SSEDV Algorithm

In the SSEDO algorithm, the scheduler uses only the ordering information of requests' deadline and does not use the differences between deadlines of successive requests. For example, suppose there are two requests in the window, and r_1's deadline is very close but r_2's deadline is far away. If r_2's position is "very" close to the current arm position, then the SSEDO algorithm might schedule r_2 first, which may result in the loss of r_1. However, if r_1 is scheduled first, then both r_1 and r_2 might get served. In the other extreme, if r_2's deadline is almost the same as r_1's, and the distance $dist_2$ is less than $dist_1$, but greater than $dist_1/\beta$, then SSEDO will schedule r_1 for service and r_2 will be lost. In this case, since there could be a loss anyway, it seems reasonable to serve the closer one (r_2) for its service time is smaller. Based on these considerations, we expect that a more intelligent scheduler might use not only the deadline *ordering* information, but also the deadline *value* information for decision making. This leads to the following algorithm: associate a priority value of $\alpha dist_i + (1 - \alpha)l_i$ to request r_i and choose the request with the minimum value for service, where l_i is the *remaining life time* of request

r_i, defined as the length of time between the current time and r_i's deadline L_i and $\alpha(0 \leq \alpha \leq 1)$ is a scheduling parameter. Again when $\alpha = 1$, this approximates the SSTF algorithm, and when $\alpha = 0$, we obtain the ED algorithm.

The performance of SSEDO and SSEDV algorithms is compared with three real-time disk scheduling algorithms proposed in the literature, ED, P-SCAN, and FD-SCAN, as well as four conventional algorithms SSTF, SCAN, C-SCAN, and FCFS. See [7] for a full description of these algorithms and their performance evaluation. An important aspect of the performance study is that the evaluation is not done in isolation with respect to the disk, but as part of an integrated collection of protocols necessary to support a real-time transaction system. The transaction system model was validated on RT-CARAT.

The main performance results are as follows:

- In a real-time system, I/O scheduling is an important issue with respect to the system performance. In order to minimize transaction loss probability, a good disk scheduling algorithm should take into account not only the *time constraint* of a transaction, but also the *disk service time*.

- The *earliest deadline* discipline ignores the characteristics of disk service time, and, therefore, does not perform well except when the I/O load is low.

- The window algorithms SSEDV and SSEDO consider two factors: *earliest deadline* and *shortest seek time*. The performance results show that SSEDV consistently outperforms SSEDO; that SSEDV can improve performance by 38% over previously-known real-time disk scheduling algorithms; and that all of these real-time scheduling algorithms are significantly better than non-real-time algorithms in the sense of minimizing the transaction loss ratio. We also showed that SSEDV algorithm performs better than SSEDO, since SSEDV uses more knowledge concerning the time constraint.

- For the SSEDV and the SSEDO algorithms, increasing the window size and the proper adjustment of parameters α and β can improve system performance, but increasing the window size beyond a particular value results in only marginal performance improvement.

- For a transaction system, if the number of operational steps for each transaction is known to the system as soon as a transaction is submitted to the system, we can define step deadlines according to the transaction's deadline and its step number. Scheduling by step deadlines is shown to be better than scheduling by transaction deadlines. This result may also have implications for cpu scheduling of tasks with precedence constraints, but with a single deadline.

- When transactions' read probability or sequential access probability are high, this improves system performance. In all cases, SSEDV and SSEDO algorithms are shown to be significantly better than the other disk scheduling algorithms considered. This conclusion also holds over a wide range of transaction deadline settings. In addition, by properly arranging the layout of the database on the disk, the SSEDV, SSEDO, and ED algorithms can improve performance to a proportionally greater degree than the other algorithms.

- The average transaction response time under SSEDV and SSEDO algorithms is higher than the SSTF and all the SCAN based algorithms, but lower than FCFS and ED.

Finally, with today's technology, the disk controller can be implemented to monitor the I/O load dynamically, and select a proper scheduling algorithm accordingly. This technique can be used with our SSEDV and SSEDO algorithms in a soft real-time environment. For example, when the I/O queue length is less than a threshold, the ED algorithm (window size 1 in SSEDV or SSEDO) might be used for scheduling, otherwise the window size would be set to 3 or 4. Alternatively, we might dynamically update the scheduling parameter α or β according to a queue length threshold. Finally, almost the entire execution time cost of executing the new algorithms can be done in parallel with disk seeks, thereby not adversely impacting disk service time.

CONCLUSIONS

In our work we have taken an integrated approach to developing algorithms for real-time transaction systems. We have developed new algorithms, implemented them on an experimental testbed called RT-CARAT, and evaluated their performance. Our main experimental results are that: (1) real-time cpu scheduling, conflict resoultion, and disk I/O scheduling are the three main factors in achieving good performance, (2) various conflict resolution protocols which directly address deadlines and criticalness can have a important impact on performance over protocols that ignore such information, (3) deadlock resolution and transaction restart policies tailored to real-time constraints seem to have negligible impact on overall performance, (4) optimistic concurrency control outperforms locking except when data contention is high, (5) basic priority inheritance should not be used in a locking-based real-time database setting, (6) real-time buffer management does not provide significant gain over typical buffer management techniques when the database is supported by local and global buffers, and (7) our new disk I/O scheduling algorithms are much more effective than others currently available.

Many important open questions remain including:

- how can soft real-time transaction systems be interfaced to hard real-time components?

- how can real-time transactions themselves be guaranteed to meet hard deadlines?

- how will real-time buffering algorithms impact real-time optimistic concurrency control?

- how will semantics-based concurrency control techniques impact real-time performance?

- how will the algorithms and performance results be impacted when extended to a distributed real-time system?

- how can correctness criteria other than serializability be exploited in real-time transaction systems?

ACKNOWLEDGMENTS

We wish to thank S. Chen, J. Huang, and W. Zhao for their work on the RT-CARAT project.

References

[1] R. Abbott and H. Garcia-Molina, "Scheduling Real-Time Trans-actions," *ACM SIGMOD Record*, March 1988.

[2] R. Abbott and H. Garcia-Molina, "Scheduling Real-Time Transactions: A Performance Evaluation," *Proceedings of the 14th VLDB Conference*, 1988.

[3] R. Abbott and H. Garcia-Molina, "Scheduling Real-Time Trans-actions with Disk Resident Data," *Proceedings of the 15th VLDB Conference*, 1989.

[4] R. Agrawal, M.J. Carey and M. Livny, "Concurrency Control Per-formance Modeling: Alternatives and Implications," *ACM Trans-action on Database Systems*, Vol.12, No.4, December 1987.

[5] A.P. Buchmann, et. al., "Time-Critical Database Scheduling: A Framework For Integerating Real-Time Scheduling and Concur-rency Control," *Data Engineering Conference*, February 1989.

[6] M. J. Carey, R. Jauhari and M. Livny, "Priority in DBMS Resource Scheduling," *Proceedings of the 15th VLDB Conference*, 1989.

[7] S. Chen, J. Stankovic, J. Kurose, and D. Towsley, "Performance Evaluation of Two New Disk Scheduling Algorithms for Real-Time Systems," *submitted for publication*, August, 1990.

[8] S. Chen, and D. Towsley, "Performance of a Mirrored Disk in a Real-Time Transaction System," to appear *Proc. 1991 ACM SIG-METRICS*, May 1991.

[9] U. Dayal, et. al., "The HiPAC Project: Combining Active Database and Timing Constraints," *ACM SIGMOD Record*, March 1988.

[10] U. Dayal, "Active Database Management Systems," *Proceedings of the 3rd International Conference on Data and Knowledge Man-agement*, June 1988.

[11] W. Effelsberg and T. Haerder, "Principles of Database Buffer Management," *ACM Transactions on Database Systems*, Vol.9, No.4, December 1984.

[12] J. R. Haritsa, M.J. Carey and M. Livny, "On Being Optimistic about Real-Time Constraints," PODS, 1990.

[13] J. R. Haritsa, M.J. Carey and M. Livny, "Dynamic Real-Time Optimistic Concurrency Control," *Proceedings of the 11th Real-Time Systems Symposium*, Dec. 1990.

[14] M. Hsu, R. Ladin and D.R. McCarthy, "An Execution Model for Active Database Management Systems," *Proceedings of the 3rd International Conference on Data and Knowledge Management*, June 1988.

[15] J. Huang, J. Stankovic, D. Towsley, and K. Ramamritham, "Experimental Evaluation of Real-Time Transaction Processing," *Proc. Real-Time System Symposium*, Dec. 1989.

[16] J. Huang and J. Stankovic, "Real-Time Buffer Management," COINS TR 90-65, August 1990.

[17] J. Huang, J. Stankovic, D. Towsley, and K. Ramamritham, "Priority Inheritance Under Two-Phase Locking," submitted for publication, Dec. 1990.

[18] J. Huang and J.A. Stankovic, "Concurrency Control in Real-Time Database Systems: Optimistic Scheme vs. Two-Phase Locking," *A Technical Report, COINS 90-66*, University of Massachusetts, July 1990.

[19] J. Huang, J.A. Stankovic, K. Ramamritham and D. Towsley, "Performance Evaluation of Real-Time Optimistic Concurrency Control Schemes," submitted for publication *VLDB*, also appears as *A Technical Report, COINS 91-16*, University of Massachusetts, Feb. 1991.

[20] J. P. Kearns and S. DeFazio, "Diversity in Database Reference Behavior," *Performance Evaluation Review*, Vol.17, No.1, May 1989.

[21] W. Kohler and B.P. Jenq, "CARAT: A Testbed for the Performance Evaluation of Distributed Database Systems," *Proc. of the Fall Joint Computer Conference*, IEEE Computer Society and ACM, Dallas Texas, November 1986.

[22] H. T. Kung and J.T. Robinson, "On Optimistic Methods for Concurrency Control," *ACM Transactions on Database Systems, Vol.6, No.2,* June 1981.

[23] K. J. Lin, "Consistency Issues in Real-Time Database Systems," *Proceedings of the 22nd Hawaii International Conference on System Sciences,* January 1989.

[24] C. D. Locke, "Best-Effort Decision Making for Real-Time Scheduling," *Ph.D. Dissertation,* Canegie-Mellon University, 1986.

[25] G. M. Sacco and M. Schkolnick, "Buffer Management in Relational Database Systems," *ACM Transaction on Database Systems,* Vol.11, No.4, December 1986.

[26] L. Sha, R. Rajkumar and J.P. Lehoczky, "Concurrency Control for Distributed Real-Time Databases," *ACM SIGMOD Record,* March 1988.

[27] S. H. Son, "Using Replication for High Performance Database Support in Distributed Real-Time Systems," *Proceedings of the 8th Real-Time Systems Symposium,* December 1987.

[28] S. H. Son and C.H. Chang, "Priority-Based Scheduling in Real-Time Database Systems," *Proceedings of the 15th VLDB Conference,* 1989.

[29] J. A. Stankovic and W. Zhao, "On Real-Time Transactions," *ACM SIGMOD Record,* March 1988.

CHAPTER 7

Concurrency Control in Real-Time Database Systems

Sang H. Son, Yi Lin, and Robert P. Cook

Department of Computer Science
University of Virginia
Charlottesville, Virginia 22903

ABSTRACT

The design and implementation of real-time database systems presents many new and challenging problems. Compared with traditional databases, real-time database systems have a distinct feature: they must satisfy timing constraints associated with transactions. Transactions in real-time database systems should be scheduled considering both data consistency and timing constraints. In addition, a real-time database system must adapt to changes in the operating environment and guarantee the completion of critical transactions. In this paper, we address some of the issues associated with scheduling and concurrency control for real-time database systems, and present an optimistic algorithm for priority-based locking.

INTRODUCTION

Real-time database systems (RTDBS) are transaction processing systems where transactions have explicit timing constraints. Typically, a timing constraint is expressed in the form of a *deadline*, a certain time in the future by which a transaction must complete its execution. RTDBS are becoming increasingly important in a wide range of applications, such as computer integrated manufacturing, aerospace, traffic control systems, nuclear power plants, robotics, military command and control applications, and program trading in the stock market.

This work was supported in part by ONR contract # N00014-88-K-0245 and by IBM Federal Systems Division.

In RTDBS, the correctness of transaction processing depends not only on maintaining consistency constraints and producing correct results but also on the time at which a transaction is completed. Transactions must be scheduled in such a way that they can be completed before their corresponding deadlines expire. For example, both the update and query operations on the tracking data for a missile must be processed within a given deadline: otherwise, the information provided could be of little value.

While traditional real-time systems research has been focused on providing a high degree of predictability in task scheduling, the problem of integrating transaction processing capabilities with timing and consistency constraints has not received much attention. Researchers identified the need for basic research in database systems that satisfy timing constraints in collecting, updating, and retrieving shared data, since traditional data models and databases are not adequate for time-critical applications. Very few conventional database systems allow users to specify or ensure timing constraints. Interest in the time-critical application domain is growing also in database community. Recently, a number of research results have appeared in the literature [1, 2, 4, 5, 7, 8, 9, 10, 11, 12, 14, 15, 17, 19, 20, 21].

It is useful to categorize transactions in RTDBS as *hard* or *soft* transactions [14]. We define hard real-time transactions as those transactions whose timing constraints must be guaranteed. Missing deadlines of this type of transaction may result in catastrophic consequences. In contrast, soft real-time transactions have timing constraints, but there may still be some justification in completing the transactions after their deadlines. Catastrophic consequences do not result if soft real-time transactions miss their deadlines. Soft real-time transactions are scheduled taking into account their timing requirements, but they are not guaranteed to make their deadlines. There are many real-time systems that need database support for both types of transactions.

Conventional database systems are typically not used in real-time applications due to two inadequacies: poor performance and lack of predictability. In conventional database systems, transaction processing requires access to a database stored on secondary storage; thus transaction response time is limited by disk access delays, which can be in the order of milliseconds. Still these databases are fast enough for traditional applications in which a response time of a few seconds is often acceptable to human users. However, those systems may not be able to provide a response fast enough for high-performance real-time applications. One approach to achieve high performance is to replace slow devices (e.g., a disk) by a high speed version (e.g., a large RAM). Another alternative is to use application-specific knowledge to increase the degree of concurrency. For example, by exploiting the semantic information associated with transactions and data, we may use the notion of correctness different from serializability. As observed by Bernstein [3], serializability may be too strong as a correctness criterion for concurrency control in database systems with timing constraints, because of the limitation on concurrency. If necessary, data consistency might be compromised to satisfy timing constraints.

In terms of predictability, current database systems do not schedule transactions to meet response-time requirements and they commonly lock data to assure consistency. Locks and time-driven scheduling are basically incompatible. Low priority transactions may block higher priority transactions, leading to timing requirement failures. Consequently, the requirements and design objectives of real-time database systems differ widely from those of conventional database systems. New techniques are necessary to manage database consistency. They should be compatible with time-driven scheduling, and meet the system response times and temporal consistency requirements. A natural question is how a conventional database system must be modified so that its performance and predictability can be guaranteed for real-time applications [19].

In RTDBS, the timeliness of a transaction is usually combined with its criticalness to calculate the priority of the transaction. Therefore, proper management of priorities and conflict resolution in real-time transaction scheduling are essential for predictability and responsiveness of RTDBS.

While the theories of concurrency control in database systems and real-time task scheduling have both advanced, little attention has been paid to the interaction between concurrency control protocols and real-time scheduling algorithms [22]. In database concurrency control, meeting the deadline is typically not addressed. The objective is to provide a high degree of concurrency and thus faster average response time without violating data consistency. In real-time scheduling, on the other hand, it is customary to assume that tasks are independent, or that the time spent synchronizing their access to shared data is negligible compared with execution time. The objective here is to maximize resources, such as CPU utilization, subject to meeting timing constraints. Data consistency is not a consideration in real-time scheduling, and hence the problem of guaranteeing the consistency of shared data is ignored. In addition, conventional real-time systems assume advance knowledge of the resource and data requirements of programs.

One of the challenges of RTDBS is the creation of a unified theory for real-time scheduling and concurrency control protocols that maximizes both concurrency and resource utilization subject to three constraints: data consistency, transaction correctness, and transaction deadlines. Several recent projects have integrated real-time constraints with database technology to facilitate efficient and correct management of timing constraints in RTDBS

[4, 14, 17, 20, 21].

There are several difficulties in achieving the integration. A database access operation, for example, takes a highly variable amount of time depending on whether disk I/O, logging, buffering, etc. are required. Furthermore, concurrency control may cause aborts or delays of indeterminate length. In this paper, we address some of the issues associated with real-time scheduling and concurrency control, and present a new optimistic protocol for priority-based locking.

SCHEDULING AND CONCURRENCY CONTROL

The goal of scheduling in RTDBS is twofold: to meet timing constraints and to enforce data consistency. Real-time task scheduling methods can be extended for real-time transaction scheduling, yet concurrency control protocols are still needed for operation scheduling to maintain data consistency. However, the integration of the two mechanisms in RTDBS is not straightforward. The general approach is to utilize existing concurrency control protocols, especially two-phase locking (2PL) [3], and to apply time-critical transaction scheduling methods that favor more urgent transactions [1, 11, 16]. Such approaches have the inherent disadvantage of being limited by the concurrency control protocol upon which they depend, since all existing concurrency control protocols synchronize concurrent data access of transactions by a combination of two measures: blocking and roll-backs of transactions. Both are barriers to meeting time-critical schedules.

Concurrency control protocols induce a serialization order among conflicting transactions. In non-real-time concurrency control protocols, timing constraints are not a factor in the construction of this order. This is obviously a drawback for RTDBS. For example, with the 2PL protocol, the serialization order is dynamically constructed and corresponds to the order in which conflicting transactions access shared data. In other words, the serialization order is bound to the past execution history with no flexibility. When a transaction T_H with a higher priority requests an exclusive lock which is being held by another transaction, T_L, with a lower priority, the only choices are either aborting T_L or letting T_H wait for T_L. Neither choice is satisfactory. The conservative 2PL uses blocking, but in RTDBS, blocking may cause *priority inversion*. Priority inversion is said to occur when a high priority transaction is blocked by lower priority transactions [11]. The alternative is to abort low priority transactions when priority inversion occurs. This wastes the work done by the aborted transactions and in turn also has a negative effect on time-critical scheduling. Various scheduling policies with lock-based concurrency control mechanisms for real-time transactions have been investigated in [1, 2].

The priority ceiling protocol, which was initially developed as a task scheduling protocol for real-time operating systems, has been extended to RTDBS [12]. It is based on 2PL and employs only blocking, but not roll-back, to solve conflicts. This is a conservative approach. For conventional database systems, it has been shown that optimal performance may be achieved by compromising blocking and roll-back [23]. For RTDBS, we may expect similar results. Aborting a few low priority transactions and restarting them later may allow high priority transactions to meet their deadlines, resulting in improved system performance. A drawback of the priority ceiling protocol is that it requires knowledge of all transactions that will be executed in the future. This is too harsh a condition for most database systems to satisfy.

For a concurrency control protocol to accommodate the timeliness of transactions, the serialization order it produces should reflect the priority of transactions [18]. However, this is often hindered by the past execution history of transactions. For example, a higher priority transaction may have no way to precede a lower priority transaction in the serialization order due to previous conflicts. The result is that either the lower priority transaction has to be aborted or the high priority transaction suffers blocking. If the information about data requirements and execution time of each transaction is available beforehand, off-line analysis can be performed to avoid conflicts [12]. This is exactly what is done in many real-time task scheduling protocols. However, such approaches may delay the starting of some transactions, even if they have high priorities, and may reduce the concurrency level in the system. This, in return, may lead to the violation of the timing constraints and degrade system performance [17].

What we need is a concurrency control algorithm that allows transactions to meet the timing constraints as much as possible without reducing the concurrency level of the system in the absence of any *a priori* information [19]. The algorithm presented in the next section meets these goals. It has the flavor of both locking and optimistic methods. Transactions write into the database only after they are committed. By using a priority-dependent locking protocol, the serialization order of active transactions is adjusted dynamically, making it possible for transactions with higher priorities to be executed first so that higher priority transactions are never blocked by uncommitted lower priority transactions, while lower priority transactions may not have to be aborted even in face of conflicting operations. The adjustment of the serialization order can be viewed as a mechanism to support time-critical scheduling. For example, T_1 and T_2 are two transactions with T_1 having a higher priority. T_2 writes a data object x before T_1 reads it. In 2PL, even in the absence of any other conflicting operations between these two transactions, T_1 has to either abort T_2 or be blocked until T_2 releases the write lock. That is because the serialization order $T_2 \rightarrow T_1$ is already determined by the past execution history. T_1 can never precede T_2 in the serialization order. In our algorithm, when such conflict occurs, the serialization order of the two transactions will be adjusted in favor of T_1, i.e. $T_1 \rightarrow T_2$, and neither is T_1 blocked nor is T_2 aborted. In addition, the algorithm is free from deadlocks.

THE ALGORITHM

The environment we assume for the implementation is a single processor with randomly arriving transactions. Each transaction is assigned an *initial priority* and a *start-timestamp* when it is submitted to the system. The initial priority can be based on the deadline and the criticality of the transaction. The start-timestamp is appended to the initial priority to form the *actual priority* that is used in scheduling. When we refer to the priority of a transaction, we always mean the actual priority with the start-timestamp appended. Since the start-timestamp is unique, so is the priority of each transaction. The priority of transactions with the same initial priority is distinguished by their start-timestamps.

All transactions that can be scheduled are placed in a ready queue, R_Q. Only transactions in R_Q are scheduled for execution. When a transaction is *blocked*, it is removed from R_Q. When a transaction is *unblocked*, it is inserted into R_Q again, but may still be waiting to be assigned the CPU. A transaction is said to be *suspended* when it is not executing, but still in R_Q. When a transaction is doing I/O operation, it is blocked. Once it completes, it is usually unblocked. The CPU scheduling policy will be discussed in the next section.

The execution of each transaction is divided into three phases: the read phase, the wait phase and the write phase. This is similar to optimistic methods [6]. During the read phase, a transaction reads from the database and writes to its local workspace. After it completes, it waits for its chance to commit in the wait phase. If it is committed, it switches into the write phase during which all its updates are made permanent in the database. A transaction in any of the three phases is called *active*. If an active transaction is in the write phase, then it is committed and writing into the database. The proposed algorithm integrates schedulers in that it uses 2PL for read-write conflicts and the Thomas' Write Rule (TWR) for write-write conflicts. The TWR *ignores* a write request that has arrived late, rather than *rejecting* it [3]. The following is the outline of a transaction:

```
transaction = { tbegin();
                read phase;
                twait();
                twrite();
              }.
```

Each procedure will be described in detail later in this section.

In our algorithm, there are various data structures that need to be read and updated in a consistent manner. Therefore we use critical sections to group the various data structures to allow maximum concurrency. We also assume that each assignment statement involving global data is executed atomically. The following are some useful notations:

read_trset:	set of transactions in the read phase
wait_trset:	set of transactions in the wait phase
write_trset:	set of transactions in the write phase
s_count:	serialization order count
ts(T):	final-timestamp of transaction T
priority(T):	priority value of transaction T
$r_i[x]$:	transaction i reads data object x.
$w_i[x]$:	transaction i writes data object x.
$pw_i[x]$:	transaction i prewrites data object x.
rlock(T,x):	transaction T holds a read lock on data object x
wlock(T,x):	transaction T holds a write lock on data object x

Read Phase

The read phase is the normal execution of a transaction except that write operations are performed on private data copies in the local workspace of the transaction instead of on data objects in the database. We call such write operations *prewrites*. One advantage of this prewrite operation is that when a transaction is aborted, all that has to be done for recovery is to simply discard the data in its local workspace. No rollback is needed because no changes have been made in the database.

The read-prewrite or prewrite-read conflicts between active transactions are synchronized during this phase by a priority-based locking protocol. Before a transaction can perform a read (resp. prewrite) operation on a data object, it must obtain the read (resp. write) lock on that data object first. If a transaction reads a data object that has been written by itself, it gets the private copy in its own workspace and no read lock is needed. In the rest of the paper, when we refer to read operations, we exclude such read operations because they do not induce any dependencies among transactions.

Each lock contains the priority of the transaction holding the lock as well as other usual information such as the lock holder id and the lock type (read/write), etc. The locking protocol is based on the principle that higher priority transactions should complete before lower priority transactions. That means if two transactions conflict, the higher priority transaction should precede the lower priority transaction in the serialization order. Using an appropriate CPU scheduling policy for RTDBS such as the one discussed in the next section, a high priority transaction can be scheduled to commit before a low priority transaction most of the time. If a low priority transaction does complete before a high priority transaction, it is required to wait until it is sure that its commitment will not cause the abortion of a higher priority transaction. Since transactions do not write into the database during the read phase, write-write conflicts need not be considered here.

Suppose active transaction T_1 has higher priority than active transaction T_2. We have four possible conflicts and the transaction dependencies they require in the serialization order as follows:

(1) $r_{T_1}[x]$, $pw_{T_2}[x]$ => $T_1 \rightarrow T_2$

(2) $pw_{T_1}[x]$, $r_{T_2}[x]$ => $T_1 \rightarrow T_2$
                                   (delayed reading)
                                     or
                                 $T_2 \rightarrow T_1$
                            (immediate reading)

(3) $r_{T_2}[x]$, $pw_{T_1}[x]$ => $T_2 \rightarrow T_1$

(4) $pw_{T_2}[x]$, $r_{T_1}[x]$ => $T_1 \rightarrow T_2$
                                     (immediate reading)
                                     or
                                 $T_2 \rightarrow T_1$
                            (delayed reading)

Case (1) meets the principle of completing high priority transactions before low priority ones. To follow the principle in case (2), we should choose delayed reading, i.e. T_2 should not read x until T_1 has committed and written x in the database. Case (3) violates our principle. In this case, unless it is already committed, T_2 is usually aborted because otherwise T_2 must commit before T_1 and thus will block T_1. However, if T_2 has already finished its work, i.e. in the wait phase, we should avoid aborting it because aborting a transaction which has completed its work imposes a considerable penalty on system performance. In the meantime, we still do not want T_1 to be blocked by T_2. Therefore when such conflict occurs and T_2 is in the wait phase, we do not abort T_2 until T_1 is committed, hoping that T_2 may get a chance to commit before T_1 commits. In case (4), if T_2 is already committed and in the write phase, we should delay T_1 so that it reads x after T_2 writes it. This blocking is not a serious problem for T_1 because T_2 is already in the write phase and is expected to finish writing x soon. T_1 can read x as soon as T_2 finishes writing x in the database, not necessarily after T_2 completes the whole write phase. Therefore T_1 will not be blocked for a long time. Otherwise, if T_2 is not committed yet, i.e. either in the read phase or in the wait phase, T_1 should read x immediately because that is in accordance with the principle.

As transactions are being executed and conflicting operations occur, all the information about the induced dependencies in the serialization order needs to be retained. To do this, we associate with each transaction two sets, *before_trset* and *after_trset*, and a count, *before_cnt*. The set *before_trset* (resp. *after_trset*) contains all the active lower priority transactions that must precede (resp. follow) this transaction in the serialization order. *before_cnt* is the number of the higher priority transactions that precede this transaction in the serialization order. When a conflict occurs between two transactions, their dependency is set and their values of *before_trset*, *after_trset*, and *before_cnt* will be changed correspondingly.

By summarizing what we discussed above, we define the locking protocol as follows:

LP1.   Transaction T requests a read lock on data object x.

        for *all transactions t with wlock(t,x)* **do**
          if *(priority (t) > priority (T)*
            or *t is in write phase)*
                /* Case 2, 4 */
        then *deny the request and* **exit;**
        endif
       enddo
       for *all transactions t with wlock(t,x)* **do**
                /* Case 4 */
       if *t is in before_trset$_T$* **then** *abort t;*
       else if *(t is not in after_trset$_T$)*
         then
            include t in after_trset$_T$;
            before_cnt$_t$:= before_cnt$_t$ + 1;
         endif
       endif

```
        enddo
        grant the lock;


LP2.    Transaction T requests a write lock on data object x.
        for all transactions t with rlock(t,x) do
            if priority (t) > priority (T)
            then  /* Case 1 */
                if (T is not in after_trset_t)
                then
                    include t in after_trset_t;
                    before_cnt_T := before_cnt_T + 1;
                endif
            else
                if t is in wait phase   /* Case 3 */
                then
                    if (t is in after_trset_T)
                            then  abort t;
                    else
                        include t in before_trset_T;
                    endif
                else  if  t is in read phase
                        then  abort t;
                    endif
                endif
            endif
        enddo
        grant the lock;
```

LP1 and LP2 are actually two procedures of the lock manager that are executed when a lock is requested. When a lock is denied due to a conflicting lock, the request is suspended until that conflicting lock is released. Then the locking protocol is invoked once again from the very beginning to decided whether the lock can be granted now. Fig. 1 shows the lock compatibility tables in which the compatibilities are expressed by possible actions taken when conflicts occur. The compatibility depends on the priorities of the transactions holding and requesting the lock and the phase of the lock holder as well as the lock types. Even with the same lock types, different actions may be taken, depending on the priorities of the lock holder and the lock requester. Therefore a table entry may have more than one block reflecting the different possible actions.

lock requested	lock held	
	read	write
read		▨
write		

lock requester has lower priority

lock requested	lock held	
	read	write
read		▨ ■
write		■

lock requester has higher priority

☐	lock granted
▨	lock requester blocked
■	lock holder aborted

Figure 1. Lock Compatibility Table

lock requested	lock held	
	read	write
read		▨
write	▨	▨

lock requester has lower priority

lock requested	lock held	
	read	write
read		■
write	■	■

lock requester has higher priority

Figure 2. Lock Compatibility Table of 2PL

With our locking protocol, a data object may be both read locked and write locked by several transactions simultaneously. Unlike 2PL, locks are not classified simply as shared locks and exclusive locks. Fig. 2 summarizes the lock compatibility of 2PL with the *High Priority* scheme in which high priority transactions never block for a lock held by a low priority transaction [1]. By comparing Fig. 1 with Fig. 2, it is obvious that our locking protocol is much more flexible, and thus incurs less blocking and fewer aborts. Note that in Fig. 1, aborting low priority transactions in the wait phase is also included. In our locking protocol, a high priority transaction is never blocked or aborted due to conflict with an uncommitted lower priority transaction. The probability of aborting a lower priority transaction should be less than that in 2PL under the same conditions. An analytical model may be used to estimate the exact probability, but that is beyond the scope of this paper.

Transactions are released for execution as soon as they arrive. The following procedure is executed when a transaction T is started:

```
tbegin = (
    before_trset := empty;
    after_trset := empty;
    before_cnt := 0;
    include T in read_trset;
    put T in the R_Q;
) .
```

Now T is in the read phase. When it tries to read or prewrite a data object, it requests the lock. The lock may be granted or not according to the locking protocol. Transactions may be aborted when lock requests are processed. To abort a transaction T, the following procedure is called:

```
tabort = (
    release all locks;
    for all transactions t in after_trset_T do
        before_cnt_t := before_cnt_t - 1;
        if before_cnt_t = 0 and t is in wait phase;
        then unblock t;
        endif
    enddo
    if T is in read phase
    then delete T from read_trset;
    else if T is in write phase
        then delete T from write_trset;
        else  if T is in wait phase
            then delete T from from wait_trset;
```

```
        endif
      endif
   endif
) .
```

Wait Phase

The wait phase allows a transaction to wait until it can commit. A transaction T can commit only if all transactions with higher priorities that must precede it in the serialization order are either committed or aborted. Since *before_cnt* is the number of such transactions, T can commit only if its *before_cnt* becomes zero. A transaction in the wait phase may be aborted due to two reasons. The first one is that since T is not committed yet and still holding all the locks, it may be aborted due to a conflicting lock request by a higher priority transaction. The second reason is the commitment of a higher priority transaction that must follow T in the serialization order. When such a transaction commits, it finds T in *before_trset* and aborts T. Once a transaction in the wait phase gets its chance to commit, i.e. its *before_cnt* goes to zero, it switches into the write phase and release all its read locks. A final-timestamp is assigned to it, which is the absolute serialization order. The wait procedure for transaction T is as follows:

```
twait = (
    include T in wait_trset;
    delete T from read_trset;
    waiting := TRUE;
    while(waiting) do
          if (before_cnt_T = 0)
          then   /* switching into write phase */
                include T in write_trset;
                delete T from wait_trset;
                ts(T) := s_count;
                s_count:= s_count + 1;
                for all t in before_trset_T do
                   if t is in read phase or wait phase
                   then abort t;
                   endif
                enddo
                waiting := FALSE
          else block;
          endif
    enddo
```

```
    release all read locks;
    for all t in after_trset_T do
          if t is in read phase or wait phase
          then   before_cnt_t := before_cnt_t−1;
                 if (before_cnt_t = 0
                        and t is in wait phase)
                 then unblock t;
                 endif
          endif
    enddo
    ).
```

Write Phase

Once a transaction is in the write phase, it is considered to be committed. All committed transactions can be serialized by the final-timestamp order. In the write phase, the only work of a transaction is making all its updates permanent in the database. Data items are copied from the local workspace into the database. After each write operation, the corresponding write lock is released. The Thomas' Write Rule (TWR) is applied here. The write requests of each transaction are sent to the data manager, which carries out the write operations in the database. Transactions submit write requests along with their final-timestamps. The write procedure for transaction T is as follows:

```
    twrite = (
        for all x in wlock(T,x)  do
             for all t in write phase do
                  if wlock(t,x) and ts(t) < ts(T)
                  then release t's write lock on x;
                  endif
             enddo
             send write request on x and wait for
             acknowledgement;
             if (acknowledgement is OK)
             then release the write lock on x;
             else  abort T;
             endif
        enddo
        delete T from R_Q;
        ).
```

For each data object, write requests are sent to the data manager only in ascending timestamp order. After a write request on data object x with timestamp n is issued to the data manager, no other write request on x with a timestamp smaller that n will be sent. The write requests are buffered by the data manager. The data manager can work with the first-come-first-serve policy or always select the write request with the highest priority to process. When a new request arrives, if there is another buffered write request on the same data object, the request with the smaller timestamp is discarded. Therefore for each data object there is at most one write request in the buffer. This, in conjunction with the procedure *twrite*, guarantees the Thomas Write Rule.

CPU SCHEDULING

Although the focal point of this paper is on concurrency control, i.e. operation level scheduling, we still need to discuss transaction scheduling, or CPU scheduling, aspect of our algorithm. In non-real-time database systems, CPU scheduling is usually done by the underlying operating system, because there are no timing constraints. Data consistency is the only concern. In real-time database systems, however, CPU scheduling should take into account the timeliness of transactions.

In our algorithm, R_Q contains all transactions that can be scheduled. These transactions can be in any phase. We need a policy to determine the CPU scheduling priority for transactions in different phases. Transactions in their wait phase are those that have finished their work and are waiting for their chance to commit. We would like to avoid aborting such transactions as much as possible. Therefore transactions in this phase are given higher CPU scheduling priority than those in the read phase so that they can commit as soon as they get the chance. Transactions in the read phase are scheduled according to their assigned priority. If there are several read phase transactions in the R_Q, the one with the highest priority is always selected to execute.

For transactions in the wait phase, the lower the priority, the higher the CPU scheduling priority. Since low priority transactions are more vulnerable to conflicts, if there is a chance, they should be committed as soon as possible to avoid being aborted later. Moreover, when a high priority transaction T_H is committed, it may have to abort a low priority transaction T_L if T_L is in T_H's *before_trset*. If T_L is also ready to commit and we allow it to commit before T_H, both T_L and T_H can be committed.

CONCLUSIONS

Time-critical scheduling in RTDBS consists of two scheduling mechanisms: transaction scheduling and operation scheduling. To find appropriate concurrency control algorithms in which timing constraints of transactions are taken into account, we have addressed issues associated with the operation scheduling aspect of time-critical scheduling.

In this paper, we have presented a concurrency control algorithm for RTDBS which integrates a priority-dependent locking mechanism with an optimistic approach. It works when no information about data requirements or execution time of each transaction is available. By delaying the write operations of transactions, the restraint of past transaction execution on the serialization order is relaxed, allowing the serialization order among transactions to be adjusted dynamically in compliance with transaction timeliness and criticality. The new algorithm allows transactions to meet timing constraints as much as possible without reducing the concurrency level of the system or increasing the restart rate significantly. In the algorithm, high priority transactions are not blocked by lower priority transactions, while low priority transactions may not have to be aborted even in face of conflicts with high priority transactions.

RTDBS of tomorrow will be large and complex. They will be distributed, operate in an adaptive manner in a highly dynamic environment, and should exhibit intelligent behavior. If the logical or timing constraints of transactions are not met, catastrophic consequences may happen. Meeting the challenges imposed by these characteristics depends on a focused and coordinated research efforts in several areas, and concurrency control of real-time transactions is one of those areas that needs further study.

References

[1] Abbott, R. and H. Garcia-Molina, "Scheduling Real-Time Transactions: A Performance Study," *VLDB Conference,* Sept. 1988, 1-12.

[2] Abbott, R. and H. Garcia-Molina, "Scheduling Real-Time Transactions with Disk Resident Data," *VLDB Conference,* Aug. 1989.

[3] Bernstein, P., V. Hadzilacos, and N. Goodman, *Concurrency Control and Recovery in Database Systems,* Addison-Wesley, 1987.

[4] Buchmann, A. et al., "Time-Critical Database Scheduling: A Framework for Integrating Real-Time Scheduling and Concurrency Control," *5th Data Engineering Conference,* Feb. 1989.

[5] Huang, J., J. Stankovic, D. Towsley, and K. Ramamritham, "Experimental Evaluation of Real-Time Transaction Processing," *Real-time*

Systems Symposium, Dec. 1989.

[6] Kung, H. and J. Robinson, "On Optimistic Methods for Concurrency Control," *ACM Trans. on Database Syst.,* vol. 6, no. 2, pp 213-226, June 1981.

[7] Korth, H., "Triggered Real-Time Databases with Consistency Constraints," *16th VLDB Conference,* Brisbane, Australia, Aug. 1990.

[8] Lin, K., "Consistency issues in real-time database systems," *Proc. 22nd Hawaii Intl. Conf. System Sciences,* Hawaii, Jan. 1989.

[9] Lin, Y. and S. H. Son, "Concurrency Control in Real-Time Databases by Dynamic Adjustment of Serialization Order," *11th IEEE Real-Time Systems Symposium,* Orlando, Florida, Dec. 1990.

[10] Rajkumar, R., "Task Synchronization in Real-Time Systems," *Ph.D. Dissertation,* Carnegie-Mellon University, August 1989.

[11] Sha, L., R. Rajkumar, and J. Lehoczky, "Concurrency Control for Distributed Real-Time Databases," *ACM SIGMOD Record 17,* 1, March 1988, pp 82-98.

[12] Sha, L., R. Rajkumar, S. H. Son, and C. Chang, "A Real-Time Locking Protocol," *IEEE Transactions on Computers,* to appear.

[13] Son, S. H., "Semantic Information and Consistency in Distributed Real-Time Systems," *Information and Software Technology,* Vol. 30, Sept. 1988, pp 443-449.

[14] Son, S. H., editor, *ACM SIGMOD Record 17,* 1, Special Issue on Real-Time Database Systems, March 1988.

[15] Son, S. H. and H. Kang, "Approaches to Design of Real-Time Database Systems," *Symposium on Database Systems for Advanced Applications,* Korea, April 1989, pp 274-281.

[16] Son, S. H., "On Priority-Based Synchronization Protocols for Distributed Real-Time Database Systems," *IFAC/IFIP Workshop on Distributed Databases in Real-Time Control,* Budapest, Hungary, Oct. 1989, pp 67-72.

[17] Son, S. H. and C. Chang, "Performance Evaluation of Real-Time Locking Protocols using a Distributed Software Prototyping Environment," *10th International Conference on Distributed Computing Systems,* Paris, France, June 1990, pp 124-131.

[18] Son, S. H. and J. Lee, "Scheduling Real-Time Transactions in Distributed Database Systems," *7th IEEE Workshop on Real-Time Operating Systems and Software,* Charlottesville, Virginia, May 1990, pp 39-43.

[19] Son, S. H., "Real-Time Database Systems: A New Challenge," *Data Engineering,* vol. 13, no. 4, Special Issue on Directions for Future Database Research and Development, December 1990, pp 51-57.

[20] Son, S. H., P. Wagle, and S. Park, "Real-Time Database Scheduling: Design, Implementation, and Performance Evaluation," *The Second*

International Symposium on Database Systems for Advanced Applications (DASFAA '91), Tokyo, Japan, April 1991.

[21] Son, S. H., C. Iannacone, and M. Poris, "RTDB: A Real-Time Database Manager for Time-Critical Applications," *Euromicro Workshop on Real-Time Systems*, Paris, France, June 1991.

[22] Stankovic, J., "Misconceptions about Real-Time Computing," *IEEE Computer 21*, 10, October 1988, pp 10-19.

[23] Yu, P. and D. Dias, "Concurrency Control using Locking with Deferred Blocking," *6th Intl. Conf. Data Engineering.*, Los Angeles, Feb. 1990, pp 30-36.

CHAPTER 8

Algorithms for Scheduling Imprecise Computations

J. W. S. Liu, K. J. Lin, W. K. Shih and A. C. Yu
Department of Computer Science
University of Illinois at Urbana–Champaign
Urbana, IL 61801

J. Y. Chung
IBM T.J. Watson Research Center
Yorktown Heights, NY 10598

W. Zhao
Department of Computer Science
Texas A&M University
College Station, TX 77843

Abstract

The *imprecise computation technique* ensures that all time–critical tasks produce their results before their deadlines by trading off the quality of the results for the computation time requirements of the tasks. This paper provides an overview of the problems in scheduling imprecise computations. It describes several workload models of imprecise computation that explicitly characterize the costs and benefits of the tradeoff and the scheduling algorithms that have been developed to achieve the desired tradeoff.

INTRODUCTION

In a (*hard*) *real–time* system, every time–critical task must meet its timing constraint, which is typically specified in terms of its *deadline*. Here, by a *task*, we mean a granule of computation that is treated by the scheduler as a unit of work to be allocated processor time, that is, *scheduled*. It is essential for every time–critical task to complete its execution and produce its result by its deadline. Otherwise, a *timing fault* is said to occur, and the result produced by the task is of little or no use. Unfortunately, many factors, such as variations in processing times of dynamic algorithms and congestion on the communication network, make meeting all timing constraints at all times difficult. An approach to minimize this difficulty is to trade off the quality of the results produced by the tasks with the amounts of processing time required to produce the results. Such a tradeoff can be realized by using the *imprecise computation technique* [1–5]. This technique prevents timing faults and achieves graceful degradation by making sure that an approximate result of an acceptable quality is available to the user whenever the exact result of the desired quality cannot be obtained in time. An example of real–time applications where one may prefer timely, approximate results, to late, exact results is image processing. It is often better to have frames of fuzzy images produced in time than perfect images produced too late. Another example is tracking. When a tracking system is overloaded and cannot compute all the accurate location data in time, one may, instead, choose to have their rough estimates that can be computed in less time.

Since the advent of the imprecise computation technique, several workload models have been developed to characterize imprecise computations. These models explicitly quantify the costs and benefits in the tradeoff between the overall result quality and the computation time requirements. Several scheduling algorithms have been developed to exploit this tradeoff. This paper gives an overview of the recent results and discusses future directions in imprecise computation scheduling.

The remainder of the paper is organized as follows. The next section briefly describes the imprecise computation technique along with ways to implement imprecise computations. We then describe a basic deterministic workload model that characterizes imprecise computations and defines the performance metrics that provide the criteria for comparison of different scheduling algorithms. The problems in scheduling imprecise computations are at least as complex as the corresponding classical real–time scheduling problems. Almost all of the problems beyond that of scheduling unit–length, dependent tasks on two processors are NP–hard [6–8], and most simple heuristic algorithms for multiprocessor scheduling of dependent tasks have unacceptably poor worst–case performance [9–11]. For this reason, the approach that we have taken in scheduling dependent tasks is to first assign the tasks statically to processors and then schedule the tasks preemptively on the individual processors using some uniprocessor scheduling algorithms. When the tasks do not depend on each other, optimal preemptive multiprocessor schedules can be obtained by a simple transformation of an optimal uniprocessor schedule. The section on scheduling to minimize total error focuses on the basic problem of scheduling imprecise computations to meet deadlines and describes two polynomial–time, optimal algorithms for preemptive scheduling on uniprocessor systems. Two variations of the basic problem, scheduling multiple–version tasks and scheduling periodic tasks, and the problem of scheduling parallelizable imprecise computations on multiprocessor systems are discussed in the following three sections. Two probabilistic formulations of the problem on scheduling to trade result quality for better average response time are then discussed. The last section is a short summary.

IMPRECISE COMPUTATION TECHNIQUE

One effective way to minimize the bad effects of timing faults is to leave less important tasks unfinished if necessary. In other words, rather than treating all tasks equally, the system views important tasks as mandatory and less important tasks as optional. It ensures that all mandatory tasks are scheduled and executed to completion before their deadlines. Optional tasks may be left unfinished during a transient overload when it is not feasible to complete all the tasks. The imprecise computation technique [1–5] uses this basic strategy but carries it one step further. In a system that supports imprecise computations, every time–critical task is structured in such a way that it can be logically decomposed into two subtasks: a mandatory subtask and an optional subtask. The mandatory subtask is the portion of the computation that must be done in order to produce a result of an acceptable quality. This subtask must be completed before the deadline of the task. The optional subtask is the portion of the computation that refines the result. The optional subtask, or a portion of it, can be left unfinished if necessary at the expense of the quality of the result produced by the task. An optional subtask that is not completed when its deadline is reached is terminated at that time.

We have the maximum flexibility in scheduling when all the time–critical computations are designed to be *monotone*. A task is said to be monotone if the quality of the intermediate result produced by it is non–decreasing as it executes longer, that is, as more processor time is spent to obtain the result. The result produced by a monotone task when it completes is the desired result. This result is said to be *precise* or exact; the *error* in the result, also referred to as the *error of the task*, is zero. If the task is terminated before it is completed, the intermediate result produced by it at the time of its termination is usable as long as the mandatory subtask is completed. Such a result is said to be *imprecise* or approximate. Again, the longer a monotone task executes before it terminates, the smaller is the error in its imprecise result. Clearly, this way of implementing imprecise computations relies on the use of monotone computational algorithms. Such algorithms exist in many problem domains, including numerical computation, statistical estimation and prediction, heuristic search, and sorting. There have been several recent efforts to develop monotone algorithms in application domains where such algorithms are still needed. Examples of the recent results of these efforts include several query processing schemes that produce monotonically improving approximate answers to standard relational algebra queries and queries in rule–based and statistical databases [12–15].

An example of programming languages in which imprecise computations can be easily implemented is FLEX [16–19], an object–oriented language that supports all the C++ constructs along with the timing–constraint and imprecision primitives. One way to return imprecise results of monotone tasks is to record the intermediate results produced by each time–critical task at appropriate instances of the task's execution. FLEX provides language primitives with which the programmer can specify the intermediate result variables to be recorded and the time instants to record them. In addition to the intermediate result variables, the programmer can also specify a set of error indicators. The latest recorded values of the intermediate result variables and error indicators are made available to the user upon premature termination of the task. By examining these error indicators, the user can decide whether an imprecise result is acceptable whenever a task is terminated before it is completed. This method for returning imprecise results is called the *milestone method*.

For some applications, it is not feasible to make all computations monotone. Trading off result quality for processing time is nevertheless possible by making use of either sieve functions or multiple versions. Sometimes, a step in a computation can be skipped in order to save time. For example, in radar signal processing, the computation step that estimates the current level of the noise in the received signal can be skipped completely; an old estimate can be used. We call a step in a computation whose sole purpose is to produce outputs that are at least as precise as the corresponding inputs a *sieve* function. In other words, when a sieve function is executed, it improves the precision of its inputs. Conversely, if it is skipped, they retain the less precise values. Thus sieves provide another means to trade off between result quality and processing time requirements. This method for producing imprecise results is called the *sieve method*. When neither the milestone method nor the sieve method can be used, we can almost always rely on the use of *multiple versions* of tasks, as suggested in [20–25]. Using this method, we need to provide, for each task, two versions: the primary version and the alternate version. The primary version of each task produces a precise result but has a longer processing time. During a transient overload, when it is not possible to complete the primary version of every task by its deadline, we may choose to schedule the alternate versions of some tasks. An alternate version has a shorter processing time but produces an imprecise, but acceptable, result.

Both the milestone and sieve methods can be easily implemented in any existing language, especially when one is willing to augment the language with sieve and milestone primitives. In addition to FLEX, we have also experimented with ways to implement these methods in Real–Time Mentat [23] and Ada [26]. The feasibility of the multiple version method has been demonstrated for both real–time computing and data communication [20,23–25]; tools and environments have been developed to support this method [20–23]. The penalty in the milestone technique is that of recording intermediate results. The penalty in the sieve technique is the higher scheduling overhead. We note that one would gain no benefit by completing a sieve in part, while incurring the cost in processing that part. Therefore, an optional subtask that is a sieve should be either executed to completion before its deadline or is not scheduled, that is, *discarded*, entirely. In this case, we say that the execution of the optional subtask satisfies the *0/1 constraint*. It will be shown in the section on scheduling with the 0/1 constraint that more complex scheduling algorithms are needed to decide whether each optional subtask should be completed or discarded. The penalty in the multiple version method is the higher overhead for the storage of multiple versions, as well as the relatively high scheduling overhead. Scheduling tasks that have two versions is essentially the same as scheduling tasks with the 0/1 constraint. For scheduling purpose, we view the alternate version of each task as a mandatory subtask. The primary version is modeled as consisting of a mandatory subtask, whose processing time is the same as that of the alternate version, and an optional subtask, whose processing time is equal to the difference between the processing times of the two versions. The optional subtask must be either scheduled and completed by its deadline, corresponding to the primary version being scheduled, or discarded entirely, corresponding to the alternate version being scheduled.

In sum, the imprecise computation approach makes meeting timing constraints in hard real–time computing systems significantly easier for the following reason. To guarantee that all timing constraints are met, the scheduler only needs to guarantee that all mandatory subtasks are allocated sufficient processor time to complete by their deadlines; it uses the leftover processor time to complete as many optional subtasks as possible. A conservative scheduling discipline with guaranteed performance and predictable behavior, such as the rate–monotone algorithm [27], can be used to schedule the mandatory subtasks. More dynamic disciplines, such as the earliest–deadline–first algorithm [27–29], that are capable of achieving optimal processor utilization but may have unpredictable behavior, can be used to schedule optional subtasks. In particular, when tasks are monotone, the decision on which optional subtask and how much of the optional subtask to schedule at any time can be made dynamically. Because the scheduler can terminate a task any time after it has produced an acceptable result, scheduling monotone tasks can be done on–line or nearly on–line.

BASIC MODEL OF IMPRECISE COMPUTATIONS

All the imprecise–computation models are extensions and variations of the following basic one. We are given a set of n tasks,

$\mathbf{T} = \{T_1, T_2, \cdots, T_n\}$. The tasks are preemptable. Each task T_i is characterized by the following parameters, which are rational numbers:

(1) *ready time* r_i' at which T_i becomes ready for execution,

(2) *deadline* d_i' by which T_i must be completed,

(3) *processing time* τ_i that is required to execute T_i to completion in the traditional sense on a single processor, and

(4) *weight* w_i that is a positive number and measures the relative importance of the task.

Logically, each task T_i is decomposed into two subtasks: the *mandatory* subtask M_i and the *optional* subtask O_i. Hereafter, we refer to M_i and O_i simply as tasks. Let m_i and o_i be the processing times of M_i and O_i, respectively. m_i and o_i are rational numbers, and $m_i + o_i = \tau_i$. The ready time and deadline of the tasks M_i and O_i are the same as that of T_i. We will return to discuss the dependency of O_i on M_i.

A *schedule* on a uniprocessor system is an assignment of the processor to the tasks in $\mathbf{T}$ in disjoint intervals of time. A task is said to be scheduled in a time interval if the processor is assigned to the task in the interval. In any valid schedule, the processor is assigned to at most one task at any time, and every task T_i is scheduled after its ready time. Moreover, the total length of the intervals in which the processor is assigned to T_i, referred to as the total *amount of processor time* assigned to the task, is at least equal to m_i and at most equal to τ_i. A task is said to be *completed in the traditional sense* at an instant t when the total amount of processor time assigned to it becomes equal to its processing time at t. A mandatory task M_i is said to be completed when it is completed in the traditional sense. The optional task O_i is dependent on the mandatory task M_i; it becomes ready for execution when M_i is completed. O_i may be terminated at any time, however, even if it is not completed at the time; no more processor time is assigned to it after it is terminated. A task T_i is said to be completed in a schedule whenever its mandatory task is completed. It is said to be terminated when its optional task is terminated. Given a schedule S, we call the earliest time instant at which the processor is assigned to a task the *start time* of the task and the time instant at which the task is terminated its *finishing time*. We note that the traditional workload model of hard real–time applications is a special case of this model in which $o_i = 0$ for all i. Similarly, the traditional soft real–time workload model is also a special case in which all tasks are completely optional, that is, $m_i = 0$ for all i.

The dependencies between the tasks in **T** are specified by their precedence constraints; they are given by a partial order relation $<$ defined over **T**. $T_i < T_j$ if the execution of T_j cannot begin until the task T_i is completed and terminated. T_j is a *successor* of T_i, and T_i is a *predecessor* of T_j, if $T_i < T_j$. In order for a schedule of **T** to be valid, all the precedence constraints must be satisfied. A set of tasks is said to be independent if the partial order relation $<$ is empty; the tasks can be executed in any order. A valid schedule is a *feasible* schedule if every task is completed by its deadline. A set of tasks is said to be *schedulable* if it has at least one feasible schedule.

It is possible that the given deadline of a task is later than that of its successors. Rather than working with the given deadlines, we use the modified deadlines that are consistent with the precedence constraints and are computed as follows. The modified deadline d_i of a task T_i that has no successors is equal to its given deadline d_i'. Let A_j be the set of all successors of T_j. The modified deadline of T_j is

$$d_j = \min \left\{ d_j', \min_{T_i \in A_j} \{d_i\} \right\}$$

Similarly, the given ready time of a task may be earlier than that of its predecessors. We modify the ready times of tasks as follows. The modified ready time r_i of a task T_i with no predecessors is equal to its given ready time r_i'. Let B_j be the set of all predecessors of T_j. The modified ready time of T_j is

$$r_j = \max \left\{ r_j', \max_{T_i \in B_j} \{r_i\} \right\}$$

A feasible schedule on a uniprocessor system exists for a set of tasks **T** with the given ready times and deadlines if and only if a feasible schedule of **T** with the modified ready times and deadlines exists. (See Section 4.2 in [6].) Working with the modified ready times and deadlines allows the precedence constraints to be ignored temporarily. If an algorithm finds an invalid schedule in which T_i is assigned a time interval later than some intervals assigned to T_j but $T_i < T_j$, a valid schedule can be constructed by exchanging the time intervals assigned to T_i and T_j to satisfy their precedence constraint without violating their timing constraints. In our subsequent discussion, by ready times and deadlines, we mean modified ready times and deadlines, respectively. We call the time interval $[r_i, d_i]$ the *feasibility interval* of the task T_i.

When the amount of processor time σ_i assigned to O_i in a schedule is equal to o_i, we say that the task O_i and, hence, the task T_i are *precisely* scheduled. The *error* ϵ_i in the result produced by T_i (or simply the error of T_i) is zero. In a *precise schedule*, every task is precisely scheduled. Only precise schedules are valid schedules in the traditional sense. Otherwise, if σ_i is less than o_i, we say that a portion of O_i of length $o_i - \sigma_i$ is discarded in the *imprecise schedule*. The error of T_i is equal to

$$\epsilon_i = E_i(o_i - \sigma_i) \tag{1}$$

where $E_i(\sigma_i)$ is the *error function* of the task T_i. This function gives the error in the imprecise result of the task. We assume throughout this paper that $E_i(\sigma_i)$ is a monotone non–increasing function of σ_i.

Depending on the applications, we may want to use different performance metrics as criteria for comparing different imprecise schedules. Consequently, there are many different imprecise scheduling problems, some of which are listed below.

Minimization of Total Error — In practice, the exact behavior of error functions $E_i(x)$ is often not known. A reasonable error function to use is the simplest one:

$$\epsilon_i = o_i - \sigma_i \tag{2a}$$

for all i. In other words, the error of a task is equal to the length of its discarded portion. For a given schedule, the *total error* of the task set **T** is

$$\epsilon = \sum_{i=1}^{n} w_i \, \epsilon_i \tag{2b}$$

Again, $w_i > 0$ are the weights of the tasks. Sometimes, we also refer to ϵ as the total error of the schedule. The basic imprecise scheduling problem is: given a set of tasks $\mathbf{T} = \{T_1, T_2, \cdots, T_n\}$, we want to find a schedule that is *optimal* in the following sense: it is feasible and has the minimum total error given by (2). An *optimal scheduling algorithm* always finds an optimal schedule whenever feasible schedules of $\mathbf{T}$ exist. The basic imprecise scheduling problem for the cases of dependent tasks on uniprocessor systems or independent tasks on multiprocessor systems is discussed later in the sections on scheduling to minimize total error and scheduling parallelizable tasks.

Minimization of the Maximum or Average Error — Two straightforward variations of the above mentioned performance metric are the average error and the maximum error. We will return to discuss the former for periodic tasks. Given a schedule of the task set $\mathbf{T}$ and the errors ϵ_i of the tasks, the maximum error of the task set is

$$\epsilon = \max_i \{ w_i \, \epsilon_i \} \tag{3}$$

For some applications, we may want to find feasible schedules with the smallest maximum error, rather than the minimum total error. Two polynomial–time algorithms for finding optimal schedules with the smallest maximum error for tasks with identical weights are described in [31]. The running times of the algorithms for the cases where the optional tasks have equal processing times and arbitrary processing times are $O(n^2)$ and $O(n^3)$, respectively.

Minimization of the Number of Discarded Optional Tasks — In a schedule that satisfies the 0/1 constraint, σ_i is either equal to o_i or 0 for every task. Often, we are concerned only with the number of discarded optional tasks. For example, it is reasonable to define an optimal schedule of tasks with multiple versions as one in which the number of tasks whose alternate versions are scheduled is a minimum. In this case, an optimal schedule is a feasible schedule in which the number of discarded optional tasks is minimum. The problem of scheduling to minimize the number of discarded optional tasks is discussed in the section on scheduling with the 0/1 constraint.

Minimization of the Number of Tardy Tasks — As long as the total error of the tasks is lower than a certain acceptable limit, its value is often not important. We may then want to minimize the number of tasks that are tardy (that is, they complete and terminate after their deadlines) for a given maximum, tolerable total error. The complexity of this problem has been studied by Leung and Wong in [32]. They presented a pseudo–polynomial–time algorithm and a fast heuristic algorithm for the preemptive scheduling, on a uniprocessor, of tasks whose feasibility intervals include each other. In the worst–case, the number of tardy tasks in a schedule found by the heuristic algorithm is approximately equal to three times that in an optimal schedule.

Minimization of Average Response Time — Given a schedule S and the finishing time of every task $f(T_i,S)$, the *mean flow time* of the tasks according to this schedule is equal to

$$F = \sum_{i=1}^{n} f(T_i,S)/n \qquad (4)$$

The mean flow time of the tasks measures the average response time, that is, the average amount of time a task waits until it completes. The tradeoff is between the average result quality and the average response time. Unfortunately, all but the simplest special cases of the problem on scheduling to minimize mean flow time subject to the constraint of a maximum acceptable total error is NP–hard [33]. In a later section, we will discusses the queuing theoretical formulations of this problem, which is a more fruitful approach to this problem.

SCHEDULING TO MINIMIZE TOTAL ERROR

We consider in this section the problem of scheduling imprecise computations to meet timing constraints and to minimize total error. The most straightforward approach to solving this problem is to formulate it as a network flow problem [34]. Optimal preemptive algorithms based on this formulation have time complexity $O(n^2 \log^2 n)$ when the tasks have identical weights and $O(n^6)$ when the tasks have different weights. We describe here two much faster algorithms, both of which make use of a modified version of the classical, earliest–deadline–first algorithm [30]. This is a preemptive, priority–driven algorithm which assigns priorities to tasks according to their deadlines; tasks with earlier deadlines have higher priorities. At every instant, the processor is assigned to the task with the highest priority among the tasks that are ready to be executed, preempting any task with a lower priority if necessary. However, according to our version, every task is terminated at its deadline even if it is not completed at the time. We call this algorithm the *ED Algorithm*. Its complexity is $O(n \log n)$. In any ED schedule produced by this algorithm, every task is scheduled in its feasibility interval.

We use the ED algorithm to test whether a task set **T** can be feasibly scheduled. The feasibility test is done by scheduling the mandatory set $\mathbf{M} = \{M_1, M_2, \cdots, M_n\}$ alone using the ED algorithm. If the resultant ED schedule of **M** is precise, then the task set **T** can be feasibly scheduled. Otherwise, no feasible schedule of **T** exists; this fact follows from the optimality of the classical earliest–deadline–first algorithm [30].

Identical–Weight Case

We note that an ED schedule of a set of entirely optional tasks is, by definition, a feasible schedule of the set. Moreover, because such a schedule is priority–driven, the processor is never left idle when there are schedulable tasks. A portion of an optional task is discarded only when it is necessary to do so. This is an intuitive explanation of

Theorem 1: The ED Algorithm is optimal if the processing times of all mandatory tasks in $\mathbf{T} = \{T_1, T_2, \cdots, T_n\}$ are zero and the tasks have identical weights.

The formal proof of this theorem can be found in [35,36]. This theorem provides the basis of the basic algorithm, called the *Algorithm F*, for optimally scheduling a set $\mathbf{T} = \{T_1, T_2, \cdots, T_n\}$ of n tasks with identical weights on a uniprocessor system. This algorithm works as follows: We decompose the set **T** into two sets, the set of mandatory tasks $\mathbf{M} = \{M_1, M_2, \cdots, M_n\}$ and the set of optional tasks $\mathbf{O} = \{O_1, O_2, \cdots, O_n\}$. Algorithm F consists of three steps:

Algorithm F

Step 1: Treat all mandatory tasks in M as optional tasks. Use the ED Algorithm to find a schedule S_t of the set **T**. If S_t is a precise schedule, stop and return the schedule. This schedule has zero error and is, therefore, optimal. Otherwise, carry out Step 2.

Step 2: Use the ED Algorithm to find a schedule S_m of the set **M**. If S_m is not a precise schedule, **T** cannot be feasibly scheduled. Stop. Otherwise, carry out Step 3.

Step 3: Transform S_t into an optimal schedule S_o that is feasible and minimizes the total error using S_m as a template.

The example shown in Figure 1 illustrates the need for Step 3. In this example, the task set consists of 6 tasks of identical weights. The schedules S_i and S_m generated in Steps 1 and 2 are shown in Figure 1(b). S_m of the mandatory set **M** is precise. Therefore, feasible schedules of **T** exist. Unfortunately, the schedule S_t obtained in Step 1 is, in general, not a feasible schedule of **T**. Because all the tasks are treated as entirely optional in Step 1, some tasks may be assigned insufficient processor time for their mandatory tasks to complete. In this example, T_4 is assigned only 2 units of processor time in S_t, which is less than m_4, the processing time of M_4. In Step 3, we transform S_t into a feasible schedule of **T** by adjusting the amounts of processor time assigned to the tasks so that every task T_i is assigned at least m_i units of processor time in the transformed schedule.

The transformation process in Step 3 has as inputs the schedules S_m and S_t. Let a_1 be the earliest start time and a_{k+1} be the latest finishing time of all tasks in the schedule S_m. We partition the time interval $[a_1, a_{k+1}]$ according to S_m into disjoint intervals such that in S_m the processor is assigned to only one task in each of these intervals and is assigned to different tasks in adjacent intervals. k denotes the number of such intervals, and a_j and a_{j+1}, for $j = 1, 2, \cdots, k$, denote the beginning and the end of the jth interval. In the example in Figure 1, there are 6 such intervals; the time instants $a_1, a_2, \cdots, a_7$ are 0, 3, 7, 9, 13, 15, and 16, respectively. Let $M(j)$ denote the mandatory task that is scheduled in the jth interval in S_m, and let $T(j)$ be the corresponding task. Step 3 of Algorithm F adjusts the amounts of processor time assigned to the tasks in S_t, using S_m as a template, in the following manner. The schedule S_t is scanned backward from its end at a_{k+2}. The segment of S_t after a_{k+1} is left unchanged. We compare in turn, for $j = k, k-1, \cdots, 1$, the total amounts $L_t(j)$ and $L_m(j)$ of processor time assigned to the tasks $T(j)$ and $M(j)$, respectively, in and after the jth interval according to S_t and S_m. If $L_t(j) \geq L_m(j)$, the segment of S_t in $[a_j, a_{j+1}]$ is left unchanged. Otherwise, let $\Delta = L_m(j) - L_t(j)$. We assign Δ additional units of processor time in $[a_j, a_{j+1}]$ to $T(j)$. These units may be originally assigned to some other tasks in S_t. We decrease the

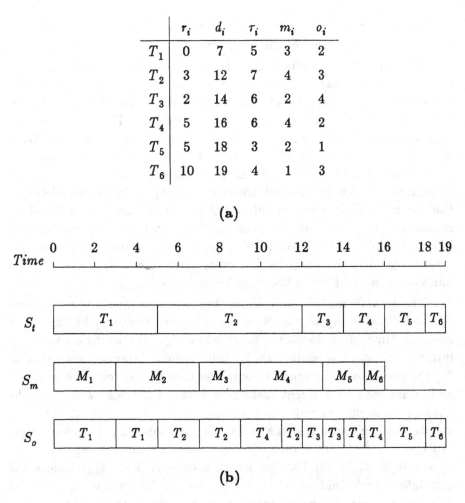

	r_i	d_i	τ_i	m_i	o_i
T_1	0	7	5	3	2
T_2	3	12	7	4	3
T_3	2	14	6	2	4
T_4	5	16	6	4	2
T_5	5	18	3	2	1
T_6	10	19	4	1	3

(a)

(b)

Figure 1. An example illustrating Algorithm F.

amounts of processor time assigned to them in this interval and update the values of $L_t(l)$, for $l = 1, 2, \cdots, j$, for all the tasks affected by this reassignment accordingly. This reassignment can always be done because Δ is less than or equal to $a_{j+1} - a_j$ and $T(j)$ is ready in the interval. In the example in Figure 1, $L_t(6)$ and $L_t(5)$ are left unchanged because they are equal to $L_m(6)$ and $L_m(5)$, respectively. $L_t(4)$ is 2 while $L_m(4)$ is 4; therefore, two additional units of processor time are assigned to $T(4)$, which is T_4. These two units of time are taken from T_2. T_2 has three units of processor time in the interval [9,13] before the reassignment and only one unit after the reassignment. The new values of $L_t(j)$ are 5, 5, 2, and 4 for $j = 1$, 2, 3, and 4, respectively. Similarly, we compare $L_t(3)$ and $L_m(3)$, and so on. The result of Step 3 is the optimal schedule S_o.

The complexity of Algorithm F is the same as that of the ED Algorithm, that is, $O(n \log n)$. The fact that Algorithm F always produces a feasible schedule of **T** as long as **T** can be feasibly scheduled follows directly from its definition. Theorem 1 ensures us that the schedule S_t obtained in Step 1 achieves the minimum total error for any set of tasks with identical weights. Since no additional idle time is introduced in Step 3, the total error remains to be minimum. Therefore, we have

Theorem 2: Algorithm F is optimal for scheduling tasks with identical weights to minimize total error.

The formal proof of this theorem, as well as the pseudo code of Step 3 in Algorithm F, can be found in [35,36]. By applying McNaughton's rule [37], it can be modified to optimally schedule independent tasks with identical weights on a multiprocessor system containing v identical processors. In this case, the complexity of Algorithm F is $O(vn + n \log n)$.

Different–Weight Case

We consider now the case where tasks in **T** have different weights, and suppose that the tasks in **T** are numbered according to their weights such that $w_1 \geq w_2 \geq \cdots \geq w_n$. Algorithm F no longer gives us optimal feasible schedules with minimum total error. An optimal algorithm for scheduling tasks with different weights is the *LWF* (*largest–weight–first*) algorithm, described by the pseudo code in Figure 2. Starting from the task with the largest weight and in the order of non–increasing weights, this algorithm first finds for every task T_i the maximum amount of processor time $\sigma_i{}^o$ that can be assigned to the optional task O_i. A feasible schedule in which the amounts of processor time assigned to all optional tasks are σ_i^o is an optimal schedule.

The procedure used in the LWF Algorithm to find σ_i^o is based on the following observation: the amount of processor time σ_i^o assigned to the only optional task in the set $\mathbf{M} \cup \{O_i\}$ in an optimal schedule (called S_o^i in Figure 2) of this set is as large as it is feasible. Let $\mathbf{T}_i = \{M_1, M_2, \cdots, M_{i-1}, T_i, T_{i+1}, \cdots T_n\}$ be a set of task in which the $i-1$ tasks with the largest weights have no optional tasks. The amount of processor time assigned to the task O_i in any optimal schedule of $\mathbf{T}_i$ is at most equal to σ_i^o. Let $\mathbf{S}_i$ be the set of optimal

---

LWF Algorithm
    Tasks are indexed so that $w_1 \geq w_2 \geq \cdots \geq w_n$
    begin
        Use the ED Algorithm to find a schedule S_m of **M**.
        If S_m is not precise, stop; **T** has no feasibly schedule.
        else
            The mandatory set $\mathbf{M}' = \mathbf{M}$
            $i = 1$
            while $(1 \leq i \leq n)$
                Use Algorithm F to find S_o^i.
                (S_o^i is an optimal schedule of $\mathbf{M}' \cup \{O_i\}$.)
                    $O_i' =$ the portion of O_i scheduled in S_o^i
                    (The processing time of O_i' is σ_i^o.)
                $M_i' = M_i \cup O_i'$
                $i = i+1$
            endwhile
            The optimal schedule sought is S_o^n
        endif
    end Algorithm LWF

Figure 2 Pseudo code of the LWF Algorithm

schedules of T_i; in each schedule in S_i, the amount of processor time assigned to O_i is $\sigma_i{}^o$.

Lemma 1: The set S_i of optimal schedules of T_i is nonempty if the amount of processor time assigned to O_i in an optimal schedule of **M** $\cup \{O_i\}$ is $\sigma_i{}^o$.

The formal proof of this lemma can be found in [36]. The LWF Algorithm makes use of this lemma. First, Algorithm F is used to schedule the set of tasks **M** $\cup \{O_1\}$. Again, T_1 is the task with the largest weight. In the resultant schedule $S_o{}^1$, the optional task O_1 is assigned the maximum possible amount of processor time $\sigma_1{}^o$. From Lemma 1, we know that there are optimal schedules of **T** in which O_1 is assigned $\sigma_1{}^o$ units of processor time. We commit ourselves to finding one of these schedules by combining M_1 and the portion $O_1{}'$ of O_1 that is scheduled in $S_o{}^1$ into a task $M_1{}'$. The task $M_1{}'$ is treated as a mandatory task in the subsequent steps. In the next step, we again use Algorithm F to schedule the task set $\{M_1{}', M_2, \cdots, M_n\} \cup \{O_2\}$. Let $O_2{}'$ be the portion of the optional task O_2 that is scheduled in the resultant optimal schedule $S_o{}^2$. $O_2{}'$ has the maximum possible amount of processor time $\sigma_2{}^o$. Again, from Lemma 1 we know that there are optimal schedules of **T** in which the amounts of processor time assigned to O_1 and O_2 are $\sigma_1{}^o$ and $\sigma_2{}^o$, respectively. We commit ourselves to finding one of these schedules by combining M_2 and $O_2{}'$ into the mandatory task $M_2{}'$. We repeat these steps for $i = 3, 4, \cdots, n$ until all $\sigma_i{}^o$ are found. The schedule $S_o{}^n$ found in the last step is an optimal schedule of **T** with the minimum total error. Indeed, we can show by induction

Theorem 3: The LWF Algorithm is optimal.

The LWF Algorithms uses Algorithm F n times. The running time of Algorithm F is $O(n \log n)$ the first time when it is used but is $O(n)$ during subsequent times. Therefore, the time complexity of the LWF Algorithm is $O(n^2)$ [36].

Figure 3 shows an example. There are four tasks, and their weights are listed in Figure 3(a). The schedule S_m of **M** $\cup \{O_1\}$ produced by Algorithm F is shown in Figure 3(b). We commit ourselves to finding an optimal schedule in which the amount of processor time assigned to O_1 is six. This schedule is an earliest–

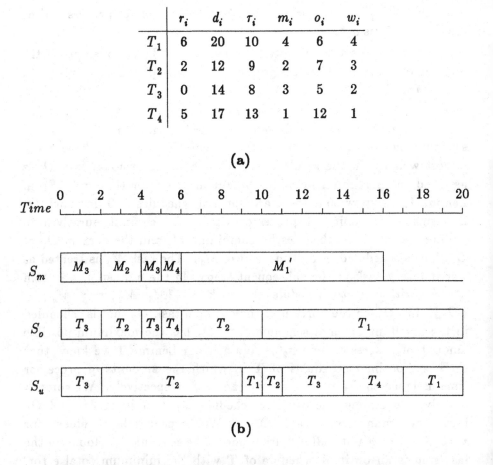

	r_i	d_i	τ_i	m_i	o_i	w_i
T_1	6	20	10	4	6	4
T_2	2	12	9	2	7	3
T_3	0	14	8	3	5	2
T_4	5	17	13	1	12	1

(a)

(b)

Figure 3. An example illustrating the LWF Algorithm

deadline–first schedule. It is used in the second step as a template to find an optimal schedule of the task set $\{M_1', T_2, M_3, M_4\}$. This resultant schedule S_o is shown in Figure 3(b). The total weighted error of the tasks is 31. Also shown is a schedule S_u that minimizes the unweighted total error, with a total weighted error of 43.

SCHEDULING WITH THE 0/1 CONSTRAINT

Again, for some applications, tasks must be scheduled so that the 0/1 constraint is satisfied. We now consider this case. In this section, the expression that an optional task O_i is scheduled means that it is assigned o_i units of processor time. As expected, the general problem of scheduling to meet the 0/1 constraint and timing constraints, as well as to minimize the total error, is NP–complete when the optional tasks have arbitrary processing times [35,36]. We describe first a polynomial–time optimal algorithm for scheduling tasks whose optional tasks have identical processing times and then discuss two heuristic algorithms for the case where the optional tasks have arbitrary processing times. In both cases, the tasks have identical weights.

Identical–Processing–Time Case

When $O_i = \delta$, for $i = 1, 2, \cdots, n$ where δ is an arbitrary rational number, a schedule that minimizes the total error also minimizes the number of discarded optional tasks. Our algorithm for scheduling with the 0/1 constraint uses the following strategy: Each task and, consequently, its optional task, are assigned a *preference*, which is an integer value determined from the feasibility intervals of the tasks in **T**. We first determine whether to schedule the optional task with the highest (that is, the largest) preference, then determine whether to schedule the optional task with the second highest preference, and so on. In particular, let p_i denote the preference given to the task T_i. For any two tasks T_i and T_j, we have

(1) $p_i > p_j$ if $r_i \leq r_j$ and $d_i > d_j$, or $r_i < r_j$ and $d_i \geq d_j$, that is, the feasibility interval of T_i contains the feasibility interval T_j;

(2) $p_i > p_j$ if $r_i < r_j$ and $d_i < d_j$, that is, the feasibility interval of T_i begins and ends before the feasibility interval of T_j; and

(3) $p_i = p_j$ if $r_i = r_j$ and $d_i = d_j$, that is, the tasks T_i and T_j have the same feasibility interval.

Here, we index the tasks in **T** such that $p_1 \geq p_2 \geq \cdots \geq p_n$.

A set **T** of tasks in which all optional tasks have the same processing time and must meet the 0/1 constraint can be optimally scheduled by the *DFS* (*Depth–first–search*) Algorithm described by the pseudo code in Figure 4. Lemma 2 provides the basis for this algorithm.

Lemma 2: There is a feasible, precise schedule of the task set $\mathbf{M} \cup \{O_i\}$ if and only if there exists an optimal schedule $S_o{}^i$ of $\mathbf{T}_i$ in which O_i is scheduled.

Here, $\mathbf{T}_i = \{M_1, M_2, \cdots, M_{i-1}, T_i, T_{i+1}, \cdots T_n\}$ is the task set in which the $i-1$ tasks with the largest preferences have no optional tasks. Obviously, if the set $\mathbf{M} \cup \{O_i\}$, containing only one optional task O_i, does not have a feasible and precise schedule in which O_i is scheduled, it is not possible to have an optimal schedule $S_o{}^i$ of $\mathbf{T}_i$ in

---

DFS Algorithm

    Assign preference p_i to tasks; the tasks are indexed such that
        $p_1 \geq p_2 \geq \cdots \geq p_n.$
    $i = 1$
    schedulables $= \phi$
    $\mathbf{M'} = \mathbf{M}$
    while $(1 \leq i \leq n)$
        Use the ED Algorithm to find a schedule $S_m{}^i$ of $\mathbf{M'} \cup \{O_i\}$.
        If $(S_m{}^i$ is a precise schedule)
            schedulables $=$ *schedulables* $\cup \{O_i\}$.
            Make the entire task T_i mandatory; $\mathbf{M'} = \mathbf{M'} \cup \{O_i\}$.
        endif
        $i = i + 1$
    endwhile
    Use the ED Algorithm to find a precise schedule
        of $\mathbf{M} \cup$ *schedulables*.
  end Algorithm DFS

Figure 4. Pseudo code of the DFS Algorithm.

which O_i is scheduled. Indeed, the fact that the set $\mathbf{M} \cup \{O_i\}$ has a feasible and precise schedule implies the existence of a non–empty subset of optimal schedules in which O_i is scheduled. This statement can be proved by contradiction [35,36].

Lemma 2 provides us with a criterion for determining whether the subset of optimal schedules in which the optional task O_1 is scheduled is empty. If it is empty, we decide to discard O_1. If it is not empty, we decide to schedule O_1. After this decision is made, we then proceed to determine whether the subset of optimal schedules in which both O_1 and O_2 are scheduled is empty. If it is, we decide to discard O_2; otherwise, we decide to schedule O_2, and so on. The DFS Algorithm works in this manner, first examining the task with the highest preference and then examining the tasks in turn in the order of non–increasing preferences. In this way, it chooses the subset of optional tasks to be scheduled and constructs a schedule of $\mathbf{T}$. The complexity of this algorithm is $O(n^2)$. We can prove by induction

Theorem 4: When the processing times of all optional tasks are equal, the DFS Algorithm is optimal for scheduling tasks with timing constraints and the 0/1 constraint to minimize the number of discarded optional tasks.

When the tasks have identical ready times, a simpler algorithm, called the *LDF* (*latest-deadline-first*) Algorithm, can be used to find optimal schedules. The complexity of the LDF Algorithm is $O(n \log n)$. Both the proof of Theorem 4 and the description of the LDF Algorithm can be found in [35,36].

Arbitrary–Processing–Time Case

When the processing times of the optional tasks are not identical, the DFS Algorithm is no longer optimal. If the criterion of optimality is the number of discarded optional tasks, regardless of their processing times, a good strategy is to try to schedule the optional tasks with the shorter processing times first. The *SPF* (*shortest-processing-time-first*) Algorithm uses this strategy. The operations of the SPF Algorithm is essentially the same as that of the DFS Algorithm. The only difference between the two algorithms is the ways they assign preferences to tasks. Specifically, the SPF algorithm assigns preferences to the tasks according to the processing times of their optional tasks; the shorter the processing time, the higher the preference. In other words, $p_i \geq p_j$ if $o_i \leq o_j$. Given a set of tasks **T**, let N_s and N_o be the numbers of optional tasks discarded in an SPF schedule and in an optimal schedule, respectively. A conjecture is that $N_s \leq 2N_o$; a complete proof of this bound remains to be completed.

When the optional tasks have difference processing times, the total error of a schedule may be a better criterion of optimality. A good strategy for scheduling tasks with the 0/1 constraint to minimize the total error is to try to schedule first the optional tasks with long processing times. This is the rational behind the assignments of preferences to tasks according to the *LPF* (*longest–processing–time–first*) Algorithm: $p_i \geq p_j$ if $o_i \geq o_j$. The operations of the LPF Algorithm is essentially the same as that of the DFS Algorithm. Again the difference between these algorithms is the ways in which they assign preference to tasks. Let ϵ_l and ϵ_o be the total error for an LPF schedule and an optimal schedule, respectively, of a task set **T**. Our conjecture is that $\epsilon_l \leq 3\epsilon$.

SCHEDULING PERIODIC JOBS

A workload model commonly used in studies on hard real–time scheduling is the periodic–job model [10,27–29,38–40]. In this model, there is a set **J** of n periodic jobs; each job consists of a periodic sequence of requests for the same computation. The *period* π_i of a job J_i in **J** is the time interval between two consecutive requests in the job. In terms of our basic model, each request in job J_i is a *task* whose processing time is τ_i. The ready time and the deadline of the task in each period is the beginning and the end of the period, respectively. Therefore, each job J_i can be specified by the 2–tuple (π_i, τ_i).

We have extended this workload model to characterize periodic imprecise computations [4,5,41,42]. As in the basic model of imprecise computations described earlier, each task in J_i is decomposed into a mandatory task, that has processing time m_i, and an optional task, that has processing time $\tau_i - m_i$ and is dependent on the mandatory task. They have the same ready time and deadline as J_i. In other words, each job $J_i = (\pi_i, \tau_i)$ is decomposed into two jobs: the mandatory job $M_i = (\pi_i, m_i)$ and the optional job $O_i = (\pi_i, \tau_i - m_i)$.

The corresponding sets of mandatory jobs and optional jobs are denoted by **M** and **O**, respectively. Let

$$U = \sum_{i=1}^{n} \frac{\tau_i}{\pi_i} \tag{5a}$$

denote the (total) *utilization factor* of the job set **J**. U is the fraction of processor time required to complete all the tasks in **J** if every task is completed in the traditional sense. Similarly, let

$$u = \sum_{k=1}^{n} \frac{m_k}{\pi_k} \tag{5b}$$

where u is the utilization factor of the mandatory set **M**.

Depending on the kind of undesirable effect caused by errors, we classify applications as either *error–noncumulative* or *error–cumulative*. Different performance metrics are appropriate for them. For any error–noncumulative application, only the average effect of errors in different periods is observable and relevant. Optional tasks are truly optional. None of them is required to be completed. Examples of this type of application include image enhancement and speech processing. In contrast, for an error–cumulative application, errors in different periods have a cumulative effect, making it necessary to generate timely, precise results sometimes. Examples of this type of application include tracking and control. In an error–cumulative job, the optional task in one period among several consecutive periods must be completed within that period and, hence, is no longer optional.

Error–Noncumulative Case

Since each periodic job can be viewed as an infinite chain of tasks, the total error defined by (2) is infinite for an imprecise schedule. A more appropriate performance measure of the overall result quality of a error–noncumulative, periodic job is the average error in the results produced in several consecutive periods. While the duration over which the average error is computed can be arbitrary, a convenient choice of this duration is π, the least common multiple of all the periods in **J**. For this duration, the average error of J_i is equal to

$$\epsilon_i = \frac{\pi_i}{\pi} \sum_{j=l}^{\pi/\pi_i} E_i\left(o_i - \sigma_{i,j} \right) \tag{6a}$$

where $\sigma_{i,j}$ is the amount of processor time assigned to the task in the jth period of J_i and $E_i(\sigma_{i,j})$ is a non–increasing function of $\sigma_{i,j}$. The average error over all jobs in **J** is

$$\epsilon = \sum_{i=1}^{n} w_i\, \epsilon_i \tag{6b}$$

where w_i is a non–negative constant weight and $\sum_{i=1}^{n} w_i = 1$.

There are several priority–driven, preemptive algorithms for scheduling error–noncumulative jobs on a single processor. Given a set of error–noncumulative jobs, these algorithms find feasible schedules that have small average error ϵ given by (6). Again, because the worst–case performance of priority–driven strategies for scheduling periodic jobs on multiprocessor systems is unacceptably poor [10], a commonly adopted approach is to first assign jobs once and for all to processors and then schedule the jobs assigned to each processor independently of the jobs assigned to other processors. The problem of finding an optimal assignment of jobs in a given set **J** to processors, making use of a minimum number of processors, can be formulated as a bin–packing problem; it is NP–hard. A heuristic job assignment algorithm with reasonably good worst–case performance is the rate–monotone next–fit (or first–fit) algorithm described in [10]. According to this algorithm, jobs in **J** are sorted in the order of increasing periods, that is, decreasing rates, and are assigned to the processors on the next–fit (or first–fit) basis. A job fits on a processor if this job and the jobs already assigned to the processor can be feasibly scheduled according to the rate–monotone algorithm [27]. (The rate–monotone algorithm is a preemptive, priority–driven algorithm that assigns priorities to jobs according to their rates: the higher the rate, the higher the priority.)

We use the rate–monotone next–fit (or first–fit) algorithm to assign individual jobs in the given set **J** to the processors in a multiprocessor system. However, in deciding whether a job can fit on a processor, we consider only the corresponding mandatory set **M**. Let $u_i = m_i / \pi_i$. Suppose that k jobs are already assigned to a processor.

Their mandatory jobs have a total utilization factor $u = \sum\limits_{i=1}^{k} u_i$. If an additional job J_{k+1} whose period is π_{k+1} and whose mandatory tasks have processing time m_{k+1} is also assigned to this processor, the total utilization factor of the $k+1$ mandatory jobs is $u + m_{k+1} / \pi_{k+1}$. J_{k+1} is assigned to the processor only if

$$u + m_{k+1} / \pi_{k+1} \leq (k+1)(2^{1/(k+1)} - 1) \tag{7}$$

Let **J** be the set of n jobs assigned to one processor in this manner. Clearly, the utilization factor of the jobs in **J** given by (5a) may be larger than $n(2^{1/n} - 1)$. Consequently, the set **J** may not be precisely schedulable to meet all deadlines according to the rate–monotone algorithm. However, the utilization factor of the mandatory set given by (5b) is less than $n(2^{1/n} - 1)$. Hence, the mandatory set **M** of **J** is always precisely schedulable [27]. Since the value of u is less than 1, (for example 0.82 for $n = 2$ and $\ln 2$ for large n), a fraction of the processor time will not be used to execute tasks in **M**. This fraction of processor time is available to execute tasks in the optional set **O**. When it is necessary to keep the average error small, we may choose to assign fewer jobs to each processor than indicated by the guideline (7) and, thus, make more processor time available for the execution of the optional set. The performance bounds and quantitative results in [5,41,42] provide the basis for such design decision.

Several heuristic algorithms for scheduling imprecise periodic jobs on uniprocessors have been designed and evaluated in [5,41,42]. They are preemptive and priority–driven, and all use the same strategy: the tasks are assigned higher priorities initially, and the priority of every task is lowered after its mandatory task has completed. Optional tasks are executed only after all ready mandatory tasks in the system have completed. Specifically, given a job set **J** and its associated mandatory set **M** and optional set **O**, all the jobs in **M** have higher priorities than all the jobs in **O**, and the jobs in **M** are scheduled precisely according to the rate–monotone algorithm. Because of the way jobs are assigned to the processor, we are ensured that the set **M** can always be feasibly scheduled. Hence, we have

Theorem 5: The strategy of assigning higher priorities to jobs in the mandatory set **M** (than jobs in **O**) and scheduling them precisely according to the rate–monotone algorithm guarantees that all the deadlines are met regardless of how the jobs in the optional set **O** are scheduled.

Figure 5 shows an example in which the job set **J** consists of four jobs. They are (2, 1), (4, 0.5), (5, 0.5) and (6, 1.5). Their mandatory tasks have processing times 0.5, 0.2, 0.1 and 1.0, respectively. The utilization factor of the job set **J** is equal to 0.975. **J** is not precisely schedulable according to the rate–monotone algorithm as shown in Figure 5(a). (The deadline of the task in the first period of J_4 is missed.) However, the mandatory set **M** consists of (2, 0.5), (4, 0.2), (5, 0.1) and (6, 1.0). Its total utilization factor is 0.4867; it is precisely schedulable according to the rate–monotone algorithm. Figure 5(b) shows a rate–monotone schedule of **M**. Black bars in Figure 5(b) indicate the time intervals during which the processor is assigned to jobs in the optional set **O**, consisting of (2, 0.5), (4, 0.3), (5, 0.4) and (6, 0.5).

The algorithms in [5,41,42] for scheduling error–noncumulative jobs differ only in the ways in which they assign priorities to optional jobs. Some of the algorithms make priority assignments based on the behavior of the error functions. Examples include

(1)   the *least–utilization* algorithm — This algorithm statically assigns higher priorities to optional jobs with smaller weighted utilization factors $(\tau_i - m_k)/\pi_i w_i$. It minimizes the average error when the error functions $E_i(x)$ are linear and when all the jobs have identical periods and weights. In this special case, this algorithm assigns higher priorities to optional jobs with shorter processing times, the same as the *shortest–job* algorithm.

(2)   the *least–attained–time* algorithm — This algorithm assigns priorities to optional tasks in the following manner: At any time when the processor is not executing tasks in **M**, the highest priority is assigned to the optional task that has attained the least processor time among all ready optional tasks. The least–attained–time algorithm tends to perform well when the error functions $E_i(x)$ are convex. Many iterative procedures converge faster during earlier iterations than later iterations; the error of the result decreases faster earlier and slower later as the computation proceeds. For this type of

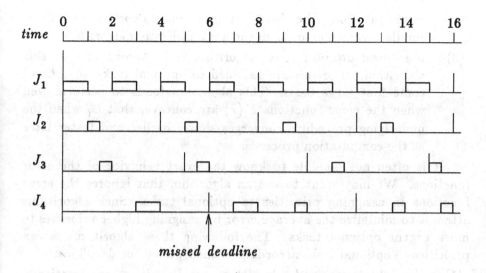

(a) A precise rate–monotone schedule.

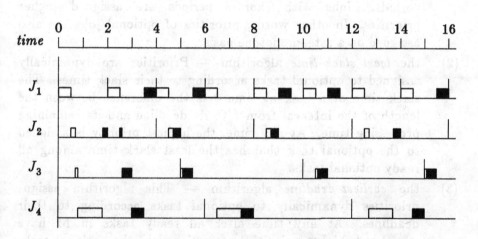

(b) A feasible schedule.

Figure 5. An example on scheduling of error–noncumulative jobs.

error function, the least–attained–time algorithm yields a smaller average error than the least–utilization algorithm.

(3)   the *most–attained–time* algorithm — According to this algorithm, priorities are assigned to optional tasks on a first–come–first–serve basis. This algorithm tends to perform well when the error functions $E_i(x)$ are concave, that is, when the underlying procedure converges slower earlier and faster later as the computation proceeds.

It is often not possible to know the exact behavior of the error functions. We may want to use an algorithm that ignores the error functions in assigning priorities to optional tasks. Such algorithms attempt to minimize the average error by assigning higher priorities to more urgent optional tasks. The following three algorithms assign priorities to optional tasks according to their periods or deadlines:

(1)   the *shortest–period* algorithm — Priorities are statically assigned to optional jobs according to the lengths of their periods. Jobs with shorter periods are assigned higher priorities. In other words, priorities of optional jobs are also assigned on a rate–monotone basis.

(2)   the *least–slack–time* algorithm — Priorities are dynamically assigned to optional tasks according to their slack times. The slack time of a task at time t is the difference between the length of the interval from t to its deadline and its remaining processing time. At any time, the highest priority is assigned to the optional task that has the least slack time among all ready optional tasks.

(3)   the *earliest–deadline* algorithm — This algorithm assigns priorities dynamically to optional tasks according to their deadlines. At any time after all ready tasks in M have completed, higher priorities are assigned to the optional tasks that have the earlier deadlines

The algorithms listed above have been evaluated for different mixtures of tasks and different types of error functions. Quantitative data on achievable average errors for different values of the total utilization factors of M and J can be found in [5,41,42]. In sum, these algorithms have the advantage of the rate–monotone algorithm: deadlines will be missed in a predictable manner during a transient overload. They also have the advantage of allowing the processor to be fully utilized like the earliest–deadline–first algorithm. They are ideally suited when transient overloads occur frequently or when the actual processing times of tasks vary widely. In most cases, the average error remains tolerably small when U becomes larger than 1 and no classical algorithm can schedule the tasks satisfactorily. Their advantages are realized at the expense of not being optimal, however. For example, these algorithms may lead to schedules with a nonzero average error for job sets that can be precisely scheduled to meet deadlines by the classical rate–monotone or earliest–deadline–first algorithms. When it is known that the total utilization factor U is less than or equal to 1 and a transient overload rarely occurs, the classical algorithms are better choices than these algorithms.

Error–Cumulative Case

We say that a schedule for a set **J** of error–cumulative jobs is a *feasible schedule* if for every job J_i in **J**, (i) every task in the mandatory job M_i is scheduled precisely and (ii) at least one optional task among every Q_i consecutive tasks in O_i is scheduled precisely. We refer to Q_i as the *cumulation rate* of J_i.

To appreciate the complexity of the problem in finding feasible schedules of error–cumulative jobs, let us examine here the simplest special case where all jobs in **J** have period π and cumulation rate Q. In this case, our problem is the same as that of finding a non–preemptive, feasible, precise schedule, on Q identical processors, of a set **R** of n independent tasks that have processing times o_i for $i = 1, 2, \cdots, n$, zero ready times and deadlines $\pi - \sum_{i=1}^{n} m_i$. This follows from the fact that every feasible schedule of **J** can be transformed into a non–preemptive, feasible, precise schedule of **R** on Q processors, and vice versa. The latter problem is known to be NP–complete [43]. A heuristic algorithm for scheduling n error–cumulative jobs with cumulation rate Q and identical periods is the *length–monotone algorithm*. This algorithm segments the time into intervals of Q periods. It schedules all the mandatory tasks in the beginning of every period. In each segment, there are Q intervals, each of length $\pi - \sum_{i=1}^{n} m_i$. During these Q intervals, the processor can be assigned to optional tasks. The length–monotone algorithm schedules one optional task from each job precisely in these intervals, using the *first–fit–decreasing* (*FFD*) algorithm [44]. The performance of this algorithm is given by

Theorem 6: A job set **J** of n error–noncumulative jobs of period π and cumulation rate Q is schedulable (i.e. a feasible schedule can always be found) using the length–monotone algorithm if

$$\frac{Q-1}{Q+1}\, u + \frac{2}{Q+1}\, U \leq 1$$

where u and U are total utilization factors of **M** and **J**, respectively, defined in (5).

The proof of this theorem can be found in [5,42].

Much work remains to be done to find effective algorithms for scheduling error–cumulative jobs. We need schedulability criteria for jobs with different periods and error cumulation rates. Workload on practical systems typically is a mixture of error–cumulative jobs, error–noncumulative jobs and aperiodic jobs. Good heuristic algorithms for scheduling such complex job mixes are needed.

SCHEDULING PARALLELIZABLE TASKS

In this section, we consider the problem of scheduling parallelizable imprecise computations to meet timing constraints and to minimize the total error. A task is said to be *parallelizable* if it can be executed concurrently, that is, in parallel, on a number of processors in order to complete in less time. The *degree of concurrency* of any task in an interval refers to the number of processors on which the task executes in parallel in the interval. In our model of parallelizable tasks, the degree of concurrency of any task may change during its execution. The parameters that characterize each parallelizable task T_i in a set **T** of n tasks include (1) its ready time r_i, (2) deadline d_i, (3) processing time τ_i, and (4) weight w_i, the parameters that characterize any sequential task in our basic model. Like sequential tasks, each parallelizable task T_i is logically decomposed into a mandatory task M_i and an optional task O_i whose processing times on a single processor are m_i and o_i, respectively. In addition to the above listed parameters, a parallelizable task has the following two parameters:

(5) *maximum degree of concurrency* C_i, that is, the task T_i can be executed in parallel on at most C_i processors, and

(6) *multiprocessing overhead factor* θ_i which is a proportional constant used to compute the overhead in the parallel execution of T_i.

Hereafter in this section, by a task, we mean a parallelizable task specifically, unless it is stated otherwise. Moreover, our attention is confined to independent tasks.

Given a task set **T**, let $\mathbf{a} = \{a_1, a_2, \cdots, a_{k+1}\}$, where $k+1 \leq 2n$, be an increasing sequence of distinct numbers obtained by sorting the list of ready times and deadlines of all the tasks in **T** and deleting duplicate entries in the list. In other words, all distinct values of r_i and d_i are in **a**. This sequence divides the time between the earliest ready time a_1 and latest deadline a_{k+1} into k intervals $I_j = [a_j, a_{j+1}]$ for $j = 1, 2, \cdots k$. A *parallel schedule* of the task set **T** on a system containing v identical processors is an assignment of the tasks to the processors in the time interval between a_1 and a_{k+1} such that, at any time, (1) each processor is assigned at most one task and (2) each task T_i is assigned to at most C_i processors. We divide the problem of finding feasible parallel schedules of **T** into two subproblems: the time allocation problem and the schedule construction problem. The former is that of deciding how many units of processor time in each of the k intervals should be allocated to each task T_i. Its solution gives us the total amounts of processor time on all the processors that are assigned to each task in the intervals I_j so that the tasks meet their timing constraints and the total error is minimum. Given this solution, we then solve the schedule construction problem to obtain a parallel schedule on v processors.

Time Allocation Problem

The factor that makes the time allocation problem differ from the problem of scheduling independent sequential tasks on multiprocessor systems considered in [34] is the multiprocessing overhead. When a task is executed in parallel on more than one processor, some processor time is wasted in carrying out interprocessor communication, synchronization, etc. We refer to this wasted time as the *multiprocessing overhead.* The multiprocessing overhead Θ_i of a task T_i in any time interval depends on the degree of concurrency c_i of the task and, consequently, on the amount of processor time allocated to the task in the interval. Clearly, when c_i is one, Θ_i is zero. Studies on scheduling parallelizable (precise) tasks typically assume that, for c_i larger than one, Θ_i is either a positive constant or a monotone non-decreasing function of c_i [45,46].

We examine now a special case where the multiprocessor overhead is a linear function of the degree of concurrency. This assumption allows us to formulate the time allocation problem as a linear programming problem and solve it using any of the well-known techniques (for example, [47,48]). In particular, the multiprocessing overhead is calculated in the following manner. Suppose that a task T_i is allocated a total of x units of processor time on all processors in an interval of length t. A rule which we follow when constructing a parallel schedule is to use as small a degree of concurrency as it is feasible. Therefore, if $x \le t$, this task is not parallelized in this interval; its multiprocessing overhead in this interval is zero. If $x > t$, the task must be executed in parallel on at least $\lceil x / t \rceil$ processors in this interval. In other words, the degree of concurrency of the task is $\lceil x / t \rceil$. Rather than making the multiprocessing overhead proportional to this non-linear function of x, we let the multiprocessing overhead of T_i in this interval be proportional to the *degree of overhead* given by

$$Y(x) = \max(x/t - 1, 0) \tag{8a}$$

with the proportional constant of T_i being θ_i. $\theta_i Y(x)$ units of processor time is wasted as the multiprocessing overhead; the actual amount of processor time available to the task in this interval for its execution towards completion is $x - \theta_i Y(x)$. We say that this amount of processor time is actually assigned to the task T_i when the total processor time allocated to the task for its execution and the multiprocessing overhead is x. Again, (2) gives us the error ϵ_i of a task T_i in terms of the amount σ_i of processor time actually assigned to its optional task O_i in all k intervals.

Let t_j denote the length of the interval $I_j = [a_j, a_{j+1}]$, and $x_i(j)$ denote the amount of processor time allocated to the task T_i in I_j.

$x_i(j)$ is zero if the feasibility interval of T_i does not include the interval I_j. Let

$$\Theta_i(j) = \theta_i \, Y(x_i(j)) \qquad (8b)$$

be the multiprocessing overhead of T_i incurred in this interval when its allocated processor time is $x_i(j)$. With the multiprocessing overheads given by (8), Figure 6 gives the linear programming formulation of the processor time allocation problem.

We want to find the set $\mathbf{X} = \{x_i(j)\}$ that minimizes the objective function, the total (weighted) error expressed here in terms of $x_i(j)$. The first set of constraints specifies that the total processor time allocated to every task in all k intervals is no more than its processing time τ_i plus its total multiprocessing overhead. These constraints ensure that no task is actually assigned more processor time than its

$$\text{minimize} \ \sum_{i=1}^{n} w_i \{ \tau_i - \sum_{j=1}^{k} [\, x_i(j) - \Theta_i(j) \,] \}$$

$$\sum_{j=1}^{k} x_i(j) \leq \tau_i + \sum_{j=1}^{k} \Theta_i(j) \qquad i = 1, 2, \ldots, n$$

$$\sum_{j=1}^{k} x_i(j) \geq m_j + \sum_{j=1}^{k} \Theta_i(j) \qquad i = 1, 2, \ldots, n$$

$$v \, t_j \geq \sum_{i=1}^{n} x_i(j) \qquad j = 1, 2, \ldots, k$$

$$(C_i - 1) \geq Y(x_i(j)) \geq 0 \qquad i = 1, 2, \ldots, n$$

$$x_i(j) \geq 0 \qquad \begin{array}{l} i = 1, 2, \ldots, n \\ j = 1, 2, \ldots, k \end{array}$$

Figure 6. Linear programming formulation

processing time. The second set of constraints specifies that the total processor time allocated to every task T_i in all k interval is no less than the sum of the processing time m_i of the mandatory task M_i and total multiprocessing overhead. These constraints ensure that sufficient processor time is actually assigned to every mandatory task for it to complete in the traditional sense. These two set of constraints together ensure that a valid schedule can be constructed from the resultant set $\mathbf{X}$ of processor time allocations. The third set of constraints requires that the total processor time allocated to all tasks in every interval I_j is no greater than the total amount of processor time available on all v processors. The fourth set of constraints gives the upper bound of the degree of overhead of each task in terms of its maximum degree of concurrency. The fifth set states that every $x_i(j)$ is non–negative.

The optimal solution for the above mentioned linear programming, if one exists, gives a set $\mathbf{X}$ of processor time allocations from which we can construct a feasible parallel schedule of $\mathbf{T}$ with the minimum total error [49]. The complexity of the linear programming formulation of the processor time allocation problem is the same as the complexity of the most efficient algorithm for linear programming [47,48]. One efficient algorithm for linear programming requires $O((\alpha + \beta)\beta^2 + (\alpha + \beta)^{1.5}\beta)$ operations where α is the number of inequalities and β is the number of variables. For our problem, α is equal to $3n + k$, and β is at most equal to nk.

Figure 7 gives an example. Figure 7(a) lists the parameters of three tasks. Their ready times and deadlines divide the time between 0 to 14 into four intervals beginning at 0, 4, 6, and 12. The values of t_j for $j = 1, 2, 3,$ and 4 are 4, 2, 6, and 2, respectively. Figure 7(b) shows the solution of the corresponding linear program. A blank entry at a row T_i and a column $x_i(j)$ indicates that the feasibility interval of T_i does not include the interval beginning at a_j and, hence, the corresponding $x_i(j)$ or $Y(x_i(j))$ is excluded from the linear programming formulation of the problem instance. To save space in the tabulation, the degree of overhead $Y(x_i(j))$ is listed simply as Y_j. In this example, the total error of the feasible schedule is 19.

	r_i	d_i	τ_i	m_i	o_i	w_i	θ_i
T_1	0	6	8	3	5	3	2
T_2	4	12	13	10	3	2	2
T_3	0	14	17	7	10	1	2

(a)

	$x_i(1)$	$x_i(2)$	$x_i(3)$	$x_i(4)$	$\sum x_i(j)$	Y_1	Y_2	Y_3	Y_4	$\sum Y_i$	$w_i \epsilon_i$
a_i	0	4	6	12		0	4	6	12		
T_1	6	2			8	0.5	0		0.5		3
T_2		2	9		11		0	0.5	0.5		6
T_3	2	0	3	2	7	0	0	0	0	0	10

(b)

Figure 7 An example of processor time allocation

Schedule Construction

The linear program solution is the set $\mathbf{X} = \{x_i(j)\}$ of processor time allocations for all n tasks and all k intervals. $\mathbf{X}$ only gives us the amount of processor time allocated to the tasks in each time interval I_j. Given $\mathbf{X}$, we still need to decide which task is to run on which processor(s) in each interval I_j so that a parallel schedule can be constructed. A straightforward approach to schedule construction is to first consider the processor time allocations $x_i(j)$ for each interval I_j independently and construct a segment of the parallel schedule for the interval. After the schedule segments in all k intervals have been constructed, we then rearrange the orders in which tasks are assigned in adjacent segments in order to reduce the total number of preemptions and migrations in the schedule. In particular, if a task is scheduled in two adjacent segments, in this rearrangement step, we move them, if necessary, so that they are scheduled contiguously on the same processor(s) in these segments after this rearrangement. An $O(n^2 \log n)$ algorithm based on a solution of the bipartite matching problem can be used to do this rearrangement. This algorithm can be found in [49].

Returning to the question of how to construct a parallel schedule segment from the processor time allocations of an interval I_j, we consider now the first interval I_1; segments in the other intervals can be constructed in the same manner. Without loss of generality, let $T_1, T_2, \cdots T_l$ be all the tasks that are allocated non–zero processor time in this interval. We refer to the portion of the task T_i that is scheduled in I_1 simply as T_i, rather than introducing a new notation here. One way to assign the tasks to the processors is as follows. The tasks are assigned to processors in the order of non–increasing amounts of allocated processor time. Specifically, suppose that $x_1(1) \geq x_2(1) \geq \cdots \geq x_l(1)$. T_1 is assigned on the first $\nu_1 = \left\lfloor x_1(1) / t_1 \right\rfloor$ processors for the entire interval of length t_1. The leftover portion of T_1 with processing time $\psi_1 = t_1 - \left\lfloor x_1(1) / t_1 \right\rfloor t_1$ is assigned on the (ν_1+1)st processor in the interval $[0, \psi_1]$. T_2 is assigned on this processor starting from ψ_1 following T_1 and, if $x_2(1)$ is larger than $t_1 - \psi_1$, on the (ν_1+2)nd processor, the (ν_1+3)rd processor, $\cdots$, until it is completely assigned. T_3 is assigned after T_2, and so on. This simple–minded scheme may fragment the tasks unnecessarily and result in a schedule containing unnecessary task preemptions and migrations. A better way is to first divide each task T_i into $\nu_i = \left\lfloor x_i(1) / t_1 \right\rfloor$ subtasks with processing time t_1 and a *fractional subtask* with processing time $\psi_i = t_1 - \left\lfloor x_i(1) / t_1 \right\rfloor t_1$. After all the subtasks with processing time t_1 are assigned on $\sum_{i=1}^{l} \nu_i$ processors, we then try to pack the l fractional subtasks on the remaining processors. This is the strategy taken in [49] where a pseudo–polynomial algorithm for the knapsack problem is used for this purpose [50].

QUEUING THEORETICAL FORMULATION

A performance metric that is commonly used for many applications is the average response time of tasks. Here, by the *average response time*, we mean the average amount of time between the instant when a task is ready and the instant at which the task is completed (and leaves the system.) In an imprecise computation system, we can trade off the average result quality for improved average response time. We described briefly in an earlier section the deterministic formulation of the problem in finding optimal schedules with the minimum average response time subject to the constraint of a maximum acceptable total error. This problem being NP–hard [33] for most cases of practical interest, the queuing–theoretical approach is a more fruitful one. This section briefly describes two queuing–theoretical formulations of this problem and summaries some the results available to date.

Two–Level Service Scheduling

Imprecise computations can be implemented by providing two versions of each task. When the primary version of a task is selected by the scheduler and is executed, we say that task is serviced at the *full level*. If its alternate version is selected and executed instead, we say that the task is serviced at the *reduced level*. When the system load is light and the response time is small, each task is serviced at the full level. When the system load becomes heavy, the overall response time of the system is reduced by servicing some tasks in the system at the reduced level. Such a scheduling scheme is called a *two–level scheduling*, or *service, scheme*.

The performance of two–level scheduling scheme in uniprocessor systems has been studied by Chong and Zhao [51–53]. In these studies, the uniprocessor system is modeled as an open Markov queue. In the simpliest case, there is only one class of task. Tasks arrive according to a Poisson process with an average rate of λ. The task processing times (that is, service times) at both the full level and the reduced level are exponentially distributed. In particular, the mean value of the full–level processing times of all tasks is $1/\mu$. The reduced–level processing time of a task is a constant fraction γ of its full–level processing time where γ is a real number between 0 and 1. Tasks are serviced according to a two–level scheduling discipline. For a given γ, a parameter of such a discipline is the threshold H. If the total number of tasks in the system is less than H, the system load is considered to be light. If the total number of tasks is equal to or larger than H, the system load is considered to be heavy. Performance data needed to guide the choice of H in uniprocessor systems can be found in [52,53]. We confine our attention here to the multiprocessor case.

A multiprocessor system with v identical processors can be modeled as an open v–server, Markov queue. Tasks arrive and join a common queue as described above. A two–level scheduling discipline that we have studied works as follows. Tasks are serviced on the first–in–first–out (FIFO) basis. The decision on whether to serve a task at the full level or the reduced level is made for each task individually. The number of tasks in the system is checked at each instant immediately before a processor begins to execute a task. The task at the head of the queue is serviced at the full level if the system load is light at the time and at the reduced level if otherwise. The number of tasks in the system is not monitored and no changes in scheduling decisions are made at any other time. Consequently, the execution of every task is never interrupted.

Let $\rho = \lambda / v \mu$ be the *offered load* of a processor in the system, that is, the fraction of time each processor would be kept busy if all the tasks are serviced at their full level. Since some tasks are serviced at the reduced level, the actual load of each processor is smaller than its offered load. It is easy to see that the system is not saturated and a stationary distribution of the number of tasks in the system exists as long as $\rho < 1/\gamma$. This simple Markov multi–server queue is analytically tractable. It does, however, model imprecise computation systems in sufficient detail to provide us with the performance data needed to guide the choices of parameters γ and H for most cases of practical interest.

In terms of the parameters of this model, the cost and benefit of the tradeoff between result quality and average response time are measured in terms of three performance metrics: (1) normalized average waiting time, (2) the average service quality, and (3) the average (processor) utilization. The average utilization gives the fraction of time each processor is busy and corresponds to the total utilization factor in our deterministic models. The *normalized average waiting time*, W, of tasks, is the average amount of time a task spends in the queue before its execution begins. W plus the average processing time of the tasks corresponds to the mean flow time F defined in (4) in the deterministic model. We normalize the average waiting time of a task with respect to its average full–level processing processing $1/\mu$. Let N_q denote the average number of tasks waiting in the queue. It follows from Little's law that $W = N_q/v\rho$. The normalized average waiting time measures the benefit of the tradeoff in providing imprecise service. It can be minimized easily by servicing every task at the reduce level. We, therefore, need another performance metric that measures the cost of this tradeoff, the quality of the service provided by the system. For this purpose, it is more convenient to use the fraction G of tasks that are serviced at the full level than the total error. This fraction is called the *average service quality*. In the steady state, G can be expressed in terms of the task parameters γ and ρ. We see that the average processing time received by departing tasks can be expressed in terms of G as $G/\mu+(1-G)\gamma/\mu$. This time can also be expressed in terms of the average utilization U of each processor, vU/λ. Therefore,

$$G = \frac{U-\gamma\rho}{(1-\gamma)\rho}.$$

The average number of tasks waiting in queue as a function of task and system parameters can be calculated numerically from the set of balance equations describing the steady–state behavior of the queue. The performance of imprecise (multiprocessor) systems was compared with that of a precise system in which all tasks are serviced at the full level, the latter modeled as an $M/M/v$ queue [54]. With an appropriate choice of H, an imprecise system with a two–level scheduling discipline performs almost as well as the corresponding precise system in terms of the average service quality, when the offered load of the system is small. When the offered load is high, the two–level scheduling scheme can significantly improve the average task waiting time by sacrificing the quality of service. This tradeoff is most effective when the offered load per processor is near one. While the average waiting time in a precise system approaches infinite, the two–level scheduling scheme keeps the average waiting time in a imprecise system small with a reasonably small degradation in the average service quality. To determine the suitable choices of H, the impact of the threshold H on performance was examined. The results in [54] show that values of H smaller than the number v of processors in the system are poor choices. In other words, the system should not sacrifice the quality of its service in order to reduce its backlog of work as long as there still are free processors available.

Monotone Imprecise Task Scheduling

The simplest model of a monotone imprecise system containing v processors is an open $M/E_{K+1}/v$ queue. Each task T_i is composed of a mandatory task M_i followed by K optional tasks $O_{i,j}$. Let $o_{i,j}$ denote the processing time of $O_{i,j}$. The processing time τ_i of the task T_i is given by $\tau_i = m_i + \sum_{j=1}^{K} o_{i,j}$ where m_i, the processing time of mandatory task M_i, and $o_{i,j}$'s are random variables. The processing times of different mandatory tasks are statistically independent and are distributed according to an exponential distribution. Similarly, the processing times of all the optional tasks are statistically independent from each other and from the processing times of the mandatory tasks. They are also exponentially distributed.

When a monotone imprecise system is overloaded, it may choose to discard some optional tasks of some tasks. The appropriate performance metrics that measure the decrease in result quality for applications where the 0/1 constraint must be satisfied include the fraction of optional tasks discarded by the system. In any time interval, this fraction is given by the ratio of the number of discarded optional tasks to the total number of optional tasks in all the tasks arriving for service in the interval. The expected value of this fraction gives a rough measure of the *average error* ϵ in the results produced by the tasks. Since the scheduler may choose to discard a variable number of optional tasks in each task, the average error does not give us a complete picture of the cost incurred. Another cost function is the *imprecision probability*, that is, the probability of any task being imprecise because some of its optional tasks are discarded. For applications where tasks are not required to meet the 0/1 constraint, the average error in the results of tasks is a more appropriate performance measure. Let l_i be the total processing time of the discarded portion of any task T_i. The error ϵ_i in the result produced by the task is roughly measured by the ratio of l_i to the total processing time of all the optional tasks in T_i.

We are current evaluating two schemes for discarding optional tasks when the system is overloaded: the responsive–service scheme and the guaranteed–service scheme. According to the *responsive–service scheme*, the total number of tasks in the queue is checked at each instant when a new task arrives and when a task begins to be executed. As long as the queue length is equal to or larger than H, x ($x \leq K$) optional tasks in each of the tasks in the system are discarded. This scheme is responsive to overload conditions. In particular, if x is equal to K, all optional tasks in the system are discarded as long as an overload condition exists. The system is doing its best possible in reducing its backlog and clearing up the overload condition. On the other hand, the quality of service is not guaranteed. A task which arrives when the system is lightly loaded may have its optional tasks discarded if the system becomes overloaded during the time the task stays in the system. In contrast, according to the *guaranteed–service scheme*, the total number of tasks in the system is examined at each arrival instant. A task arriving at the system when there are H or more tasks in the queue is tagged to receive reduced service; x of its optional tasks are discarded as long as the overload condition lasts. The tasks already in the system before the overload condition occurs are not tagged; they continue to be fully serviced to completion. When the queue length becomes less than H, all tasks are fully serviced again. Using this scheme, an imprecise system does not respond as quickly as possible to correct the overload condition. However, the quality of results produced by tasks arriving to the system when it is not overloaded is guaranteed to be good.

SUMMARY

This paper has presented an overview of different approaches for scheduling imprecise computations in hard real–time environments. The imprecise computation technique prevents timing faults by making sure that an approximate result of an acceptable quality is available to the user whenever the desired result cannot be obtained in time. We have described several models of imprecise computations that explicitly quantify the costs and benefits in the tradeoff between the result quality and computation time requirements. An imprecise computation scheduler must balance the benefit in enhanced system response with the cost in reduced result quality. For different types of applications, these costs and benefits are more appropriately measured by different criteria. Consequently, there are many different imprecise scheduling problems. We have presented statements of the different imprecise scheduling problems, the recent progress we have made towards solving some of these problems and the directions we plan to take in our future work.

ACKNOWLEDGEMENT

The authors wish to thank Susan Vrbsky for her comments and suggestions. This work was partially supported by the U. S. Navy ONR contracts No. NVY N00014 87–K–0827 and No. NVY N00014 89–J–1181.

REFERENCES

[1] J. W. S. Liu, K. J. Lin and C. L. Liu, "A Position Paper for the IEEE 1987 Workshop on Real–Time Operating Systems," Cambridge, Mass, May, 1987.

[2] K. J. Lin and S. Natarajan, "Concord: A System of Imprecise Computations," *Proceedings of the 1987 IEEE Compsac*, pp. 75–81, Tokyo, Japan, October 7–9, 1987.

[3] K. J. Lin, S. Natarajan, J. W. S. Liu, "Imprecise Results: Utilizing Partial Computations in Real–Time Systems," *Proceedings of the IEEE 8th Real–Time Systems Symposium,* San Jose, California, December 1987.

[4] J. W. S. Liu, K. J. Lin and S. Natarajan, "Scheduling Real–Time, Periodic Jobs Using Imprecise Results," *Proceedings of the 8th Real–Time Systems Symposium*, pp. 252–260, San Jose, California, December 1–3, 1987.

[5] J. Y. Chung, J. W. S. Liu, and K. J. Lin, "Scheduling Periodic Jobs that Allow Imprecise Results," *IEEE Transactions on Computers,* Vol.19, No.9, pp. 1156–1173, September 1990.

[6] E. L. Lawler, J. K. Lenstra, A. H. G. Rinnooy Kan, and D. B. Shmoys, "Sequencing and Scheduling: Algorithms and Complexity," Centre for Mathematics and Computer Science, Amsterdam, 1989.

[7] E. G. Coffman, Jr., and R. L. Graham, "Optimal Scheduling for Two–Processor Systems," *Acta Informatica*, vol. 1, pp. 200–213, 1972.

[8] M. R. Garey, D. S. Johnson, B. B. Simons, and R. E. Tarjan, "Scheduling Unit–Time Tasks with Arbitrary Release Times and Deadlines," *SIAM J. Comput.* 1981 vol. 10–2, pp. 256–269.

[9] R. L. Graham, "Bounds on Multiprocessing Timing Anomalies," *SIAM J. Appl. Math.*, vol. 17, pp. 263–269, 1969.

[10] S. K. Dhall and C. L. Liu, "On a Real–Time Scheduling Problem," *Operations Research*, Vol. 26, No. 1, pp. 127–140, 1978.

[11] D. Gillies and J. W. S. Liu "Greed in Resource Scheduling," *Proceedings of the 10th IEEE Real–Time Systems Symposium*, pp. 285–294, Los Angeles, California, December 1989.

[12] K. P. Smith, and J. W. S. Liu, "Monotonically Improving Approximate Answers to Relational Algebra Queries," *Proceedings of COMPSAC '89*, Orlando, Florida, October 1989.

[13] S. Vrbsky, K. P. Smith, and J. W. S. Liu, "An Object–Oriented Semantic Data Model to Support Approximate Query Processing," *Proceedings of IFIP TC2 Working Conference on Object–Oriented Database Semantics*, July 1990.

[14] P. Buneman, S. Davidson, and A. Watters, "A Semantics for Complex Objects and Approximate Queries," *Proceedings of the Seventh Symposium on the Principles of database Systems*, pp. 305–314, March 1988.

[15] G. Ozsoyoglu, Z. M. Ozsoyoglu, and W. Hou, "Research in Time– and Error–Constrained Database Query Processing," *Proceedings of the 7th IEEE Workshop on Real–Time Operating Systems and Software*, Charlottesville, VA, May 1990.

[16] K. J. Lin and S. Natarajan, "Expressing and Maintaining Timing Constraints in FLEX," *Proceedings of the IEEE 9th Real–Time Systems Symposium*, Huntsville, Alabama, December 1988.

[17] S. Natarajan and K. J. Lin, "FLEX: Towards Flexible Real–Time Programs," *Proceedings of IEEE International Conference on Computer Languages*, October 1988.

[18] S. Natarajan, "Building Flexible Real–Time System," Ph.D. thesis, Department of Computer Science, University of Illinois, August 1989.

[19] K. J. Lin and K. Kenny, "Implementing Timing Constraint in FLEX," submitted to *IEEE Trans. Software Engineering*.

[20] A. L. Liestman and R. H. Campbell, "A Fault–Tolerant Scheduling Problem," *IEEE Transactions on Software Engineering*, vol. SE–12, No. 10., pp. 1089–1095, Oct. 1986.

[21] K. Kenny and K. J. Lin, "Structuring Real–Time Systems with Performance Polymorphism," *Proceedings of the 11th IEEE Real–Time Systems Symposium*, Orlando, Florida, December 1990.

[22] P. Gopinath and R. Gupta, "Applying Compiler Techniques to Scheduling in Real–Time Systems," *Proceedings of the 11th IEEE Real–Time Systems Symposium*, Orlando, Florida, December 1990.

[23] A. S. Grimshaw, J. W. S. Liu and A. Silberman, "Real–Time Mentat, A Data–Driven, Object–Oriented System," *Proceedings of IEEE Globecom*, pp. 141–147, Dallas, Texas, November 1989.

[24] B. Kim and D. Towsley, "Dynamic Flow Control Protocols for Packet–Switching Multiplexers Serving Real–Time Multipacket Messages," *IEEE Transactions on Communications*, Vol.COM–34, No.4, April 1986.

[25] Y. Yemini, "A Bang–Bang Principle for Real–Time Transport Protocols," *Proc. SIGCOMM '83 Symp. Commun. Architect. Protocols*, pp. 262–268, May 1983.

[26] G. J. Gregory and K. J. Lin, "Building Real–Time Imprecise Computations in Ada," *Proceedings of Tri–Ada*, Baltimore, December 1990.

[27] C. L. Liu and J. W. Layland, "Scheduling Algorithms for Multiprogramming in a Hard Real–Time Environment," *J. Assoc. Comput. Mach.*, vol. 20, pp. 46–61, 1973.

[28] A. K. Mok, "Fundamental Design Problems of Distributed Systems for the Hard Real–Time Environment," Ph.D. Thesis, Department of Electrical Engineering and Computer Science, M.I.T., 1983.

[29] J. Y.–T. Leung and M. L. Merrill, "A Note on Preemptive Scheduling of Periodic, Real–Time Tasks," *Information Processing Letters*, vol. 11, no. 3, pp. 115–118, November, 1980.

[30] E. L. Lawler and J. M. Moore, "A Functional Equation and Its Application to Resource Allocation and Scheduling Problem," *Management Science*, Vol. 16, pp. 77–84, 1969.

[31] W. K. Shih and J. W. S. Liu, "Minimization of the Maximum Error of Imprecise Computations." manuscript in preparation.

[32] J. Y–T. Leung and C. S. Wong, "Minimizing the Number of Late Tasks with Error Constraints," *Proceedings of the 11th Real–Time Systems Symposium*, Orlando, Florida, December 1990.

[33] J. Y–T. Leung, T. W. Tam, C. S. Wong, and G. H. Wong, "Minimizing Mean Flow Time with Error Constraints," *Proceedings of the 10th IEEE Real–Time Systems Symposium*, December 1989.

[34] W. K. Shih, J. W. S. Liu, J. Y. Chung and D. W. Gillies, "Scheduling Tasks with Ready Times and Deadlines to Minimize Average Error," *ACM Operating Systems Review*, July 1989.

[35] W. K. Shih, J. W. S. Liu, and J. Y. Chung, "Fast Algorithms for Scheduling Tasks with Ready Times and Deadlines to Minimize Total Error," *Proceedings of the 10th IEEE Real–Time Systems Symposium*, December 1989.

[36] W. K. Shih, J. W. S. Liu, and J. Y. Chung, "Algorithms for Scheduling Imprecise Computations with Timing Constraints," to appear in *SIAM Journal of Computing*.

[37] R. McNaughton, "Scheduling with Deadlines and Loss Functions," *Management Science*, Vol. 12, pp. 1–12, 1959.

[38] A. A. Bertossi and M. A. Bonuccelli, "Preemptive Scheduling of Periodic Jobs in Uniform Multiprocessor Systems," *Information Processing Letters*, vol. 16, pp. 3–6, January, 1983.

[39] Leung, J. Y.–T. and J. Whitehead, "On the Complexity of Fixed–Priority Scheduling of Periodic, Real–Time Tasks,"

Performance Evaluation, vol. 2, pp. 237–250, 1982.

[40] Lawler, E. L. and C. U. Martel, "Scheduling Periodically Occurring Tasks on Multiple Processors," *Information Processing Letters*, vol. 12, no. 1, pp. 9–12, February, 1981.

[41] Chung, J. Y. and J. W. S. Liu, "Performance of Algorithms for Scheduling Periodic Jobs to Minimize Average Error," *Proceedings of the IEEE 9th Real–Time Systems Symposium*, Huntsville, Alabama, December 1988.

[42] Chung, J. Y., "Scheduling Periodic Jobs Making Use of Imprecise Results," Ph.D. Thesis, Department of Computer Science, University of Illinois, May 1989.

[43] Garey, M. R. and D. S. Johnson, *Computers and Intractability: A Guide to the Theory of NP–Completeness*, W. H. Freeman and Company, New York, 1979.

[44] E. G. Coffman, Jr., M. R. Garey, and D. S. Johnson, "An Application of Bin–Packing to Multiprocessor Scheduling," *SIAM J. Comput.*, vol 7, no. 1, pp. 1–17, February, 1978.

[45] C. Han and K. J. Lin, "Scheduling Parallelizable Real–Time Jobs on Multiprocessors," *Proceedings of the 10th IEEE Real–Time Systems Symposium*, December 1989.

[46] J. Du and J. Y–T. Leung, "Complexity of Scheduling Parallel Task Systems," Technical Report UTDCS 6–87, University of Texas at Dallas, Dallas, TX, 1987.

[47] N. Karmarker, "A New Polynomial–Time Algorithm for Linear Programming," *Combinatorica*, vol. 4, pp. 373–395, 1984.

[48] L. G. Khanchian, "Polynomial Algorithms in Linear Programming," *Zhurnal Vychislitelnoi Mathematiki Matematicheskoi Fiziki*, vol. 20, pp. 53–72, 1980.

[49] A. C. Yu and K. J. Lin, "Scheduling Parallelizable Imprecise Computations on Multiprocessors," submitted for publication.

[50] E. L. Lawler, "Fast Approximation Algorithms for Knapsack Problems," *Math. of Operations Research*, vol.4, pp. 339–356, November 1979.

[51] E. K. P. Chong and W. Zhao, "Performance Evaluation of Scheduling Algorithms for Imprecise Computer Systems," submitted for publication. Also as Tech. Report, Department of

Computer Science, University of Adelaide, SA 5006, Australia, September 1988.

[52] E. K. P. Chong and W. Zhao, "Task Scheduling for Imprecise Computer Systems with User Controlled Optimization", *Proc. of International Conference on Computers and Information*, May 1989.

[53] W. Zhao and E. K. P. Chong, "Performance Evaluation of Scheduling Algorithms for Dynamic Imprecise Soft Real–Time Computer Systems", *Australian Computer Science Communications*, Vol. 11, No. 1, 1989, pp 329—340.

[54] W. Zhao and J. W. S. Liu, "An Analytical Model for Multi-Server Imprecise Systems", Tech. Report, Department of Computer Science, University of Adelaide, July 1990.

CHAPTER 9

Allocating SMART Cache Segments
for Schedulability

David B. Kirk, Jay K. Strosnider, and John E. Sasinowski
Department of Electrical and Computer Engineering
Carnegie Mellon University, Pittsburgh, Pennsylvania 15213

Abstract

Since they were first introduced in the IBM 360/85 in 1969, the primary application of cache memories has been in the general purpose computing community. Thus, it is no surprise that modern cache designs are optimized for average case performance. This optimization criterion has opened a wide gap between the average case performance which is important to general purpose computing and the worst case performance that is critical to real-time computing. This has delayed the adoption of caches by the real-time community. The SMART (Strategic Memory Allocation for Real-Time) cache design approach narrows the gap between this worst case performance, and the impressive average case performance provided by conventional caches. This paper focuses on an analytical approach to cache allocation which minimizes task set utilization while guaranteeing schedulability. An overview of the SMART caching strategy is presented, as well as an algorithm which optimally allocates cache segments to a set of periodic tasks using rate monotonic scheduling. This algorithm uses dynamic programming to reduce an exponential search space to a polynomial one. Results which show SMART caches narrowing the gap between average and worst case performance to less than 10% are then presented.

INTRODUCTION

Cache Memories and Real-Time Computing

Cache memories are small, fast buffers, placed between the CPU and main memory, which provide the functionality of main memory at the speed of the CPU. The general purpose computing community has been very successful in using caches to take advantage of the program properties of temporal and spatial locality. By exploiting these properties, the cache attempts to ensure that information, local both in time and in space to the current information, is readily available [15]. When successful, the memory request results in a *cache hit*, and the access is performed at the speed of the cache. When it fails, the request results in a *cache miss*, and the access is performed at the speed of main memory - often three or four times slower than cache. For more information on caches (line sizes, replacement policies, write policies, prefetch policies, and more), an excellent summary is provided in [14] and [3]. A good discussion on placement policies (associativity) is found in [6]. Cache coherence snooping and directory schemes are discussed in [1], and the write-once scheme is discussed in [4] and [17].

Real-time systems are used in environments that impose tight timing constraints on the worst case response times of individual tasks. Unlike general purpose computing environments where notions of average performance are sufficient, the usefulness of results in real-time computing environments is a function of both its accuracy and the time at which the result is produced. Failure to meet required timing constraints can have severe consequences for many real-time applications. In order to guarantee that the timing constraints of individual tasks are met, systems must be designed for worst case performance and not average case performance.

The adoption of caches by the real-time computing community has been slow due to the unpredictable task execution times that they introduce. This is particularly true for multi-tasking, interrupt-driven environments which are typical of most real-time applications. In such cases, wide swings in individual task execution times arise from the interactions of real-time tasks and the external environment via the operating system. Although the effects of preemption and associated overhead can be predictably accounted for in the absence of caches, preemptions modify the cache contents and thereby cause nondeterministic cache hit behavior which translates into unpredictable task execution times.

Currently, real-time systems that do include caches perform their timing analysises as if the caches were not present and either disable the cache or use it to handle transient overloads. This is the case in the U.S. Navy's AEGIS Combat System. The AN/UYK-43 computer, which provides the central computing power to the system, has a 32K-word cache that is partitioned for instructions and data. However, due to unpredictable cache performance, all module (task) utilizations are calculated as if the cache were turned off (cache bypass option). As a result, the theoretically overutilized CPU is often underutilized at run-time when the cache is enabled.

The goal of this research has been to develop cache designs that narrow the gap between the worst case performance required for real-time computing, and the impressive average case performance provided by conventional caches. The SMART (Strategic Memory Allocation for Real-Time) cache design approach [10, 9] has been developed to exploit the performance advantages of caches in real-time computing environments. Hardware requirements and resulting cache access delay times of implementations of SMART cache designs in the MIPS R3000 were presented in [11].

This paper focuses on an analytical treatment of the cache segment *Allocation* component of the SMART caching strategy. For this reason, a brief overview of SMART caching is presented in Section . Section then introduces the problem of optimally allocating the cache segments to a set of periodic tasks. A technique is presented for reducing the exponential search space to a polynomial search space through the use of dynamic programming. Minimized task set utilization and the scheduling constraints imposed by the rate monotonic framework[1] are considered. Section presents initial simulation results which show that SMART caches narrow the gap between average and worst case performance to less than 10 percent. Finally, Section highlights conclusions that can be drawn from this research.

SMART CACHE PARTITIONING OVERVIEW

The SMART cache design strategy is a software controlled partitioning technique which provides predictable cache performance while requiring minimal hardware costs and resulting in very little overhead during context switching. The following sections review how the cache is partitioned, and how it is controlled. Section presents the performance gains achieved using SMART caching. For a more detailed discussion of SMART caching, see [7], [9], and [11].

---

[1]Although the rate monotonic algorithm was chosen due to its wide acceptance [13] in both government and industry, the SMART design strategy is beneficial in any priority-based preemptive scheduling environment.

The Partitioning Approach

Under the SMART cache partitioning scheme, a cache of size C is divided into S segments. These segments are then allocated to the N tasks in an active task set, where N may be greater than, equal to, or less than S. The cache is partitioned so that a portion of the segments are contained in one partition referred to as the *shared partition*, and the remainder of the segments form the *private partitions* that are assigned to the performance-critical tasks (see Figure 1). The shared partition services aperiodics, interrupts and other miscellaneous tasks, as well as providing for coherent caching of shared data structures. This paper is concerned with the optimal allocation of cache segments to the private partitions of periodic tasks scheduled by the rate monotonic algorithms.

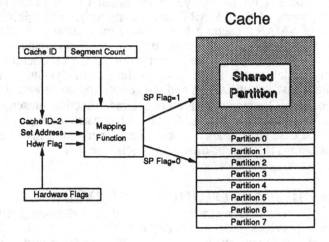

Figure 1: SMART Cache Partitioning

Segments within a private partition can only be accessed by the task that owns it and are consequently protected from preemption-induced cold-starts and the associated low hit rates. Each task owning segments in a private partition is also free to use the shared partition to limit collisions within the private partition or to store shared data. Since the shared partition is accessed by multiple tasks, it is not protected across preemptions, and the resulting cache hits are not guaranteed. Therefore, references to the shared partition by tasks which own private partitions should be limited. Systems which employ split data and instruction caches can use the shared instruction partition as a read only memory which stores commonly used library functions. References to this shared partition would then result in predictable cache hits.

Private partitions can also be allocated to a group of tasks if they share the same preemption level (i.e. are not permitted to preempt one another).

The AEGIS Tactical Executive System (ATES) implements such a scheduling scheme. ATES supports 64 priority levels, divided into 4 preemption levels. Priorities within a preemption category are used to determine which active task will be serviced at the next task completion boundary. Once a task is running, only tasks in a higher preemption category can cause a context switch. If one partition is used by interrupt routines, one is used for the operating system, and one partition is used for each of the four preemption levels, the entire task set can be serviced with six cache partitions.

Controlling the Partitions

The following discussion assumes a set-associative cache, but the same conclusions hold for a direct-mapped cache (a comprehensive discussion of the differences appears in [6]). A segment count field and cache ID are used to identify how many segments a task owns, and which they are. A hardware flag determines whether the shared partition or the private partition is active. The cache ID, segment count field, and hardware flag(s) for the active task are loaded during the context swap. During memory accesses, the set address for the cache is combined with the cache ID and the hardware flag as shown in Figure 1. The delay in the cache access path due to the additional SMART hardware is minimized by restricting the partition sizes to powers of two.

The shared partition hardware flag is toggled by instructions embedded in the execution code either as additional instructions (vertical insertion), or as additional bits in the present instructions (horizontal insertion). Maintaining internal cache coherence for shared data structures, handling interrupts, and servicing aperiodics are topics discussed in [9].

CACHE SEGMENT ALLOCATION

This section discusses the problem of determining the optimal scheme for allocating cache segments to a set of periodic tasks. Optimality in this context refers to finding the minimal task set utilization among the set of all schedulable combinations of tasks and allocations. A technique for reducing the exponential search space to a polynomial search space through the use of dynamic programming is presented.

Understanding Execution Times

The SMART cache partitioning scheme divides a cache into S equal-sized segments which are then allocated to individual tasks, as well as to the shared partition. Before discussing the allocation of these cache segments, it is useful to understand the impact of cache induced nondeterministic execution times on the schedulability analysis. Consider periodic tasks $\tau_1, \tau_2, ..., \tau_N$ with corresponding run-times $C_1, C_2, \cdots, C_N$ and periods $T_1 \leq T_2 \leq \cdots \leq T_N$.

The total utilization is given by

$$U_{total} = \sum_{i=1}^{N} \frac{C_i}{T_i}.$$

Using the rate monotonic algorithm, the tasks are ordered by priority with τ_1 having the highest priority and τ_N having the lowest priority. Because this discussion is only concerned with comparing the effects of memory reference delays on execution times, the run-time requirement is only dependent on time spent fetching data and instructions. Therefore, we assume instruction execution is pipelined and occurs in parallel with the memory references.

Cache misses cause the processor to stall while data is fetched from main memory and loaded into the cache. Therefore, any task execution time can be divided into to two components: $C_{i_{ideal}}$, the minimum time required to fetch all instructions and data; and $C_{i_{stall}}$, the time the processor is stalled while waiting for main memory accesses to complete. $C_{i_{ideal}}$ is the execution time for τ_i when running with an infinite size cache which never misses. The U_{total} can thus be rewritten as

$$U_{total} = \sum_{i=1}^{N} \frac{C_{i_{ideal}} + C_{i_{stall}}}{T_i}.$$

Factoring out the stall component, we have

$$U_{total} = U_{total_{ideal}} + U_{total_{stall}}$$

where

$$U_{total_{stall}} = \frac{C_{i_{stall}}}{T_i}.$$

It is the stall component of the execution time that is unpredictable in multi-tasking, interrupt-driven environments. Assigning private partitions does not eliminate the stall component, but it does make it predictable. As the number of segments allocated to a task's private partition increases, its stall component monotonically decreases since miss rates diminish with cache size.

From the above analysis, it would seem clear that cache segments should be allocated to periodic tasks so that the *stall* utilization is minimized. This results in a minimum total utilization since the *ideal* component is constant. However, Section will demonstrate that schedulability constraints must be factored into the analysis. For now, we will concern ourselves with determining the cache allocation scheme that yields the minimum task set utilization.

Clearly the *stall* utilization of any task can be minimized by allocating the task enough cache segments to ensure that its entire working set fits in cache. Only intra-task cache line collisions would cause misses under this allocation policy. While this results in the minimum execution time for that particular task, it may deprive other tasks of needed cache segments since there is a limited number of cache segments to allocate. As a result, the total task set utilization would most likely not be minimized.

Before cache segments can be handed out to any one task, the reduction in execution time provided by each task must be considered. In addition, this benefit must be weighted by the frequency of the task, since a reduction of 1*ms* in execution time in a task which runs every 10*ms* is more significant than a reduction of 1*ms* in a task which runs every 100*ms*. The segment allocation must address the reduction of the total execution times over a fixed interval and not just those of the individual tasks. One way to do this is to measure the number of hits provided by each task in all legal partition sizes and then to weight these counts by the task's frequency. This weighting provides the number of cache hits that the task returns over a fixed interval of time in each legal partition size, thereby allowing comparisons of the performance of different cache allocations.

The results of this procedure are tabulated as shown in the example in Figure 2. This table shows two values for each table entry. One entry is the weighted number of hits, and the other is the resulting execution time.

Assuming that the schedulability checks will be addressed later, the goal of the allocation process is to select one entry from each row (making sure that the total number of segments allocated is less than or equal to S) so that the sum of the resulting scores is as large as possible. The resulting segment allocation provides the maximum total cache hit count and minimizes both the composite task execution time and the task set utilization. The next section describes a technique for determining the number of possible allocations that must be considered.

Segments

	0	1	2	4	...	S
Task 1	Scr1,0	Scr1,1	Scr1,2	Scr1,4		Scr1,S
	Time1,0	Time1,1	Time1,2	Time1,4		Time1,S
Task 2	Scr2,0	Scr2,1	Scr2,2	Scr2,4		Scr2,S
	Time2,0	Time2,1	Time2,2	Time2,4		Time2,S
Task 3						
.						
.						
Task N	ScrN,0	ScrN,1	ScrN,2	ScrN,4		ScrN,S
	TimeN,0	TimeN,1	TimeN,2	TimeN,4		TimeN,S

Scr n,s = Weighted Hits for Task *n* with *s* segments

Time n,s = Exec Time for Task *n* with *s* segments

Figure 2: Example Score Table

Calculating Total Combinations

Understanding the size of a problem is helpful in finding its solution. However, the problem size can be difficult to calculate. In the case of segment allocation, the number of unique allocations of segments to tasks depends on both the total number of segments available for allocation and the number of segments previously assigned to other tasks.

The number of allocations of S segments to tasks $\tau_1, \tau_2, \ldots, \tau_N$ will be represented by $A_{N,S}$. To compute the value of $A_{N,S}$, we can use an incremental approach. To start, suppose we only have one task and an arbitrary number of segments, S. Due to the hardware implementation constraints [11], the legal allocations of segments for this task must either be zero or powers of two. The resulting number of choices is $\lfloor \log_2(S) \rfloor + 2$, since there are $\lfloor \log_2(S) \rfloor + 1$ choices of powers of two segments in S and a choice of zero segments. The one exception to this formula is for $S = 0$, since $\log_2(0)$ is undefined, and it is only possible to allocate zero segments. Therefore, for $N=1$, we have:

$$A_{1,S} = \begin{cases} 1 & \text{if } S = 0 \\ \lfloor \log_2(S) \rfloor + 2 & \text{otherwise} \end{cases}$$

Next, consider a case with two tasks, τ_1 and τ_2. Each allocation that τ_2

makes will leave some segments for τ_1. If τ_2 is given S segments and takes k of them, then τ_1 has $S-k$ segments available. To compute the number of allocations of S segments to τ_1 and τ_2, we need to find $A_{2,S}$. For each assignment k that τ_2 can make, there are $A_{1,S-k}$ possible assignments that τ_1 can make. From this, we can get:

$$A_{2,S} = A_{1,S} + A_{1,S-1} + A_{1,S-2} + A_{1,S-4} + \cdots$$

$$= A_{1,S} + \sum_{i=0}^{\lfloor \log_2(S) \rfloor} A_{1,S-2^i}.$$

The first term represents τ_2 taking no segments, and the summation term covers all cases of τ_2 taking 2^i segments, and passing $S-2^i$ segments to τ_1.

Now, consider the more general case. Suppose we are looking at S segments to be assigned to $\tau_1, \ldots, \tau_j$. Determining the number of possible allocations to these tasks is analogous to the case for τ_1 and τ_2. We are looking for $A_{j,S}$. τ_j can only choose a number of segments that are either zero or a power of 2. After τ_j takes k segments, the remaining $S-k$ segments are available to the other tasks. The number of possible allocations if τ_j takes k segments is the number of ways that $\tau_1, \ldots, \tau_{j-1}$ (the remaining tasks) can allocate $S-k$ segments. This gives us:

$$A_{j,S} = A_{j-1,S} + \sum_{i=0}^{\lfloor \log_2(S) \rfloor} A_{j-1,S-2^i}.$$

Summarizing this, we get:

$$A_{j,S} = A_{j-1,S} + \sum_{i=0}^{\lfloor \log_2(S) \rfloor} A_{j-1,S-2^i} \qquad (1)$$

$$\text{with} \quad A_{1,S} = \begin{cases} 1 & \text{if } S = 0 \\ \lfloor \log_2(S) \rfloor + 2 & \text{otherwise} \end{cases}$$

For clarification, consider the following example. Suppose we have τ_1, τ_2, and τ_3 to which we want to allocate 8 segments. Using the equation 1), we need $A_{3,8}$:

$$A_{3,8} = A_{2,8} + A_{2,7} + A_{2,6} + A_{2,4} + A_{2,0}$$

Computing the $A_{2,s}$ terms:

$$A_{2,8} = A_{1,8} + A_{1,7} + A_{1,6} + A_{1,4} + A_{1,0}$$
$$A_{2,7} = A_{1,7} + A_{1,6} + A_{1,5} + A_{1,3}$$
$$A_{2,6} = A_{1,6} + A_{1,5} + A_{1,4} + A_{1,2}$$

$$A_{2,4} = A_{1,4} + A_{1,3} + A_{1,2} + A_{1,0}$$
$$A_{2,0} = A_{1,0}$$

Now evaluating the $A_{1,s}$ terms:

$$A_{1,8} = \lfloor \log_2(8) \rfloor + 2 = 5 \qquad A_{1,7} = \lfloor \log_2(7) \rfloor + 2 = 4$$
$$A_{1,6} = \lfloor \log_2(6) \rfloor + 2 = 4 \qquad A_{1,5} = \lfloor \log_2(5) \rfloor + 2 = 4$$
$$A_{1,4} = \lfloor \log_2(4) \rfloor + 2 = 4 \qquad A_{1,3} = \lfloor \log_2(3) \rfloor + 2 = 3$$
$$A_{1,2} = \lfloor \log_2(2) \rfloor + 2 = 3 \qquad A_{1,0} = 1$$

This gives us:

$$A_{3,8} = 60$$

It is important to note that this expression for the number of possible assignments was derived independently from any specific allocation algorithm, and simply specifies the total number of combinations that must be considered to provide an optimal solution.

Tree Traversal

One approach to finding the optimal segment assignment is to generate a tree of all possible assignment combinations. An example tree is shown in Figure 3. The root node represents τ_N with S segments available. The arcs out of the root node represent the possible allocation choices for τ_N. Each such arc represents the choice of τ_N taking k segments and passing the remaining $S-k$ segments to τ_{N-1}. Each of the children of the root node is now the root of a subtree which represents the ways that τ_{N-1} can allocate the segments that are passed to it. This process continues until τ_1 is passed k segments. Since all the other tasks have considered their possible allocations, τ_1 cannot pass any unused segments to another task. The nodes for τ_1 are therefore the bottommost nodes in the tree. Each level in the tree contains the nodes for the possible allocations for one task, and each complete assignment scheme is represented by the a path through the tree.

> **Theorem 1:** Each path in the tree represents a unique assignment of cache segments.
>
> **Proof: By contradiction:** Assume for the moment that two different paths P_i and P_j represent identical segment assignments. For some number of levels L, both P_i and P_j traverse the same path. As a minimum, the root is common to both paths. Furthermore, since P_i and P_j are different paths, there must be a node at level $L+1$ where the paths diverge. However, since the tree structure

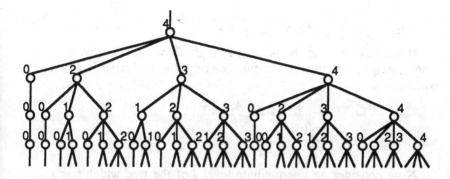

Figure 3: Tree-based Search Algorithm.

defines that each branch out of a node corresponds to a different assignment of segments to a particular task, P_i and P_j must have different assignments at level $L+1$ and therefore represent different segment assignments. Thus, paths P_i and P_j cannot represent identical segment assignments.

Since each path through the tree represents a unique segment assignment and terminates at a leaf, determining the best path through the tree is reduced to selecting the leaf with the highest score. Calculating the score for each leaf is straightforward. Scores are assigned to each leaf by summing the weighted scores associated with each branch along the path from the root to the leaf. Since each path represents a complete segment allocation, the score recorded at the leaf represents the score for that assignment. The leaf with the highest score represents the best path through the tree. The following proof shows that this algorithm considers all possible cache assignments, so it must find the highest possible score.

Theorem 2: The tree-based algorithm considers all possible cache assignment combinations.

Proof: We will show this by demonstrating that the number of unique paths considered by the tree traversal is equivalent to the total number of unique allocations as derived in Section . Therefore, selection of the path in the tree that produces the highest score must also represent the highest score for any possible combination of cache segment allocations.

Starting with the nodes of height 1, we see that the number of assignments generated at a node that is passed s segments is given by:

$$A_{1,s} = \begin{cases} 1 & \text{if } s = 0 \\ \lfloor \log_2(s) \rfloor + 2 & \text{otherwise.} \end{cases}$$

If we next look at the nodes of height 2, we see that when a node is passed s segments, the number of paths evaluated is given by:

$$A_{2,s} = A_{1,s} + A_{1,s-1} + A_{1,s-2} + A_{1,s-4} + \cdots$$

$$= A_{1,s} + \sum_{i=0}^{\lfloor \log_2(s) \rfloor} A_{1,s-2^i}.$$

Now consider an intermediate level j of the tree which has s segments to allocate. T_j can only take a number of segments that is either zero or a power of 2. After τ_j takes k segments, the remaining segments s-k are available for the other tasks below it in the tree. The number of possible allocations when τ_j takes k segments is the number of ways that $\tau_1, \ldots, \tau_{j-1}$ (the tasks below τ_j in the tree) can allocate s-k segments. This gives us:

$$A_{j,s} = A_{j-1,s} + \sum_{i=0}^{\lfloor \log_2(s) \rfloor} A_{j-1,s-2^i}$$

Summarizing this, we get:

$$A_{j,s} = A_{j-1,s} + \sum_{i=0}^{\lfloor \log_2(s) \rfloor} A_{j-1,s-2^i}$$

where $A_{1,s} = \begin{cases} 1 & \text{if } s = 0 \\ \lfloor \log_2(s) \rfloor + 2 & \text{otherwise.} \end{cases}$

If we assume there are S segments to allocate, the number of combinations checked by the tree-based algorithm is identical to the total number of combinations derived in Section . Since all paths were shown to be unique by Theorem 1, the algorithm considered all possible combinations.

There is another way to traverse the tree which also finds the optimal solution. This technique stores the highest total score that a node and its subtree can earn if passed a certain number of segments. It starts in the bottom level and moves up to the root. At each node in the lowest row, it compares the scores earned by making legal moves, selects the highest one, and stores it in the node, along with the number of segments that are needed to earn that score. At each node in the other levels, it adds the score earned by each legal allocation for that node to the score earned by passing the remaining segments to the previous task. This represents the score for τ_j

taking k segments, and passing on s-k (where s is the number of segments passed to τ_j). It compares these sums, selects the highest score, and stores it in the node along with the segment allocation that earns that score. It repeats this process for each level in the tree. The score assigned to the root node represents the highest possible score for allocating S cache segments to the N tasks.

Although the tree traversal technique finds the optimal solution, the number of calculations grows exponentially with the number of tasks. However, much of this is wasted work. Notice that in any given level L, two nodes that are passed the same number of segments always have the same score because the subtrees below them are identical. The paths are only different in the assignments made above level L, which do not effect the score at level L. Therefore, each of these nodes need only be calculated once. In the tree traversal algorithm, however, they are recalculated at every node. There are at most $S+1$ unique nodes in each row, because there is one unique node for each number of segments that could be passed from the previous level. Since the size of the tree grows exponentially with the number of tasks, the number of repeated nodes grows exponentially as N gets large.

The next section discusses a technique for using this information to reduce the number of calculations that are needed to find the optimal allocation.

Dynamic Programming Algorithm

Dynamic programming is a bottom-up programming technique. The underlying idea of dynamic programming is to avoid calculating the same thing twice, usually by keeping a table of known results which is filled up as subinstances of the problem are solved. Dynamic programming algorithms generally start with the smallest, and hence simplest, subinstances. Solutions to larger instances are formed by combining the solutions to the smaller instances, until the original problem is solved [2].

Several characteristics of the tree-search algorithm can be exploited to create a dynamic programming algorithm that runs in polynomial time. Since the repeated nodes compute the same value, there is no need to calculate them multiple times. If there are S segments available to the set of tasks, then each level can have at most $S+1$ nodes, one for each possible number of segments that can be passed from the previous level. There are cases when there are fewer than $S+1$ nodes, but the analysis will be easier if we assume that $S+1$ nodes need to be computed on each level. This assumption will not affect the order of the execution time of the algorithm. Since there are N tasks, the number of nodes that need to be computed is $N(S+1)$.

The next property of the tree that we can exploit is that if all the children of a particular node have been computed, then that node can compute its value by looking no further than the values of its children.

From this information, we formulate the following dynamic programming algorithm. We need some tables to store information. All of them have N rows and $S+1$ columns. We need a table of the weighted scores that each task gets in each legal partition size called $Score[i, j]$. To make the discussion simpler, let Score[i, j] be the score that τ_i gets from running in j segments if j is a legal cache size and 0 otherwise. We also need $Total[i, j]$ to store the computed score of each node, which is the highest possible score for $\tau_1, \tau_2, \ldots, \tau_i$ if τ_i is passed j segments. In addition, we need another table $Alloc[i, j]$ to store the number of segments allocated by τ_i to get $Total[i, j]$ if passed j segments. This will allow us to read out the final allocation strategy when the computation is finished.

The process of filling up the tables proceeds as follows. Start with the first row, which corresponds to the bottom level in the tree. Any segments that are not taken by the nodes in this row are unused, so the score for passing any segments is zero. Therefore, the scores in the first row are computed by considering all legal assignments when passed j segments and selecting the highest resulting score. The score is recorded, as well as the minimum number of segments required to achieve that score. In other words,

$$Total[1,j] = max(Score[1,s]), \text{ where } s \in \{ \text{ legal partition sizes } \leq j\}$$

$Alloc[1,j] = k,$ where k is the minimum number of segments

that τ_1 must take to get $Total[1,j]$.

Once a row is complete, the next one can be processed. Any segments that are not taken by the nodes in this row are passed to the nodes in the previous row, who have already determined the best possible score for any number of segments passed to them. Therefore, to calculate $Total[i, j]$, we need to add the score for any legal assignment k to $Total[i-1, j-k]$, which is the highest score earned by passing the remaining segments on. The highest sum is assigned to $Total[i, j]$ and represents the best score for τ_i given j segments. The number of segments that need to be allocated to τ_i to get this score is stored in $Alloc[i, j]$. In other words,

$$Total[i,j] = max(Score[i,k], + Total[i-1,j-k]),$$

where $k \in \{ \text{ legal partition sizes } \leq j\}$,

$Alloc[i,j] = s_{min},$ where s_{min} is the minimum number of

segments that τ_i must take to get $Total[i,j]$.

This process continues until the last row is filled. When the last row is complete, the maximum score is contained in $Total[N,S]$.

Now we know the highest possible score we can get. What we really need is the segment allocation scheme that gives us that score. Recall that $Alloc[i, j]$ is the number of segments that τ_i would take to get the highest possible score (*Total[i, j]*) if it were passed *j* segments . These values act as pointers that we can use to trace out the segment allocation scheme. For example, *Alloc[N, S]* is the number of segments that τ_N would take if given *S* segments to get *Total[N, S]*. We want to get a total score of *Total[N, S]*, so τ_N should be given *Alloc[N, S]* segments. Now we need to find the rest of the allocations. Since we know *Alloc[N, S]*, we can figure out how many segments to allocate to τ_N. Since there were *S* segments passed to τ_N, there must be *S - Alloc[N, S]* segments passed to τ_{N-1} to get the highest total score. Therefore, τ_{N-1} should be allocated *Alloc[N-1, S - Alloc[N, S]]* segments. If we refer to the number of segments passed to τ_i along the optimum allocation path as p_i and the number of segments allocated to τ_i along this same path as a_i, we have:

$$a_i = Alloc[i, p_i], \; p_i = \begin{cases} S & \text{if } i = N \\ p_{i+1} - a_{i+1} & \text{otherwise} \end{cases}$$

Earlier we claimed that the dynamic programming algorithm is inherently faster than the tree-based search algorithm which runs in exponential time. We will now show that the dynamic programming algorithm runs in polynomial time. Using the add/compare step as our basic operation, an upper bound of the tree-traversal algorithm can be found by assuming that every node in the tree has $\lfloor \log_2(S) \rfloor + 2$ children. Using this assumption, the order of the tree-traversal algorithm is given by:

$$O(tree) = (\lfloor \log_2(S) \rfloor + 2)^N$$

Now let us look at the order of the dynamic programming approach. The number of operations needed to compute *Total[i, j]* depends upon the number of combinations that *Total[i, j]* needs to consider, which depends upon the value of *j*. The number of steps required to compute *Total[i, j]* is given as:

$$STEPS_{i,j} = \begin{cases} 1 & \text{if } j = 0 \\ \lfloor \log_2(j) \rfloor + 2 & \text{otherwise} \end{cases}$$

For each row of *Total[i, j]*'s in the table, the number of such operations is then:

$$1 + \sum_{i=1}^{S} (\lfloor \log_2(i) \rfloor + 2)$$

Since *S* is always a power of 2, we get:

$$1 + \sum_{j=0}^{\log_2(S)-1} 2^j(j+2) \; + \log_2(S) + 2.$$

If we define $Z = \log_2(S) - 1$, we have

$$1 + \sum_{j=0}^{Z} j2^j + 2\sum_{j=0}^{Z} 2^j + \log_2(S) + 2. \tag{2}$$

It can be shown that

$$2\sum_{j=0}^{Z} 2^j = 2(2^{Z+1} - 1) = 2(S - 1). \tag{3}$$

To solve the other summation, we use the fact that

$$\sum_{j=0}^{n} jx^{j-1} = \frac{d}{dx}\sum_{j=0}^{n} x^j = \frac{d}{dx}\frac{1 - x^{n+1}}{1 - x} = \frac{nx^{n+1} - (n+1)x^n + 1}{(1 - x)^2}.$$

Substituting 2 for x and changing the limits of the summation we get

$$\sum_{j=0}^{Z} j2^j = 2\sum_{j=0}^{Z} j2^{j-1},$$

which, when expanded, gives

$$\sum_{j=0}^{Z} j2^j = 2[Z2^{Z+1} - (N+1)2^Z + 1]$$

$$= 2[(\log_2(S) - 1)2^{\log_2[S]} - (\log_2(S))2^{\log_2[S] - 1} + 1],$$

$$= 2[S\log_2(S) - S - \frac{1}{2}S\log_2(S) + 1]$$

$$= S\log_2(S) - 2S + 2. \tag{4}$$

Therefore, when we substitute equations 3 and 4 into equation 2, we get the number of computations in each row which is

$$1 + \log_2(S) + 2 + 2(S - 1) + S\log_2(S) - 2S + 2$$
$$= 3 + \log_2(S) + S\log_2(S).$$

There are N rows of totals, so it takes $N[3 + \log_2(S) + S\log_2(S)]$ operations to find the highest score. Determining the final segment allocation scheme takes N steps, since there are N tasks and determining the allocation for each task only involves a subtraction of indices and a couple of variable assignments.

Therefore, the total execution time is:

$$N[3 + \log_2(S) + S\log_2(S)] + N = N[4 + \log_2(S) + S\log_2(S)],$$

which gives us:

$$O(dynamic) = O(N \cdot S \cdot \log_2(S)).$$

As you can see, the dynamic programming algorithm runs in polynomial time, whereas the tree-based search ran in exponential time. This is why the dynamic programming algorithm is so much faster than the tree-based approach.

We ran implementations of both the tree-based algorithm and the dynamic programming algorithm[2] on a DecStation 3100. There were thirty-two segments available to a task set consisting of eight tasks. The tree-based search took 1,961,220,666 cycles, while the dynamic programming search ran in 521,501 cycles.

Schedulability

The allocation algorithms discussed thus far minimized the task set utilization. The example provided in the next section shows that minimizing the total utilization of a task set is insufficient. The lack of schedulability of the minimum utilization partitioning solution does not necessarily imply that no schedulable partitioning solution exists. The following example illustrates such a case.

Schedulability Example. Consider a task set composed of three tasks. The task workloads are specified in memory operations, and the computation times are given in cycles which are divided into the *ideal* and *stall* components discussed in Section . We assume that a cache hit takes 1 cycle, and a cache miss (and main memory access) takes 4 cycles. The task information is summarized in Figure 4.

Task Set Definition			
Task	Period (cycles)	Relative Frequency	Workload (memory operations)
τ_1	T1 = 100	14	10
τ_2	T2 = 140	10	18
τ_3	T3 = 1400	1	60

Figure 4: Task Set: Workload in Memory Operations

Assume that there are 4 cache segments to allocate. The table shown in Figure 5 shows the cache hits provided by each task in the legal size cache partitions, along with the associated weighted score in parentheses. The weighted scores are computed by multiplying the hit counts by the relative frequencies of the tasks. In this case the relative weighting factors (relative to the lowest frequency task) are 14, 10, and 1 corresponding to τ_1 having a

---

[2]The implementation of the dynamic programming algorithm included the schedulability checks described in section

frequency 14 times higher than τ_3 and τ having a frequency 10 times higher than that of τ_3.

Unweighted Hit Counts and Weighted Scores in Parentheses				
Task	0 Segs	1 Seg	2 Segs	4 Segs
τ_1	0	0	0	0
τ_2	0	0	3 (30)	4 (40)
τ_3	0	0	20 (20)	20 (20)

Figure 5: Unweighted hit counts and Weighted Scores

To achieve the highest possible weighted score of 50 and thereby minimize the total utilization, no segments are given to τ_1, 2 segments are given to τ_2, and 2 segments are given to τ_3. This gives us $0 + 30 + 20 = 50$. No other legal allocation scheme has a higher total score. The resulting execution times are shown in Figure 6.

Computation Times After Mimimized Utilization		
Task	Computation Time (cycles) *Ideal*	Computation Time (cycles) *Stall*	Computation Time (cycles) *Total*
τ_1	$C_{1_{ideal}} = 10$	$C_{1_{stall}} = 30$	$C_{1_{total}} = 40$
τ_2	$C_{2_{ideal}} = 18$	$C_{2_{stall}} = 45$	$C_{2_{total}} = 63$
τ_3	$C_{3_{ideal}} = 60$	$C_{3_{stall}} = 120$	$C_{3_{total}} = 180$

Figure 6: Task Set: Computation times for first allocation

Task τ_1 never hits in cache. As a result, all of its memory accesses require four cycles: one execution cycle and three stall cycles. Its 10 memory operations require 40 cycles. Task τ_2 is allocated 2 cache segments, hitting on 3 of its 18 memory references. The 15 misses cause 45 stall cycles to be added to the 18 ideal execution cycles for a total of 63 machine cycles. Task τ_3 is also allocated 2 cache segments, hitting on 20 of the 60 memory operations. The 40 misses cause 120 stall cycles to be added to the 60 ideal cycles for a total of 180 machine cycles for τ_2 to execute. No other segment allocation has a lower task set utilization. The total execution time required over the maximum task period of 1400 cycles is given by:

$$(14 \times 40) + (10 \times 63) + 180 = 1370 \text{ cycles},$$

of which

$$(14 \times 30) + (10 \times 45) + (120) = 990 \text{ cycles}$$

are stall cycles. The total utilization is thus 96%.

Applying the rate monotonic scheduling check [12] shows that τ_2 will miss a deadline at 140 cycles because it won't complete its first execution until 143 cycles. If the allocation algorithm had been aware of scheduling constraints and had instead allocated all 4 cache segments to τ_2, the tasks would have had the computation times shown in Figure 7.

Computation Times After Allocation for Scheduling			
Task	Computation Time (cycles) *Ideal*	Computation Time (cycles) *Stall*	Computation Time (cycles) *Total*
τ_1	$C_{1_{ideal}} = 10$	$C_{1_{stall}} = 30$	$C_{1_{total}} = 40$
τ_2	$C_{2_{ideal}} = 18$	$C_{2_{stall}} = 42$	$C_{2_{total}} = 60$
τ_3	$C_{3_{ideal}} = 60$	$C_{3_{stall}} = 180$	$C_{3_{total}} = 240$

Figure 7: Task Set: Computation times considering scheduling

Task τ_2 is now allocated 4 cache segments, hitting on 4 of its 18 memory references. The 14 misses cause 42 stall cycles that must be added to the 18 ideal execution cycles for a total of 60 machine cycles required for τ_2's execution. Task τ_3 is now allocated no cache segments, and therefore never hits in cache. Its 60 memory references thus require 240 machine cycles. By computing the total number of execution cycles required during the maximum period of 1400, we get

$$(14 \times 40) + (10 \times 60) + 180 = 1400 \text{ cycles},$$

of which

$$(14 \times 30) + (10 \times 42) + (180) = 1020 \text{ cycles}$$

are stall cycles. The task set utilization has increased from 96% to 100%. Checking the schedulability of the task set using equations from [12] shows the task set to be schedulable.

Although the utilization has gone to from 96% to 100%, the task set has become schedulable. The remainder of this section discusses building scheduling checks into the allocation algorithm presented earlier. The resulting scheme finds the allocation with the lowest utilization from the set of all schedulable partitionings.

Checking Schedulability. Although the following discussion deals with the Rate Monotonic Scheduling (RMS) algorithm, the allocation procedures presented in this paper do not preclude the use of alternate scheduling algorithms. The procedures detailed by Liu and Layland in [13] provide a method for determining the worst case lower bound on processor utilization. This bound for n tasks is given as n $(2^{1/n} - 1)$. This, however, describes the worst case lower bound, and is unnecessarily pessimistic for most task sets. Lehoczky, Sha and Ding defined a set of equations for determining if any set of N tasks is schedulable using the RMS algorithm [12].

These equations, discussed briefly in the previous section, define a technique which incrementally determines the schedulability of the entire task set. If we assume critical phasing of tasks at time $t=0$, then τ_i's deadline is met if there is a time $t_j \leq T_i$ when the sum of the total workloads of tasks τ_1 through τ_i is $\leq t_j$. The total workload contributed by each task is determined by multiplying the actual workload requirement of the task, by the maximum number of request it would generate up to, but not including time t_j. The original set of tasks checked for schedulability contains only the highest priority task. After each schedulability check, the remaining task with the highest priority is added to the set, and the schedulability test is repeated. For more details see [12].

Integrating Scheduling Into Allocation

The next issue we are faced with is how to integrate the schedulability checks into the search algorithms. We will confine our discussion to the dynamic search algorithm since it is inherently faster. By ordering the tasks so that τ_1 is the highest priority task and τ_N is the lowest priority task, the Lehoczky, Sha, and Ding procedure can easily be incorporated into the allocation algorithm. When evaluating the entries in the ith row, $\tau_1, \ldots, \tau_{i-1}$ are all tasks with priorities higher than τ_i. Also, when we fill in row i, all the previous rows have been filled in. This means that the optimum segment allocations, and thus the execution times, of the higher priority tasks in all possible cache sizes are already known, so we now have all the information that we need to run schedulability checks. Suppose we are filling in the entry *Table[i, j]*. When we evaluate each of the possible segment assignments, we also test for schedulability. We do not consider allocations that create unschedulable task sets to be legal. At each stage we therefore only consider allocations that are schedulable. When we have filled in *Table[N, S]*, we will know the segment assignment that results in the smallest utilization while remaining schedulable.

There are several optimizations that can be made to speed up the schedulability checks. First of all, we need another table, *Util[N, S]*. *Util[i, j]* contains the utilization of $\tau_1, \ldots, \tau_i$ if there were *j* segments passed to τ_i. The entry *Util[i, j]* is computed when the corresponding entries in *Table* and *Alloc* are filled in. This table allows us to reduce the number of times we have to use the Lehoczky, Sha, and Ding test, which is the more time consuming schedulability check. There are two quick tests that can be performed. The first allows trivial rejection: if the total utilization exceeds 100%, then the task set cannot be schedulable. The second is the corresponding test for trivial acceptance: if the total utilization is below the Liu and Layland worst case lower bound for *i* tasks, then the task set must be schedulable. Only if we cannot decide schedulability based upon these two tests do we use the Lehoczky, Sha, and Ding test. We have found that the two quick tests allow us to decide schedulability in about 2/3 of the cases. This makes sense, because the Liu and Layland bound is quite high for the first few tasks, and a large task set is not likely to exceed that. On the other hand, tasks sets that have high utilizations are more likely to exceed 100% utilization towards the end of the assignment process.

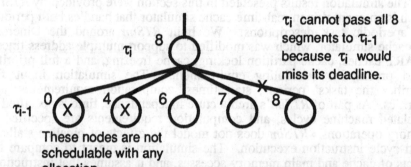

Figure 8: Example of scheduling constraints during segment allocation

There are several other optimizations. An entry in the table for which there are no schedulable assignments can be flagged so that the next task won't consider passing segments to it. In addition, a task that is not schedulable with *k* segments must also not be schedulable with fewer than *k* segments, so these possibilities can be marked as not schedulable. These enhancements are illustrated in Figure 8.

SIMULATION RESULTS

As discussed in [16], 16K caches often provide hit rates above 90%, while 4K caches typically achieve hit rates approaching 90% for a range of program traces including database management, scientific applications and batch jobs. In addition, [8] and [16] have shown that caches as small as 256 words typically achieve hit rates of 75%. The impact of caches in real-time applications was tested using a MIPS R3000 and the CSALI (Core Set of Assembly Language Instructions) benchmarks. These benchmarks were developed to evaluate the USAF RH-32 (Radiation Hardened 32-bit) processor. The suite of nine routines, which ranged from implementing a Kalman filter to performing a shell sort, were first run with no cache and then with an 8K data / 8K instruction cache with 4 word block refill. An average speedup of 5.45 was measured by the simulator, which corresponds to a utilization reduction of 82% over the non-cached implementation, thus substantiating the significant performance gains possible with a cache. The simulation results presented in the this section further substantiates these performance speedups. Small cache sizes are used to highlight the differences in the various cache models simulated.

SONAR Scenario

The simulation results presented in this section were provided by *RTSim*, which is an event-driven real-time cache simulator that handles both periodic and aperiodic task descriptions. We built *RTSim* around the DineroIII [5] cache simulator, which was modified to support multiple address traces, SMART caches, cache partition locking, cache freezing, and a full priority-based preemptive scheduling environment. The simulation input file describes the tasks' periods, start times, computation requirements, and priorities. As part of *RTSim*'s architecture independence, time is specified in simulated machine cycles, and computation requirements are specified in memory operations. *RTSim* does not model the effects of pipeline stalls or multi-cycle instruction execution. The simulation is meant to compare the effects of cache and main memory accesses, and it assumes that instructions execute in parallel with the required memory operations. During execution, cache hits advance the clock one cycle, while cache misses advance the clock by a value dependent on many factors, some of which are: cache linesize; memory bus widths; write buffers; dirty verses clean cache line; copyback verses write-through cache policy; and subsector (sub-block) support.

We simulated six cache scenarios to determine the benefits and costs of SMART caching. The first cache model is an *ideal cache* which is a preloaded, infinite cache which never misses. The second cache model is the *normal cache* used in most general purpose computers. The third is the *SMART cache* model which simulates the SMART caching scheme described throughout this paper. The *locked cache* model is based on the SMART partitioning strategy but has the added ability to lock and unlock the contents of each cache partition individually. The *frozen cache* model simulates a cache whose entire contents can be frozen and unfrozen, but, unlike the *locked* model, provides no partitions. Finally, simulation was performed using no cache.

The SONAR scenario developed at the Carnegie Mellon Software Engineering Institute provides guidelines for task periods and utilizations. Due to security and confidentiality constraints, no actual code was available with the SONAR description. Address traces with similar characteristics to the underlying SONAR signal processing functions were substituted. The resulting utilization figures were decomposed into two components: U_{ideal}, which represents the minimum utilization component as discussed in Section , and U_{stall}, which gives the utilization component due to processor stalls during fetches from main memory. For example, if a single memory reference missed in cache and then took three additional cycles to fetch the data from main memory, the total cycle count would be four cycles. Of this time, one cycle is spent doing real work, and three are spent in stall cycles. Clearly, we would like as much of it as possible to be the U_{ideal} component. Figure 9 shows the results of this simulation.

Of the four predictable cache models (*SMART, locked, frozen, no cache*), SMART partitioning provides the highest utilization. Furthermore, there is only a 7% difference between the performance of the unpredictable cache model with no partitioning and the predictable SMART cache model. The unpredictable execution times resulting from the *normal cache* design strategy far exceeded the execution times recorded for tasks in a cold cache, which led to missed deadlines. This shows how execution times in the *normal cache* can actually increase after the cache is initialized due to preemptions and interrupts, often negating the effects of the warm cache.

The locked and frozen cache models, in addition to returning lower U_{ideal} figures, are also very susceptible to performance losses due to variations in the execution paths. Once the cache contents have been locked (or frozen) there is no benefit when the execution path results in a different set of addresses. The utilization figures presented above always assume that the same execution path was taken. The *lock* and *freeze* models suffer when this assumption is invalid, because the alternate execution paths are probably not in the cache. SMART partitioning, however, functions as a normal cache, and allows the new working set to be loaded in cache as the execution path varies.

While each of the predictable caching strategies (*SMART, Locked and Frozen*) help narrow the 61% utilization gap between *Normal* caches and the *NoCache* model (often used for worst case scheduling analysis), the SMART cache model has consistently provided the highest performance gains while maintaining the full flexibility of conventional cache designs.

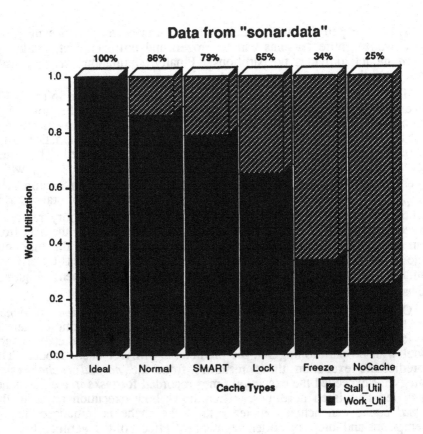

Figure 9: SONAR scenario cache simulation results

CONCLUSION

The nondeterministic execution times introduced by cache memories have deterred the use of caches in multi-tasking, interrupt-driven, real-time systems. This paper discussed the reasons for these unpredictable execution times, and provided an overview of the SMART cache design which eliminates this nondeterminism and narrows the gap between the impressive average case performance provided by conventional caches and the worst case performance used in real-time environments. With the SMART caching scheme, cache *segments* are allocated to private partitions owned by individual tasks. This paper presented the issues surrounding the selection of an optimal segment allocation for a set of periodic tasks. We showed that the complexity of the segment allocation problem mapped to a search tree requiring exponential time to traverse. We then presented a dynamic programming solution which runs in polynomial time, namely $O(dynamic)=O(N \cdot S \cdot \log_2(S))$, where N is the number of tasks in the task set and S is the number of segments available for allocation. We next demonstrated that minimum utilization is a necessary but not sufficient for real-time computing by showing an example where the minimum utilization solution was not schedulable, and a higher utilization solution produced a schedulable task set. We then integrated schedulability checks into the dynamic programming algorithm to ensure that the schedulability constraints were met. Finally, simulation results of a typical real-time application showed that the SMART caching strategy provides deterministic execution times at utilizations which differ from conventional (nondeterministic) caches by less than 10%.

References

[1]   A. Agarwal, R. Simoni, J. Hennessy, and M. Horowitz. An Evaluation of Directory Schemes for Cache Coherence. In *The 15th Annual International Symposium on Computer Architecture Conference Proceedings*, pages 280-289. IEEE, Hoholulu, Hawaii, May, 1988.

[2]   Gilles Brassard and Paul Bratley. *Algorithmics: theory and practice*. Prentice-Hall, Englewood Cliffs, NJ, 1988.

[3]   D. W. Clark, B. W. Lampson, and K. A. Pier. The memory system of a high performance personal computer. *IEEE Transactions on Computers* TC-30(10):715-733, October, 1981.

[4]   James R. Goodman. Using Cache Memory to Reduce Processor-Memory Traffic. In *The 10th Annual International Symposium on Computer Architecture Conference Proceedings*, pages 124-131. IEEE, Hoholulu, Hawaii, June, 1983.

[5]   Mark D. Hill. *Dinero III Cache Simulator: Version 3.1* Computer Science Dept, Univ. of Wisconsin, Madison, WI, 1985.

[6]   Mark Hill. A Case for Direct Mapped Caches. *IEEE Computer* 21(12):25-40, December, 1988.

[7]   David B. Kirk. SMART (Strategic Memory Allocation for Real-Time) Cache Design. PhD Thesis Proposal. December, 1988 Carnegie-Mellon University.

[8]   David B. Kirk. Process Dependent Static Cache Partitioning for Real-Time Systems. In *Proceedings of the Real-Time Systems Symposium*, pages 181-190. IEEE, Huntsville, AL, December, 1988.

[9]   David B. Kirk. SMART (Strategic Memory Allocation for Real-Time) Cache Design. In *Proceedings of the Real-Time Systems Symposium*, pages 229-237. IEEE, Santa Monica, CA, December, 1989.

[10]   David B. Kirk. *Predictable Cache Design for Real-Time Systems*. PhD thesis, Carnegie Mellon University, December, 1990.

[11]   David B. Kirk, Jay K. Strosnider. SMART (Strategic Memory Allocation for Real-Time) Cache Design Using the R3000. In *Proceedings of the Real-Time Systems Symposium*. Orlando, FA, December, 1990.

[12]   J. P. Lehoczky, L. Sha, and Y. Ding. The Rate Monotonic Scheduling Algorithm --- Exact Characterization and Average Case Behavior. In *Proceedings of the Real-Time Systems Symposium*, pages 166-171. IEEE, Santa Monica, CA, December, 1989.

[13]   C. L. Liu and James W. Layland. Scheduling Algorithms for Multiprogramming in a Hard-Real-Time Environment. *Journal of the Association for Computing Machinery* 20(1):46-61, January, 1973.

[14]   Alan J. Smith. Cache Memories. *ACM Computing Surveys* 14(3):473-530, September, 1982.

[15]   Alan J. Smith. Cache memory design: an evolving art. *IEEE Spectrum* 24(12):40-44, December, 1987.

[16]   Kimming So, Rudolph N. Rechtschaffen. Cache Operations by MRU Change. *IEEE Transactions on Computers* 37(6):700-709, June, 1988.

[17]   Paul Sweazy and Alan Smith. A Class of Compatible Cache Consistency Protocols and their Support by the IEEE Futurebus. In *The 13th International Symposium on Computer Architecture Conference Proceedings*, pages 414-423. IEEE, Tokyo, Japan, June, 1986.

CHAPTER 10

Scheduling Strategies Adopted in Spring: An Overview *

Krithi Ramamritham and John A. Stankovic
Department of Computer and Information Science
University of Massachusetts
Amherst, MA 01003, USA

Abstract

In managing the tasks and resources in a real-time system, there are three phases to consider:

- *allocation* – the assignment of the *tasks* and *resources* to the appropriate nodes or processors in the system,

- *scheduling* – ordering the execution of tasks such that their timing constraints are met and the consistency of resources is maintained, and

- *dispatching* – executing the tasks in conformance with the scheduler's decisions.

Whereas a large part of our work deals with scheduling, more recently we have begun to examine allocation and dispatching issues in the context of our scheduling approach. To date, the main results of our work include (i) the adoption and development of *guarantee*, a notion fundamental to predictable scheduling, (ii) algorithms for the guarantee of dynamically arriving tasks, (iii) an analysis of the quality of the schedules produced by the basic version of our algorithm, (iv) the schemes for reclaiming unused time and resources when tasks complete early, (v) distributed scheduling and meta-level control techniques, and (vi) algorithms for the static allocation and scheduling of safety-critical tasks. These results form the basis for predictable, adaptable, and flexible scheduling support for complex real-time systems.

*This work was supported by ONR under contract NOOO14-85-K-0389, by NSF under grant DCR-8500332, and by a grant from Texas Instruments.

INTRODUCTION

The complexities of next generation real-time systems arise from a number of factors including different types of time constraints, different types of time granularities, the presence of tasks with complex characteristics such as resource requirements, precedence constraints, importance factors, and fault tolerance requirements, the dynamic and distributed nature of the environment, and, finally, the long lifetimes of the complex systems being designed today [20], [19].

These complex systems call for resource and task management strategies that are not only *predictable*, i.e., provide assurances that time constraints will be met, but are also *adaptable* and *flexible*. Adaptability calls for approaches that can deal with the dynamics and uncertainties of the environment effectively while flexibility demands approaches that can accommodate changes to the requirements as well as modification to the hardware and software structures. In managing the tasks and resources in a real-time system, there are three phases to consider:

- *allocation* – the assignment of the *tasks* and *resources* to the appropriate nodes or processors in the system,

- *scheduling* – ordering the execution of tasks such that their timing constraints are met and the consistency of resources is maintained, and

- *dispatching* – executing the tasks in conformance with the scheduler's decisions.

Each of the above phases cannot be dealt with in total isolation, since the mechanism used in one phase may greatly affect the performance of others. For example, the scheduling algorithm used influences the design of the allocation scheme, how well the allocation is done affects the run-time performance of the scheduling algorithm, and whether and how time and resources allocated to a task are reclaimed (when it finishes early) affects the correctness as well as the performance of the scheduling algorithm.

In providing support for the three phases, it is important to take into consideration the nature and characteristics of tasks in a given system.

In a system interacting with an environment that is dynamic, large, complex, and evolving, many types of tasks exist. These can be categorized based on their interaction with and impact on the environment. *Critical* tasks are those real-time tasks which must make their deadline, otherwise a catastrophic result might occur. It must be shown *a priori* that these tasks will always meet their deadlines subject to some specified number of failures. Thus, resources must be allocated and scheduling decisions must be made such that these tasks will always meet their deadlines. The number of truly critical tasks (even in very large systems) is likely to be small in comparison to the total number of tasks in the system. *Essential* tasks are tasks that are important to the operation of the system, have specific timing constraints, and will degrade the performance of the system if their timing constraints are not met. However, essential tasks will not cause a catastrophe if they are not finished on time. There are a large number of such tasks and the importance levels of these essential tasks may differ. It is necessary to treat such tasks in a dynamic manner as it is impossible to reserve enough resources for all contingencies with respect to these tasks. *Non-essential* tasks, whether they have deadlines or not, execute when they do not impact critical or essential tasks. Many background tasks, long range planning tasks, and maintenance functions fall into this category.

Whereas a large part of our work deals with scheduling, more recently, we have begun to examine allocation and dispatching issues in the context of our scheduling approach. Specifically, to date, the main results of our work include:

- *The adoption and development of guarantee, a notion fundamental to predictable scheduling.* A task is guaranteed by constructing a plan for task execution whereby all guaranteed tasks meet their timing constraints. A task is guaranteed subject to a set of assumptions, for example, about its worst case execution time, and the nature of faults in the system. If these assumptions hold, once a task is guaranteed it *will* meet its timing requirements. The guarantee notion is elaborated and its benefits are outlined in "The Notion of Guarantee and its Benefits".

When essential tasks with different levels of importance are considered, we will find a need for the notion of "conditional guarantee" where a task's guarantee is predicated upon the non-arrival of tasks with higher importance.

- *Algorithms for the guarantee of dynamically arriving tasks.* The basic version of our guarantee algorithm deals with independent, non-preemptable, equally important tasks that have deadlines and resource requirements. It is capable of dealing with both uniprocessors and multiprocessors. Extensions of the basic algorithm deal with precedence relationships among tasks, tasks with varying importance levels, tasks with different fault tolerance requirements, and tasks that are preemptable. The section entitled "Scheduling Tasks on a Multiprocessor Node" is devoted to various aspects of dynamic task scheduling on a multiprocessor node.

- *Analysis of the quality of the schedules produced by the basic version of our algorithm.* Both the *ability* to generate feasible schedules and the *quality* of the generated feasible schedules, expressed in terms of the schedule length, are important metrics for scheduling algorithms. Our theoretical analysis identified several ways in which the basic algorithm can be improved even further. The results of the analysis are discused under "Analysis of the Basic Scheme and the Improvements Motivated by it".

- *Reclaiming unused time and resources when tasks complete early.* The guarantees are based on worst case computation times, but when a task finishes early, as would typically be the case, the unused CPU and resource time may be reclaimed and used. This reclamation is considered in the dispatching phase and the reclaimed time is taken into account by the scheduler for subsequent guarantees. The section entitled "Reclaiming Unused Time and Resources" provides an outline of the scheme.

- *Distributed scheduling and meta-level control.* A suite of distributed scheduling algorithms has been developed and evaluated. We have also hypothesized the usefulness of a *meta-level controller* that can select the heuristic appropriate for a given system (state). Details can be found under "Scheduling Tasks in a Distributed System" and "Meta-Level Control".

- *Static allocation and scheduling of safety-critical tasks.* We have developed an algorithm that is suitable for the static allocation and scheduling of complex, safety-critical periodic tasks. Besides periodicity constraints, tasks handled by the algorithm can have resource requirements and can possess precedence, communication, as well as fault tolerance constraints. Details of the algorithm as well as the extensions necessary to accommodate dynamic non-periodic arrivals are presented in the penultimate section of this paper.

The notion of guarantee is aimed at achieving *predictability. Adaptability* and *flexibility* are supported by a collection of dynamic task management techniques. These include dynamic guarantees with task characteristics identified at invocation time, distributed scheduling, meta-level control, and resource reclaiming.

Many practical instances of scheduling algorithms have been found to be NP-complete [23], [24]. A majority of scheduling algorithms reported in the literature perform static scheduling, and hence, have limited applicability since not all task characteristics are known *a priori* and further, tasks arrive dynamically. For dynamic scheduling, in single processor systems with independent preemptable tasks, the earliest deadline first algorithm and the least laxity first algorithm are optimal. For dynamic systems with more than one processor, and/or tasks that have mutual exclusion constraints an optimal scheduling algorithm does not exist [6]. These negative results point out the need for heuristic approaches to solve scheduling problems in such systems. In the rest of this paper we provide the details of our approaches.

THE NOTION OF GUARANTEE AND ITS BENEFITS

The notion of guarantee underlies our approach to achieving predictability.

Since all safety-critical tasks must meet their timing constraints, they must be guaranteed statically. Thus, all critical tasks are guaranteed *a priori* and resources are reserved for them. In addition, scheduling decisions for these tasks are also made *a priori*. While *a priori* dedicating resources to critical tasks is, of course, not flexible, due to the importance of these tasks, we have no other choice! On the positive side, recall that the ratio of critical tasks to essential tasks is typically very small.

Given the large numbers of essential tasks and the extremely large number of their possible invocation orders, preallocation of resources to essential tasks is not possible due to cost, nor desirable due to its inflexibility. Hence, such tasks are guaranteed dynamically when they arrive, in the context of the current load. Specifically, if a set S of tasks has been previously guaranteed and a new task T arrives, T is guaranteed if and only if a feasible schedule can be found for tasks in the set $S \bigcup \{T\}$.

The basic notion and properties of guarantee for essential tasks have the following characteristics:

- A task is guaranteed by planning the task executions. When a task is being guaranteed, the scheduler attempts to plan a schedule for it and the previously guaranteed tasks so that all tasks can make their deadlines. This enables our system to understand the total load of the system and to make intelligent decisions when a guarantee cannot be made. This is in contrast with other real–time scheduling algorithms which have a myopic view of the set of tasks. That is, these algorithms only know *which task to run next* and have no understanding of the total load or current capabilities of the system. This planning is done on the system processor in parallel with the execution of previously guaranteed tasks and so it must account for those tasks which may be completed before it itself completes.

- At any point in time the system knows exactly which tasks have been guaranteed to make their deadlines, and what, where and when spare resources exist. The on-line guarantee for essential tasks is an *instantaneous* guarantee with respect to the current state. This presents a *macroscopic* view that *all* critical tasks will make their deadlines and *exactly* which essential tasks will make their deadlines given the current load[1].

- Planning during guarantee *avoids* conflicts over resources. This

---

[1] It is also possible to develop an overall quantitative, but probabilistic assessment of the performance of essential tasks. For example, given expected normal and over-load workloads, we can compute the average percentage of essential tasks that are guaranteed to make their deadlines.

eliminates the random nature of waiting for resources found in timesharing operating systems (this same feature also tends to minimize context switches since tasks are not being context switched to wait for resources). Basically, resource conflicts are resolved at guarantee time by scheduling tasks to execute in different time intervals if they contend for a given resource.

Current real–time scheduling algorithms schedule the CPU independently of other resources. For example, consider a typical real–time scheduling algorithm, earliest deadline first. Scheduling a task which has the earliest deadline does no good if it subsequently blocks because a resource it requires is unavailable. Our approach integrates CPU scheduling and resource allocation so that this blocking never occurs.

By integrating CPU scheduling and resource allocation at run time, we are able to understand (at each point in time), the current resource contention and completely control it so that task performance with respect to deadlines is predictable, rather than letting resource contention occur in a random pattern resulting in an unpredictable system.

- Guarantee can be subject to computation time requirements, deadline or periodic time constraints, resource requirements where resources are segmented, fault tolerance requirements, importance levels for tasks, precedence constraints, and I/O requirements. Specific guarantee algorithms can be designed depending on the task and resource characteristics.

- Dynamic guarantee allows use of dynamic task information. Information about tasks is retained at run time and includes formulas describing worst case execution time, deadlines or other timing requirements, importance level, precedence constraints, resource requirements, fault tolerance requirements, etc. This is utilized to guarantee timing and other requirements of the system. In other words, significant amounts of semantic information about a task can be utilized at run time.

- Guarantees and dispatching can be done independently allowing these system functions to run in parallel. The dispatcher is always working with a set of tasks which have been previously guaranteed to make their deadlines and the guarantee routine operates on the set of currently guaranteed tasks plus any newly invoked tasks.

- Attempt to guarantee provides early notification. By performing the guarantee calculation when a task arrives there may be time to reallocate the task to another node of the system. Early notification also has *fault tolerance* implications in that it is now possible to run alternative error handling tasks early, before a deadline is missed.

- Guarantee can be designed to support the co-existence of real–time and non-real–time tasks, and note that this is non-trivial when non-real–time tasks might use some of the same resources as real–time tasks.

- Even though a task is guaranteed with respect to its worst case computation time and resource requirements, it is possible to re-claim unused resources, including time, when it completes early.

Even if it is not guaranteed on a node in a distributed system, it may still meet its deadline. This could coour in several different ways. First, it could receive idle cycles at this node, and, in parallel, there can be an attempt to get the task guaranteed on another node of the system subject to location dependent constraints. Consequently, it might either complete at this node or be guaranteed elsewhere. Second, based on the fault tolerance and correctness semantics of the task, an alternative task with smaller computation time, reduced resource needs, or larger deadline could be invoked and hence might get guaranteed.

DYNAMIC SCHEDULING

Scheduling Tasks on a Multiprocessor Node. A guarantee algorithm must consider many issues including the presence of periodic tasks, preemptable tasks, precedence constraints (which is used to handle task groups), multiple importance levels for tasks, and fault tolerance requirements. We first describe a basic version of the algorithm that handles task deadlines and resource requirements. Subsequently, we discuss the extensions required to handle the other considerations.

The Basic Algorithm. The basic algorithm attempts to guarantee non-preemptable tasks given their arrival time T_A, deadline T_D or period T_P, worst case computation time T_C, and resource requirements $\{T_R\}$. A task uses a resource either in shared mode or in exclusive mode and holds a requested resource as long as it executes. The guarantee algorithm computes the earliest start time, T_{est}, at which task T can begin execution. T_{est} accounts for resource contention among tasks. It is a key ingredient in our scheduling strategy.

The heuristic scheduling algorithms we use try to determine a full feasible schedule for a set of tasks in the following way. It starts at the root of the search tree which is an empty schedule and tries to extend the schedule (with one more task) by moving to one of the vertices at the next level in the search tree until a full feasible schedule is derived. To this end, we use a heuristic function, H, which synthesizes various characteristics of tasks affecting real-time scheduling decisions to actively direct the scheduling to a plausible path. The heuristic function, H, is applied to at most k tasks that remain to be scheduled at each level of search. The task with the smallest value of function H is selected to extend the current schedule.

While extending the partial schedule at each level of search, the algorithm determines if the current partial schedule is *strongly-feasible* or not. A partial feasible schedule is said to be *strongly-feasible* if *all* the schedules obtained by extending this current schedule with any one of the remaining tasks are also feasible. Thus, if a partial feasible schedule is found not to be *strongly-feasible* because, say, task T misses its deadline when the current schedule is extended by T, then it is appropriate to stop the search since none of the future extensions involving task T will meet its deadline. In this case, a set of tasks can not be scheduled given the current partial schedule. (In the terminology of branch-and-bound techniques, the search path represented by the current partial schedule is *bound* since it will not lead to a feasible complete schedule.)

However, it is possible to backtrack to continue the search even after a non-strongly-feasible schedule is found. Backtracking is done by discarding the current partial schedule, returning to the previous partial schedule, and extending it using a different task. The task chosen is the one with the *second* smallest H value. Even though we allow backtracking, the overheads of backtracking can be restricted either by restricting

the maximum number of possible backtracks or by restricting the total number of evaluations of the H function. We use the latter scheme
because we found it to be more effective.

The algorithm works as follows: It starts with an empty partial schedule. Each step of the algorithm involves (1) determining that the current
partial schedule is strongly-feasible, and if so (2) extending the current
partial schedule by one task. In addition to the data structure maintaining the partial schedule, tasks in the task set S are maintained in the
order of increasing deadlines. This is realized in the following way: When
a task arrives at a node, it is *inserted*, according to its deadline, into a
(sorted) list of tasks that remain to be executed. This insertion takes at
most $O(n)$ time where n is the task set size. Let $n_k = \min(k,$ number of
tasks yet to be scheduled). Then when attempting to extend the schedule
by one task, three steps must be taken: (1) strong-feasibility is determined with respect to the first (still remaining to be scheduled) n_k tasks
in the task set, (2) if the partial schedule is found to be strongly-feasible,
then the H function is applied to the first n_k tasks in the task set (i.e.,
the n_k remaining tasks with the earliest deadlines), and (3) that task
which has the smallest H value is chosen to extend the current schedule.
Given that only n_k tasks are considered at each step, the complexity
incurred is $O(n \times k)$ since only the first n_k tasks are considered each
time. If the value of k is constant (and in practice, k will be small when
compared to the task set size n), the complexity is linearly proportional
to n, the size of the task set [9]. While the complexity is proportional
to n, the algorithm is programmed so that it incurs a fixed worst case
cost by limiting the number of H function evaluations permitted in any
one invocation of the algorithm. Also, see [11] for a discussion on how
to choose k.

Given a partial schedule, for each resource, the earliest time the resource is available can be determined. This is denoted by EAT. Then the
earliest time that a task that is yet to be scheduled can begin execution
is given by

$$T_{est} = Max(\text{T's start time}, EAT_i^u)$$

where u = s or e if T needs resource R_i in shared or exclusive mode,
respectively.

The heuristic function H can be constructed by simple or integrated
heuristics. The following is a list of simple and integrated heuristics that

we have tested:

- Minimum deadline first (Min_D): $H(T) = T_D$
- Minimum processing time first (Min_C): $H(T) = T_C$
- Minimum earliest start time first (Min_S): $H(T) = T_{est}$
- Minimum laxity first (Min_L): $H(T) = T_D - (T_{est}+T_C)$
- Min_D + Min_C: $H(T) = T_D + W * T_C$
- Min_D + Min_S: $H(T) = T_D + W * T_{est}$

The first four heuristics are considered simple heuristics because they treat only one dimension at a time, e.g., only deadlines, or only resource requirements. The last two are considered to be integrated heuristics. W is a weight used to combine two simple heuristics. Min_L and Min_S need not be combined because the heuristic Min_L contains the information in Min_D and Min_S.

Extensive simulation studies of the algorithm for uniprocessor and multiprocessors show that the simple heuristics do not work well and that the integrated heuristic (Min_D + Min_S) works very well and has the best performance among all the above possibilities as well as over many other heuristics we tested [26] [28] [29], [9], [11]. For example, combinations of three heuristics were shown not to improve performance over the (Min_D + Min_S) heuristic.

Analysis of the Basic Scheme and the Improvements Motivated by it. Both the *ability* to generate feasible schedules and the *quality* of the generated feasible schedules, expressed in terms of the schedule length bound, are important metrics for scheduling algorithms. Our analysis [25] showed that in the worst case, on a multiprocessor with m processors, the length of the schedules produced by the basic algorithm (called H_1 here) will be m times of the length of an optimal schedule. List scheduling, which is not as successful in finding feasible schedules, has a worst case schedule length bound, of $(m + 1)/2$, almost half of the worst case schedule length bound of H_1. The two algorithms differ in the following way. In H_1, a task's H value consolidates the task's deadline and resource requirement information. Our algorithm selects a task with the minimum H value among all unscheduled tasks, while list scheduling selects a task with the minimum H value among the unscheduled tasks which have the same earliest start time. Thus, in list scheduling the task's deadline is only a secondary factor. Hence, we developed algorithm H_2 that uses a task selection procedure that has elements from both H_1 and list scheduling. It selects a task to keep at least two processors busy whenever possible, otherwise its behavior is similar to H_1. This change was motivated by the fact that in general, list scheduling keeps more processors busy at a given time than H_1. H_2 has a better worst-case schedule length bound, namely $(m + 1)/2$. At the same time, it has almost the same success as H_1 in finding feasible schedules. Further, H_2 can be implemented so that its scheduling overhead is not higher than that of H_1.

Can the bound of H_2 be reduced further by increasing the (polynomial time) complexity of the scheduling algorithm? Partly motivated by this question, we developed H_s, a generalized version of H_2, which keeps at least s processors busy whenever possible. It turns out that the added time complexity of H_s does not help to reduce the bound $((m + 1)/2)$. The reason is that, in the worst case, there may be some tasks with very small computation times which contribute significantly to the number of tasks running in parallel at scheduling decision points, but they do not contribute much to the schedule length. If the ratio between the shortest task and the longest task in a task set is close to 1, the bound of H_s is likely to be smaller than $(m + 1)/2$. In the extreme case, the ratio is one and in this case, in systems where the number of resources is larger than the number of processors, the bound of H_s reduces from $(m + 1)/2$ to $m/s + \sum_{j=2}^{s} 1/j$. In practice, it is also very important to choose a proper s to balance the time overhead and the achieved bound.

One of the next steps we envisage is to better characterize the worst-case task characteristics that produce the above bounds. This will help avoid the pessimistic bounds.

Extensions to the Basic Algorithm. Recall that the basic algorithm takes tasks' computation time, timing constraints, and resource requirements into account. In this section, we present the extensions necessary to deal with periodic tasks, tasks that have fault tolerance requirements, tasks with different importance levels, tasks that have precedence constraints, and preemptable tasks.

Periodic Tasks: In what follows, we discuss several ways of guaranteeing periodic tasks in the presence of nonperiodic tasks. Depending on whether periodic and nonperiodic tasks need access to a common set of resources, one or more options will be applicable to a given system. We have yet to test the effectiveness of the various options.

We assume that when a periodic task is guaranteed, every instance of the task is guaranteed.

Consider a system with only periodic tasks. A schedule can be constructed using the basic algorithm described in the previous section. Specifically, we can assign start time and deadline constraints to the periodic task instances based on the periods and guarantee a periodic task only if all instances of the periodic tasks can be guaranteed. In fact, we need only construct a schedule whose length is equal to the least common multiple of all the periods. This can serve as a template according to which all periodic task instances are executed.

When a periodic task arrives dynamically, an attempt can be made to construct a new template. If the attempt succeeds, the new task is guaranteed, otherwise not.

Suppose periodic tasks *and* nonperiodic tasks occur in a system. If the resources needed by periodic tasks and nonperiodic tasks are disjoint then a subset of the processors in a node can be earmarked for periodic tasks. A template can be constructed to execute the periodic task instances on just these processors. The remaining processors are used for nonperiodic tasks guaranteed using our dynamic guarantee scheme. If however, periodic and nonperiodic tasks have common resources, more complicated schemes are needed.

If a periodic task arrives in a system consisting of previously guaranteed periodic and nonperiodic tasks, an attempt is made to construct a new template. If this fails, the new task is not guaranteed. If the attempt succeeds, we can immediately guarantee the task provided this will not jeopardize other guaranteed nonperiodic tasks. Otherwise, introduction of the periodic task into the system has to be delayed until the guaranteed nonperiodic tasks complete or at least until its introduction will not affect the remaining guaranteed tasks.

Suppose a new nonperiodic task arrives. In the presence of the template for periodic tasks, the task can be guaranteed in the idle slots identified by the template. More flexibility can be gained by using the following scheme. Given that we can assign start time and deadline constraints to the periodic task instances based on the periods, applying our dynamic guarantee scheme, we can guarantee a nonperiodic task if all instances of the periodic tasks and all previously guaranteed nonperiodic tasks can also be guaranteed. In this scheme, the number of tasks that have to be considered in guaranteeing a new nonperiodic task (in the presence of periodic tasks) is higher and hence can involve high scheduling overheads.

Tasks with Fault Tolerance Requirements: When a task is not guaranteed a *timing fault* is forecast. In this situation, an alternative task which has a shorter computation time or less resource needs can be invoked. If the latter is guaranteed, the timing fault is masked from the next higher level. If not, the next higher level can decide whether some other activity should be performed instead of the original nonguaranteed task.

If a node with a guaranteed tasks fails, the guarantees do not hold. The problem of node failures and the reallocation of tasks guaranteed on that node is studied in [21]. Here reallocation is done so as to maximize the number of tasks that can still meet their deadlines.

If guarantees are required in spite of node failures, guarantees have to be provided on multiple nodes. Specifically, if a task is nonperiodic and does not share resources with other tasks, or if a task is an instance of a periodic task and shares resources only with other instances of the same task, then guaranteed execution with respect to t fail-stop node failures can be achieved by guaranteeing the execution of the task at $t+1$ nodes. When a task does not share resources, the following scheme reduces the overheads of executing $t+1$ copies of a task at all times: Start times of a task's replicates are staggered so that the ith replicate is guaranteed with respect to a start time of $(s + (i-1)m)$ and a deadline of $(d - (t+1-i)m)$ where s and d are the start time and deadline of the task, respectively, and m is the communication delay. The idea is to avoid executing as many task replicates as possible. The first replicate to complete successfully, informs all others, and as a result, the following replicates stop further processing of the task. The assumption here is that all interactions with the environment take place when a replicate completes successfully. Obviously, this scheme is applicable only when communication delays and task computation times are small compared to task deadlines.

These techniques also apply when guaranteeing in spite of processor failures. To guarantee a task on a node in spite of t processor failures, its execution is guaranteed on $t + 1$ processors. $t + 1$ staggered executions of a task can be scheduled on different processors within a node. To handle transient processor failures when nodes are not fail-stop, the latter scheme can be applied to a single processor. Once a task completes successfully, as determined by specified acceptance tests, subsequent replicates of the task are deleted and their time reclaimed.

Tasks with Different Levels of Importance: The two main task parameters, deadline and importance, may sometimes be in conflict with each other. That is, tasks with very short deadlines might not be very important, and vice versa. This causes a dilemma in choosing the next task to execute. Also, the semantics of guarantee needs to be refined when tasks with differing importance values are present. Suppose a task has been guaranteed and a task with a higher importance arrives. Also suppose that the new task can be guaranteed only if the lower importance task is removed from the guaranteed list, i.e., the guarantee is withdrawn. In this case the initial guarantee is not absolute but conditional upon the non-arrival of higher importance tasks which conflict with it. In most applications it is important to meet the deadlines of higher importance tasks even if that implies the withdrawal of guarantees to other (lower importance) tasks. The concept of 'guarantee' as *conditional* rather than *absolute* is found to be superior in terms of adaptiveness and responsiveness to changing system conditions.

We have proposed and evaluated two dynamic scheduling algorithms [2]. They integrate importance and deadline such that, not only do the more important tasks meet their deadlines, but many other less important tasks also meet their deadlines. Overall, their goal is to maximize the net worth of the executed tasks to the system.

Both the algorithms first attempt to guarantee an incoming task according to its deadline, ignoring its importance. If the task is guaranteed then the scheduling is successful.

However, if this first attempt at scheduling fails, then there is an attempt to guarantee the new task at the expense of previously guaranteed, but less critical tasks. If enough less critical tasks can be found then the new task is guaranteed at this node and the removed tasks are transferred to alternative sites. If there are not enough less critical tasks, or the deadline of the new task is such that the removal of any such tasks does not allow the new task to meet its deadline, then the *new task* is not guaranteed.

The two algorithms differ only in how they remove previously guaranteed low importance tasks. In the first algorithm lower importance tasks are removed one at a time and in strict order from low to high importance. The second algorithm also only removes tasks of lower importance, but does not follow the strict order found in the first algorithm. Rather, it removes any task with lower importance, starting from tasks with the largest deadline.

Surprisingly, both the algorithms have the same performance for almost all system conditions and task parameters. We have also observed that at low loads pure deadline based algorithms tend to perform better than pure importance based algorithms. At high loads, the situation is reversed and pure importance based algorithms outperform pure deadline based algorithms. Also, we show that our algorithms outperform the pure deadline and importance based baselines since they combine the advantages of both the deadline and importance based algorithms.

We are beginning to evaluate an alternative scheme. This scheme adds another factor into $H(T)$. The goal is to produce a feasible schedule biased with the most important tasks first. Thus important tasks are likely to be scheduled earlier than unimportant ones.

Tasks with Precedence Constraints: Precedence constraints between tasks are used to model end-to-end timing constraints both for a single node and across nodes.

A task group is a collection of simple tasks that have precedence constraints among themselves, but have a single deadline. Each task acquires resources before it begins and can release the resources upon its completion. For task groups, it is assumed that when the task group is invoked the worst case computation time and resource requirements of each task can be determined. In [3], an algorithm for guaranteeing tasks groups in distributed systems was developed and evaluated. This algorithm first clusters tasks in a group; each cluster is expected to be scheduled on a single node. From the deadline for the task group, deadline for individual clusters are identified. If a set of nodes, each of which commits to executing tasks within a cluster by the deadline, is found, then the task group is guaranteed. Given the communication involved in such a scheme, this is applicable to task groups with large laxities.

Considering a task group that executes within a multiprocessor node, it is possible to extend our basic scheme to deal with precedence constraints. We have identified, but are yet to test, a number of strategies. When tasks with precedence constraints are considered, a task becomes eligible to execute only when all of its ancestors are scheduled. Hence, at a given point in the search for a feasible schedule, the H function is applied only to tasks whose ancestors have already been scheduled and whose scheduled finish times have occurred. Also, another factor is added to the heuristic function in order to provide a positive bias to those eligible tasks that lie along the critical path.

Currently, we are also studying precedence related tasks where tasks may have different importance levels. In this case, it is necessary to schedule the tasks such that not only are task deadlines satisfied, but the value of executed tasks is also maximized.

Preemptable Tasks: In scheduling a set of preemptable tasks on a multiprocessor, a *schedule S* for a set of preemptable tasks can be viewed as consisting of a sequence of *slices* $S_k, k = 1, ...,$ number of slices in the schedule S. A slice S_k is associated with a *slice start time*, a *slice length*, and a subset of tasks which can run in parallel in that slice. A task is said to be *preempted* between slices S_k and S_{k+1} if it is in slice S_k, does not complete in that slice, and is not in slice S_{k+1}.

With this view, scheduling decisions have to be made about the length of slices and about the tasks that belong to a slice. The slice length is chosen to be no more than the minimum remaining processing time of a task in the slice. Also, it should be no more than the minimum of the laxities of the remaining tasks. Thus, it is the smaller of the above two quantities. In the context of our dynamic search for a feasible schedule, the core of the algorithm lies in effectively and correctly identifying the subset of tasks associated with a new slice. Let us first understand the basis for including a task in a slice. Considering just the timing constraint, it is well known that both earliest-deadline-first and smallest-laxity-first scheduling schemes produce optimal preemptive schedules. Given that in addition to timing constraints there are resource constraints, we need to include resource considerations in scheduling. Hence, we construct a slice with one primary and one or more secondary tasks. The primary task is selected based purely on timing considerations: one with the smallest laxity among tasks that have not completed is selected. Then we use a heuristic function similar to the one used for nonpreemptive scheduling to select the secondary tasks. Ideally, this function should consider both timing and resource constraints and select as many secondary tasks as possible to execute in parallel with the primary task. Thus, the heuristic function is applied to all the candidate tasks. The task with the minimum value returned by the function is selected for the slice. This process is repeated until no more tasks can be included in the slice. In [27] we identify and evaluate different heuristic functions. In addition to the considerations involved in the basic algorithm, here the heuristic function should also consider preemption costs as well as resource usage and their effect of preempting a task at the end of a slice.

Reclaiming Unused Time and Resources. In order to guarantee that hard real-time tasks will meet their deadlines in the worst case, most real-time scheduling algorithms schedule tasks with respect to their worst case computation times. In reality, this worst case computation time is only an upper bound and the actual execution time may vary between some minimum value and this upper bound, depending on various factors, such as the system state, the amount and value of input data, the amount of resource contention, and the types of tasks. *Resource reclaiming* refers to the problem of *correctly* and *effectively* utilizing the resources unused by a task when a task executes less than its worst case computation time, or when a task is deleted from the current schedule. Task deletion occurs either during an operation mode change [14], or when one of the copies of a task completes successfully in a fault-tolerant system.

We have designed two versions of a resource reclaiming algorithm that (1) avoid any run time anomalies, (2) effectively reclaim the unused portions of resource time and processor time, and (3) have time complexities independent of the number of tasks in the given schedule. The last requirement arises due to the fact that resource reclaiming will have to be done on every task completion and, hence, reclamation costs are added to task dispatching costs.

A feasible multiprocessor schedule provides task ordering information that is *sufficient* to guarantee the timing and resource requirements of tasks in the schedule. If two tasks overlap in time on different processors in a schedule, then we can conclude that no matter which one of them will be dispatched first at run time, they will never jeopardize each other's deadlines. On the other hand, if two tasks do not overlap in time, we cannot make the same conclusion without re-examining resource constraints or without total re-scheduling. Assume each task is assigned a scheduled start time sst and a scheduled finish time sft in the given feasible schedule, our resource reclaiming algorithms utilize this information to do *local* optimization at run time, while preserving the correct relative ordering among the scheduled tasks, thus ensuring the original guarantee. This local optimization is accomplished by reasoning only about the first m tasks in the schedule, m being the number of processors. By doing so, we avoid explicitly examining the availability of each of the resources needed by a task in order to dispatch a task when reclaiming occurs. Thus, the complexity of the algorithms is independent of the number of tasks in the schedule.

Each of our resource reclaiming algorithms consists of two steps. A task is removed from the schedule only upon its completion. In the first step, upon completion of a task, we try to identify idle periods on all processors and resources by computing a function $reclaim\_\delta = min(sst_i) - current\_time$; where sst_i is the scheduled start time of the current first task for processor i in the schedule, $1 \leq i \leq m$. The computational complexity of this function is $O(m)$. Any positive value of $reclaim\_\delta$ indicates the length of the idle period. The cumulative value of these idle periods is stored in θ. This first step is identical for the two versions of our algorithm. In the second step of the algorithm, the basic version of our resource reclaiming algorithm computes the *actual start time* $(= sst - \theta)$ for the next task scheduled on the processor in question. The task will be dispatched if the *actual start time* equals the current time. In the extended version of our algorithm, we first compute a Boolean function $can\_start\_early = sst_i < sft_j, \forall j$ such that $j \neq i$ and $1 \leq j \leq m$, where sst_i is the scheduled start time of the first task on processor i and sft_j is the scheduled finish time of the first task on processor j. This function identifies parallelism between the first task on processor i and the first tasks on all other processors and has a complexity $O(m)$. The task will be dispatched if the value of *can_start_early* is true. If it is false, *actual start time* is computed as in the basic version. Whenever a positive value of *reclaim_δ* is obtained in the first step of the algorithm, the second step of the algorithm must be executed for all currently idle processors. Thus the complexity of the basic version is: $O(m) + m * O(1) = O(m)$, while the extended version has a complexity of $O(m) + m * O(m) = O(m^2)$.

We have demonstrated the effectiveness of the two versions of the resource reclaiming algorithms through simulation [15]. Even though the extended version incurs a higher run time cost, it still performs much better than the basic version in most parameter settings of the simulation. Only when the resource conflict probability is very high, or when the system is either extremely overloaded or lightly loaded, the basic version demonstrates the same effectiveness as the extended version.

One of the positive fallouts of reclaiming is that now we can afford to be pessimistic about the computation times of tasks. This is because even if the dynamic guarantees are done with respect to tasks' worst case computation times, since any unused time is reclaimed, the negative effects of pessimism are considerably eliminated.

Scheduling Tasks in a Distributed System

As alluded to earlier, when a task arrives at a node, the scheduler at that node attempts to guarantee that the task will complete execution before its deadline, on that node. If the attempt fails, the scheduling components on individual nodes cooperate to determine which other node in the system has sufficient resource surplus to guarantee the task. In [10], four algorithms for cooperation are evaluated. They differ in the way a node treats a task that cannot be guaranteed locally:

- The *random scheduling algorithm*: The task is sent to a randomly selected node.

- The *focussed addressing algorithm*: The task is sent to a node that is estimated to have sufficient surplus to complete the task before its deadline.

- The *bidding algorithm*: The task is sent to a node based on the bids received for the task from nodes in the system.

- The *flexible algorithm*: The task is sent to a node based on a technique that combines *bidding* and *focussed addressing*.

Simulation studies were performed to compare the performance of these algorithms relative to each other as well as with respect to two baselines. The first baseline is the non-cooperative algorithm where a task that cannot be guaranteed locally is not sent to any other node. The second is an (ideal) algorithm that behaves exactly like the bidding algorithm, but incurs no communication overheads. We examined the relative performance of the various algorithms with respect to the system state, specifically, the system load, the load distribution among nodes, and the communication delays. They showed that:

- Distributed scheduling improves the performance of a hard real-time system. This is attested by the better performance of the flexible algorithm compared to the non-cooperative baseline under all load distributions.

- The performance of the flexible algorithm is better than both the focussed addressing and bidding algorithms. However, the performance difference between the bidding algorithm and the flexible algorithm under small communication delays is negligible. The same can be said about the performance difference between the focussed addressing algorithm and the flexible algorithm at large communication delays.

- The random algorithm performs quite well compared to the flexible algorithm, especially when system load is low as well as when system load is high and the load is unevenly distributed. Under moderate loads, its performance falls short by a few percentage points which may be significant in a hard real-time system.

Our studies showed that no algorithm outperforms all others in all system states. Though the flexible algorithm performs better than the rest in most cases, it is more complex than the other algorithms.

Details of the distributed scheduling algorithms can be found in [7], [10], and [18]. The stability of these algorithms is discussed in [17].

Meta Level Control

Any algorithm used for scheduling in complex real-time systems must be *adaptive*. That is, decisions made by the scheduling components must adapt to changes in the state of the system. Changes include availability of nodes, variations in task arrival rate, characteristics of tasks, load on individual nodes, and delays in the communication network.

As our discussion of distributed scheduling algorithm illustrates, no single scheduling algorithm can be effective under all situations, even if the parameters that control the behavior of the algorithm are fine-tuned.

Reexamining the flexible algorithm, one notices that, depending on the current state of the nodes and the communication network as well as the task characteristics, it elects to resort to focussed addressing alone, bidding alone, or attempts both in parallel. In one sense, what it does, albeit in a limited manner, is *control the scheduling*. Since scheduling is the control of task executions, we term this control of scheduling as *meta-level control*. The prime motivation for such control is *adaptability*.

We envisage each node having a component of the *Meta-Level Controller* (MLC) where the components cooperate in making meta-level control decisions. We propose to use the meta-level controller primarily for the following [8]:

- Controlling the choice of algorithm(s) used for the various scheduling components in a given situation. The primary components are the *local scheduler* and the *distributed scheduler*.

- Controlling the values of scheduling parameters used in the chosen algorithm(s). For example, one of the crucial set of parameters is the set of weights that govern the behavior of the (heuristic) *guarantee algorithm* invoked by the local scheduler; these weights determine the importance to be given to the deadline and resource requirements of a set of tasks in determining a schedule for these tasks. Important parameters used in global scheduling include the minimum surplus a node should have to be a candidate for focussed addressing and the minimum surplus a node should have for it to respond to a request-for-bids.

- Controlling the reallocation of periodic tasks to nodes. Through such a reallocation, loads on nodes can be adjusted such that the number of nonperiodic tasks that are sent to other nodes can be reduced. Periodic tasks exist for reasonably long intervals of time. Instances of a periodic task execute on the same node until the periodic task is reassigned. Thus periodic task assignment determines the *basic* load on a node. If we assume that the distribution of dynamic task arrivals on each node is determined by the external world and thus we are not able to control it, then one solution to obtain a new "balance" of node loads is to dynamically reallocate the periodic tasks subject to constraints such as the resource needs of these tasks.

The potential benefits of meta-level control are clear. But we have not yet investigated are the cost/benefits tradeoffs.

STATIC ALLOCATION AND SCHEDULING OF COMPLEX PERIODIC TASKS

Resources needed to meet the deadlines of safety-critical tasks are typically preallocated. Also, these tasks are usually statically scheduled such that their deadlines will be met even under worst-case conditions. We have developed an algorithm that is suitable for the static allocation and scheduling of complex, safety-critical periodic tasks. Besides *periodicity constraints*, tasks handled by the algorithm can have *resource requirements* and can possess *precedence, communication*, as well as *fault tolerance constraints* [12].

Given a set of periodic tasks, the algorithm attempts to assign subtasks of the tasks to nodes in a distributed system and to construct a schedule of length L where L is the least common multiple of the task periods. A real-time system with the given set of tasks then repeatedly executes its tasks according to this schedule every L units of time.

The algorithm consists of four steps. Step-I constructs the *comprehensive graph* containing all instances of the tasks that will execute in an interval of length L. In Step-II, the comprehensive graph is embellished with replicates of the subtasks that have fault-tolerance requirements. This results in the addition of some subtasks and some arcs to the graph. Step-III involves clustering subtasks in the comprehensive graph. Specifically, based on the amount of communication involved between a pair of communicating subtasks and the computation time of the subtasks, a decision is made as to whether the two subtasks should be assigned to the same node, thereby eliminating the communication costs involved. The algorithm makes its decision based on whether the fraction $\frac{sum\ of\ the\ computation\ time\ of\ the\ two\ subtasks}{cost\ of\ communication}$ is lower than a tunable parameter called the *communication factor*, CF. Applying the above scheme to *every pair* of communicating subtasks in the comprehensive graph derived in Step-II, a *communication graph* is generated with the current value of CF. Step-IV allocates the subtasks to nodes in the system, allocates the communication (between subtasks) to the time slots in the communication channel, and if possible, determines a feasible schedule. This is done using a heuristic search technique that takes into account the various task characteristics, in particular, subtask computation times, communication costs, deadlines, and precedence constraints. It allocates a subtask to a node, determines the order in which each node processes its subtasks, and schedules communication. The allocation and scheduling decisions are made in a coordinated fashion. Specifically, allocation and scheduling decisions about a subtask are made only after all its predecessors have been allocated and scheduled. Of course, these decisions take into account the communication and computational needs of the subtasks that follow. If at the end of Step-IV, a feasible allocation and schedule is not possible, the value of CF is altered, and Steps III and IV are repeated. In [12], we provide details of each of these steps.

Our experiments indicate that the algorithm conducts the search path so effectively that if the initial path does not lead to a feasible schedule for a given set of tasks, chances are high that we have an infeasible task set. This is attested by our test results which show that even a large number of additional backtracks produces only a small marginal improvement in performance.

Integrating Dynamic Task Management with Static Task Scheduling

The primary criterion in the static scheduling of periodic tasks is *feasibility*, i.e., determining a feasible schedule wherein all tasks meet their timing requirements, precedence constraints, etc. Under static allocation and scheduling, exactly when and where instances of a task will execute are fixed. But, if both periodic tasks as well as nonperiodic tasks exist in a system, provision should be made during static scheduling to cater to the needs of dynamic arrivals. Some leeway should be provided such that the static schedules can be dynamically modified for better nonperiodic task schedulability while retaining the feasibility of the critical task set.

Suppose we consider a distributed system of multiprocessor nodes. When static schedules for distributed or multiprocessor systems are examined, two types of phenomena can be observed. The first relates to the computational loads imposed on the individual nodes or processors. Typically, there exists a load imbalance within the processors on a node as well as across the nodes. The second relates to the idle times on individual nodes or processors. Often, these occur in a clustered fashion towards the end of the schedule, that is, idle times are not evenly spread across the schedule. Both of these are to be avoided if the idle time and resources are to be used to better accommodate dynamic arrivals. In particular, we would like to balance the loads not only across individual nodes and processors within a node but also along the time axis.

We have investigated two approaches to address this issue. One involves defining a limit to the load imposed on a node during the allocation of tasks to processors and nodes. The other forces an idle time interval following the scheduled execution of a task. Effect of different limits on the loads and fixed length idle times as well as task execution time dependent idle times have been studied [13]. The experiments indicate that these very simple techniques can be used to enhance the responsiveness to dynamic arrivals without jeopardizing the schedulability of the static periodic tasks. In addition, more flexibility can be gained by modifying the start times of the components of a critical tasks allocated to a node. If this modification is done such that the ancestors of these components on other nodes are not delayed or that task deadlines are not missed, more dynamic arrivals can be guaranteed. [13] discusses such modifications as well.

SUMMARIZING REMARKS AND OUTSTANDING ISSUES

In this paper we have surveyed some of the significant aspects of scheduling research done within the Spring project. We have endeavored to examine task and system characteristics that are likely to be encountered in next generation real-time systems and provide a flexible and adaptable, and yet predictable scheduling support for these systems.

We believe that our solutions are well integrated. Some examples of this integration are the ability to deal with dynamic arrivals of periodic as well as nonperiodic tasks, to schedule tasks under timing, resource, precedence, as well as fault tolerance constraints, to accommodate the orthogonal characteristics of deadlines and importance levels, and to cater to dynamic arrivals within static schedules.

Given that most scheduling problems are computationally intensive, the Spring scheduling algorithms are driven by heuristics. Our simulation studies have demonstrated the efficacy of the heuristics and in many cases have suggested possible enhancements. Certain possibilities for improvements to the dynamic guarantee algorithm also came to light when mathematical analysis of the algorithm was done. The basic dynamic guarantee algorithm and the reclaiming algorithms have been implemented as part of the Spring kernel [5] [22]. Many race conditions that occur in a multiprocessor environment manifested themselves when this implementation was carried out. In particular, this necessitated schemes that allowed the dispatchers on individual processors to access system data structures while the scheduler was guaranteeing new arrivals.

Some of the extensions to the guarantee algorithm are yet to be implemented. Also we are currently addressing the problem of initial allocation of tasks and resources. The goal of the allocation algorithm, in the context of the integrated treatment of CPU and resources, is to partition the set of *tasks* and *resources* among processors to maximize the inherent concurrency. How well the allocation of tasks and resources is done directly influences the performance of the dynamic on-line scheduling of the real-time tasks. Hence we have developed algorithms using various heuristics to solve this allocation problem and are in the process of evaluating them in context of our scheduling algorithms.

Acknowledgements

Many people have worked on scheduling as part of the Spring Project. W. Zhao contributed significantly to the basic scheduling concepts. We also wish to thank K. Arvind, S. Biyabani, S. Cheng, E. Gene, J. Huang, L. Molesky, E. Nahum, M. Kuan, D. Niehaus, C. Shen, P. Shiah, F. Wang, and G. Zlokapa for their work in this area.

REFERENCES

[1] S. Biyabani, "The Integration of Deadline and Criticalness in Hard Real–Time Scheduling," Masters Thesis, Univ. of Mass., August 1987.

[2] S. Biyabani, J.A. Stankovic, and K. Ramamritham, "The Integration of Deadline and Criticalness in Hard Real–Time Scheduling," *Proc. Real-Time Systems Symposium*, December 1988.

[3] S. Cheng, J.A. Stankovic, and K. Ramamritham, "Dynamic Scheduling of Groups of Tasks with Precedence Constraints in Distributed Hard Real-Time Systems," *Real-Time Systems Symposium*, December 1986.

[4] S. Cheng, "Dynamic Scheduling Algorithms for Distributed Hard Real-Time Systems," *Ph.D. Thesis*, University of Massachusetts, May 1987.

[5] L.D.Molesky, K. Ramamritham, C. Shen, J.A.Stankovic, and G. Zlokapa. "Implementing a Predictable Real-time Multiprocessor Kernel – the Spring Kernel", *7th IEEE Workshop on Real-time Operating Systems and Software*, May 1990.

[6] A. K. Mok, "Fundamental Design Problems of Distributed Systems for the Hard Real-Time Environment", *Ph.D. Dissertation, Department of Electrical Engineering and Computer Science, MIT, Cambridge, Mass.*, May 1983.

[7] K. Ramamritham and J. A. Stankovic, "Dynamic Task Scheduling in Distributed Hard Real-Time Systems," *IEEE Software*, 1(3), 1984.

[8] K. Ramamritham, J. Stankovic, W. Zhao, "Meta-Level Control in Distributed Real-Time Systems," *Intl. Conference on Distributed Computing Systems*, September 1987.

[9] K. Ramamritham, J. Stankovic, P. Shiah, "O(n) Scheduling Algorithms for Real-Time Multiprocessor Systems," *International Conference on Parallel Processing Systems*, August 1989.

[10] K. Ramamritham, J. Stankovic, and W. Zhao, "Distributed Scheduling of Tasks With Deadlines and Resource Requirements," *IEEE Transactions on Computers*, Vol. 38, No. 8, August 1989, pp. 1110-1123.

[11] K. Ramamritham, J. Stankovic, and P. Shiah, "Efficient Scheduling Algorithms for Real–Time Multiprocessor Systems," *IEEE Transactions on Parallel and Distributed Systems*, Vol. 1, No. 2, April 1990, pp. 184-194.

[12] K. Ramamritham, "Scheduling Complex Periodic Tasks", *Intl. Conference on Distributed Computing Systems*, June 1990.

[13] K. Ramamritham and J. M. Adan, "Load Balancing During the Static Allocation and Scheduling of Complex Periodic Tasks", COINS Technical Report, October 1990.

[14] L. Sha, R. Rajkumar, J. Lehoczky and K. Ramamritham, "Mode Change Protocols for Priority-Driven Preemptive Scheduling", *Real-Time Systems*, pp. 243-264, Vol. 1, No. 3, December 1989.

[15] C. Shen, K. Ramamritham, and J. Stankovic, Resource Reclaiming in Real-Time, *Proc Real-Time System Symposium*, December 1990.

[16] P. Shiah, "Real-Time Multiprocessor Scheduling Algorithms," MS Thesis, Univ. of Mass., January 1989.

[17] J.A. Stankovic, "Stability and Distributed Scheduling Algorithms," *IEEE Trans. on Software Engineering*, Vol. SE-11, No. 10, October 1985.

[18] J.A. Stankovic, K. Ramamritham, and S. Cheng, "Evaluation of a Flexible Task Scheduling Algorithm for Distributed Hard Real-Time Systems," *IEEE Transactions on Computers*, December 1985, pp. 1130-1143.

[19] J. A. Stankovic, "Misconceptions About Real-Time Computing," *IEEE Computer*, October 1988.

[20] J. A. Stankovic and K. Ramamritham, *Hard Real–Time Systems*, Tutorial Text, IEEE Press, 1988.

[21] J.A. Stankovic, "Decentralized Decision Making for Task Allocation in a Hard Real-Time System" *IEEE Transactions on Computers*, March 1989.

[22] J. A. Stankovic and K. Ramamritham, "The Spring Kernel: A New Paradigm for Real–Time Systems," *IEEE Software*, May 1992. pp. 54-71.

[23] J. D. Ullman, "Polynomial Complete Scheduling Problems", *Operating System Review*, Vol. 7, No. 4, October. 1973.

[24] J. D. Ullman, "NP-Complete Scheduling Problems", *Journal of Computer and System Science*, October. 1975.

[25] F. Wang, K. Ramamritham, and J.A. Stankovic, "Bounds on the Schedule Length for Some Heuristic Scheduling Algorithms for Hard Real-time Tasks", submitted for publication, September 1990.

[26] W. Zhao, "A Heuristic Approach to Scheduling with Resource Requirements in Distributed Systems," *Ph.D. Thesis*, February 1986.

[27] W. Zhao, K. Ramamritham and J. A. Stankovic, "Preemptive Scheduling under Time and Resource Constraints," *IEEE Trans. on Computers*, August 1987, pp. 949-960.

[28] W. Zhao, K. Ramamritham and J. A. Stankovic, "Scheduling Tasks with Resource Requirements in Hard Real-Time Systems," *IEEE Trans. on Software Engineering*, SE-12(5), May 1987.

[29] W. Zhao and K. Ramamritham, "Simple and Integrated Heuristic Algorithms for Scheduling Tasks with Time and Resource Constraints," *Journal of Systems and Software*, Vol 7, 1987, pp. 195-205.

CHAPTER 11

Real-Time, Priority-Ordered, Deadlock Avoidance Algorithms

Robert P. Cook
Lifeng Hsu
Sang H. Son

Department of Computer Science
Thornton Hall
University of Virginia
Charlottesville, VA 22903

ABSTRACT

The StarLite integrated programming environment is designed to support research in real-time database, operating system, and network technology. This paper discusses the results of experiments, using the capabilities of StarLite, to test the applicability of deadlock avoidance algorithms for real-time resource management. We extend existing algorithms to include priority inheritance and we introduce a new class of algorithms embodying a specification-ordered safety test. These new algorithms have the potential for improved efficiency and great flexibility in meeting user requirements. We also present a resource manager design that is amenable to hardware implementation.

INTRODUCTION

The goal of this paper is to illustrate the effectiveness of the StarLite programming environment[1] to support real-time systems research. The problem that we have chosen as an example is to determine the applicability of traditional deadlock avoidance algorithms[2,3] for real-time resource management.

The StarLite integrated programming environment is designed to facilitate research in real-time database, operating system, and network technology. The StarLite library synthesizes intellectual effort in the form of software components that can be transferred, examined, learned, or experimented with by the community at large. Thus, an abstraction, such as a resource manager, may be associated with interfaces, implementations, performance ratings, text, hypertext, video animations, sample programs, test cases, formal specifications, modification history, etc.

StarLite has been used to implement a real-time UNIX (Phoenix)[4], a real-time distributed database system[5], a parallel programming library[6] that extends the WorkCrews[7] interface for the DEC SRC FireFly, and network protocols. StarLite has also been used to support graduate and undergraduate courses in operating systems and database technology. The StarLite components include a Modula-2 compiler, an interpreter-based runtime, a SunView/X graphics package, a viewer, a simulation package, movie system, profiler, browser, Prolog interpreter, relational database system, and a software reuse library (250 modules, 100,000 lines). New tools under development include a modeling system, an algorithm animation package, and a remote execution package.

One of the interests of the StarLite project is resource management for real-time systems. Because of the project's emphasis on software reuse, one of the goals is to design generic interfaces that are invariant across a broad spectrum of application requirements and technology options. For example, the resource management interface described later is designed so that it can be implemented either as a chip or by using a co-processor.

The requirements and rationale for this interface are discussed in Section 2. In Section 3, we present the Banker's[2] deadlock avoidance algorithm and its extension proposed by Munch-Andersen and Zahle[8]. In Section 4, we extend Munch-Andersen's algorithm for real-time resource management and detail the results of the experiments that we ran using the StarLite environment. In Section 5, we summarize our observations and plans for future work.

THE BANKER INTERFACE

One of the goals of the StarLite project is to define interface standards for the abstractions represented in the module library. A "good" interface should have low coupling with respect to other abstractions, should be useable across a wide range of application requirements and technological restrictions, and should be functionally complete. Furthermore, every StarLite interface defines an abstract data type. As a result, the "Banker" interface declares a type "Manager" that can be instantiated to create managers for disjoint sets of resources, such as for a distributed system. The final requirement for the resource manager is that the design be amenable to a hardware implementation.

The best way to view the design (as listed in Figure 1) is as a hardware chip. As such, a manager has control inputs, control and status outputs, as well as retained state information. Processes are denoted by integer tags and it is the operating system's responsibility to maintain the relationship between its own process structures and process tags. Typically, the tag is stored as a field in each process' context block. The control inputs reflect process state transitions, such as process creation/death, resource requests/releases, priority changes, and canceling a resource request that is blocking a process. The control outputs are represented by up-level procedure calls to a "Guard" procedure in the Modula-2 interface, but these could just as easily be implemented as interrupts in a hardware realization. The control outputs are used to block/unblock a process and to change a process' priority.

The status outputs are represented by the Available and Request procedures. The Available procedure determines the number of allocable units of a resource while the Request procedure encodes a non-blocking resource allocation. If a request cannot be satisfied, the routine returns a count of the number of resources that would have to be released before the Request could proceed.

A resource manager can be created with different "class" selections to identify the management policy to be followed. Thus, to run the experiments described later in the paper, we used the same test programs with different "class" selections. We ran a more diverse set of experiments than those reported herein, but we have included those that seemed to be the most interesting. None of the changes to priority calculation, management policy, or scheduling algorithm affected the interface, once we got it right. We will admit, however, that it took several iterations until the final design was achieved.

DEADLOCK AVOIDANCE

Perhaps the most widely-known, deadlock-avoidance algorithm for resource management is the Banker's algorithm, developed by Dijkstra[2] and Habermann[3]. To avoid deadlock, we need to have information about the future. Obviously, if a perfect knowledge of the future exists, the existence or absence of deadlock is predetermined. The more common case is the existence of partial information. For the Banker's algorithm, the future actions of a process are restricted by its current resource holdings and its *maximal claim* specification. The maximal claim is a resource vector that indicates the maximum number of units of each resource that might be used by a process. However, resources are not allocated until actually requested

definition module Banker;

type   Tag = **cardinal**;
        Mgr; (* Manager *)
        Guard = **procedure** (Mgr, Tag, **cardinal, integer**);
   (* Manager, Process, Action=Block/UnBlock on Resource, Set Priority *)

procedure Open(**var** r:Mgr; N, M, class: **cardinal; var** limit: **array of cardinal**);
  (* Create resource Manager for N processes, M resources with "limit" units *)
  (* The "class" parameter selects different resource management policies *)

procedure Close(**var** r:Mgr);
  (* Kill a resource Manager *)

procedure Request(r:Mgr; process:Tag; resource, amount: **cardinal**): **integer**;
  (* The return value is <0 if request exceeds available by -value units;
    0 if request exceeds maximum claim; 1 if unsafe state; 2 if success *)

procedure Block(r:Mgr; process:Tag; res,amt: **cardinal**; p:Guard): **boolean**;
  (* res = resource, amt = amount *)
  (* Blocks until request can be safely granted; returns **true** if blocked *)
  (* **Note**: block can be called multiple times for a "blocked" process. *)

procedure Cancel(r:Mgr; process:Tag; resource, amount: **cardinal**);
  (* Used to cancel a currently blocked request; doesn't call the Guard *)

procedure Available(r:Mgr; resource: **cardinal**): **cardinal**;
  (* Returns the number of available units of the selected resource *)

procedure Release(r:Mgr; process:Tag; resource, amount: **cardinal**);
  (* Free the selected amount of the resource *)

procedure Process(r:Mgr; **var** maxClaim: **array of cardinal**):Tag;
  (* Create a process with an optional resource claim list *)

procedure Kill(r:Mgr; **var** process:Tag);
  (* Kill a process and release all its resources *)

procedure Priority(r:Mgr; process:Tag; newPriority: **integer**);
  (* Used by the operating system to signal a change in status *)

end Banker.

Figure 1. The Resource Management Interface

by a process. Therefore, better resource utilization is possible than with typical prevention algorithms, such as collective request.

The Banker's algorithm solves the problem of avoiding deadlock with only a restricted knowledge (maximal claim) of the future by examining all possible future states in the context of current resource holdings. In other words, the current set of processes is examined to see if their resource requests can eventually be satisfied. The assumption is that a process not blocked on a resource will eventually terminate. If there is at least one sequence of resource actions that would allow all current processes to satisfy their maximal claims and in doing so to terminate, the system is said to be in a *safe* state. If no such sequence is possible, the system is in an *unsafe* state.

Notice that the existence of a safe state does not imply the absence of unsafe states in the future. Remember that the definition states "at least one". If the actual execution sequence does not follow the sequence we found, unsafe states can occur. In a similar fashion, an unsafe state does not imply eventual deadlock since the algorithm assumes the worst case; that is, maximal claims will occur. If all processes were in an unsafe state and made no more resource requests, they might still terminate. Notice that any resource request can direct the system down a poor execution path. Therefore, the avoidance algorithm must be applied for every request and for "free" operations when a blocked process' request is reconsidered. This overhead is the price that is paid for greater potential resource utilization.

An Example

The next example illustrates a safe state and its safe execution sequences (SES). We examine a system composed of three processes and a single resource of ten units. The "[]" represents the "maxClaim" minus "allocation" value, or the limit on future requests. A "()" value denotes an unsatisfied resource request. A value of "[0]" means that a process can request no more resources. In the example, Process 2 (P2) has 3 units of the resource, has requested one more, and could request three more units at which point its maximal claim would be satisfied. The question is "can the request be granted?".

A SAFE STATE

Process	1	2	3	Available	total
Resource					
1	1+[4]	3+(1)+[4]	3+[2]	3	10

Safe Execution Sequences = (P3, P1, P2), (P3, P2, P1)

P1 cannot have its maximal claim satisfied; therefore, it is not eligible to begin a SES. Even though process two could have its request satisfied, it would still have a three-unit claim remaining. There would only be two units available so process two is ruled out as well. Finally, process three is examined; a safe execution sequence (two in fact) is found; and the request is granted. At this point, the operating system grants process two's request.

Now let us assume that process one requests two additional units.

AN UNSAFE STATE

Process	1	2	3	Available	total
Resource					
1	1+(2)+[4]	4+[3]	3+[2]	2	10

No Safe Execution Sequences Exist If The Request Is Granted.

If the request by process 1 were granted and all three processes then requested an additional resource, the system would be deadlocked. Of course, it is just as likely that no more resources are requested and that all processes terminate.

The Banker's algorithm has the very desirable property of maintaining the independence of the scheduler from the resource allocator. Resources are granted so long as safety can be guaranteed and the scheduler chooses processes to execute; both decisions are made independently.

However, there are problems with the Banker's algorithm. First, since resources are given away as long as safety can be guaranteed, the system can gridlock. As stated by Lausen[9] in the case when a system is heavily loaded: "so many resources are granted away that very few feasible sequences remain, and as a consequence, the processes will be executed sequentially one by one". Secondly, the safety algorithm must examine a resource vector of size m for each of n processes and this must occur for each of the n schedule steps. Thus, the algorithm may require m*n*n operations.

This is too time-consuming to execute on every resource operation. Finally, the priorities of the processes are not taken into account.

The Priority-Ordered, Liberal Granting Algorithm

The safety test of the Banker's Algorithm is too time consuming. An alternative algorithm (termed Liberal Granting), which was proposed by Munch-Anderson and Zahle[8], imposes a linear ordering, which we term a Linear Resource Order (LRO), on the system's processes with respect to resource allocation. The ordering is defined such that it is always "safe" and new requests are considered only with respect to the safety of the existing order. As a result, the computational cost of the safety check can be reduced to a constant time operation because only one of the many possible execution sequences is examined. The disadvantage is that the Banker's algorithm may grant requests that the Liberal Granting Algorithm would not. (At this point, we point out that both algorithms were previously used only for time-sharing systems with no real-time constraints.)

For the Liberal Granting Algorithm, the safety test reduces to checking whether an allocation will invalidate the claim of a process' predecessor in the schedule. If the processes preceding the requesting process can satisfy their maximal (worst-case) claims one at a time, the state is safe. Consider the following example with 5 units of the resource initially available.

PROCESSES	5	4	3	2	1
INITIAL STATE	(1)+[2]	(1)+[2]	(1)+[2]	(1)+[1]	(1)+[2]
BANKERS	1+[1]	1+[1]	1+[1]	1+[0]	1+[1]
LIBERAL	1+[1]	1+[1]	1+[1]	1+[0]	(1)+[2]

Assume that the LRO equals 5, 4, 3, 2, 1. For the Liberal Granting Algorithm, Process 1 remains blocked because granting its request would conflict with the claim of Process 5. The Banker's algorithm allocates all the resources because it finds the safe execution sequence beginning with Process 2. Notice that the Banker's algorithm gave away all the resources; for this reason, which typifies its performance, it is referred to as the Most Liberal granting algorithm. At the other extreme, the collective request prevention algorithm is the Most Conservative.

Munch-Anderson and Zahle also extended the Liberal Granting Algorithm to include priority by defining an operation that we term *promotion*. A process may be *promoted* over a lower priority process in the LRO if the action results in a safe state.

The algorithm assumes that a LRO exists. When a process is created, the LRO is scanned from low to high priority until an insertion point for the new process is found that is consistent with its priority and the liberal granting policy. For example, assume that the system has 6 units of a single resource type, and the LRO is determined by the priority of the processes.

At time 0:
Suppose that the following four processes arrive and the state after their initial requests are satisfied is

LRO	7	5	2	0	Available
	1+[2]	1+[1]	1+[2]	1+[2]	2

At time 1:
A priority 3 process arrives with a claim of 3 units.

LRO	7	5	2	0	3	Available
	1+[2]	1+[1]	1+[2]	1+[2]	[3]	2

Notice that even if the new process arrives with an initial request of 1 unit, the request still cannot be granted because the system has to reserve enough resources to cover the maximum claims of all preceding processes.

At time 2:
A priority 8 process arrives with a claim of 5 units.

LRO	7	5	3	2	8	0	Available
	1+[2]	1+[1]	[3]	1+[2]	[5]	1+[2]	2

Notice the situation that occurs in the example. Process 8, although it has the highest priority, has to be placed after process 2 because the processes at priorities 7, 5 and 2 are holding the resources that the priority 8 process needs for completion. This situation, when a high priority task is suspended while waiting for a low priority task to execute, is called priority inversion[10].

REAL-TIME RESOURCE MANAGEMENT

In this section, we discuss the problems associated with real-time resource management, extend Munch-Anderson's algorithm for real-time use, and discuss several experiments that were performed using the StarLite environment. We begin with some definitions.

The basic differences between real-time and traditional resource management are the notions of time and predictability. Time is important because real-time tasks typically include some function of time in their specification. Predictability is important because engineers are required to guarantee with some confidence level (typically high) that a system will meet its specification.

A task in a real-time system can be characterized as having the following attributes: arrival time, start time, slack time, execution time and deadline. The arrival time is the time when a task enters the system. The start time (release time[11]) is the earliest time when the resources can be used and is usually the arrival time. The slack time is an estimate of how long a task can afford to delay its execution. The execution time is the amount of time that a task requires each resource. The deadline is the time by which a process has to complete its task. A task incurs a "miss" if it can not complete by its deadline. A deadline can be defined as hard or soft. A hard deadline cannot be missed, for if it is, the system fails. A soft deadline normally implies that good response time is desired, but, missing some soft deadlines is tolerable. We may also be given information on a task's resource holding times; however, in the absence of this information, the assumption is that the hold time is the same as the execution time. For the purposes of our experiments, we also assume that maximal claim information is available.

Tasks can be periodic, sporadic, or aperiodic in nature[12]. Periodic tasks enter the system at regular intervals, and each instance of a periodic task has to be completed by the arrival time of the next instance of the task. Sporadic tasks are asynchronous tasks that have a minimum inter-arrival time between instances of the task, and may have hard deadlines. Aperiodic tasks enter the system at irregular intervals, and normally have soft deadlines.

Many papers on real-time processing use criticalness, or criticality, and/or priority in the discussions of real-time scheduling. Criticalness (criticality) means the degree of importance of the task itself. Priority refers to the scheduling priority which is derived from task or system characteristics. For example in rate monotonic[13] systems, a task with a shorter period is assigned a higher priority. However, this short-period task may not be more important than a long-period task. Therefore, the scheduling priority in real-time systems may not correspond to the degree of importance of the task.

Priority assignment is said to be dynamic if the priority of any task may change during its execution. When criticality is used with priority, the criticality value is assigned statically and the priority is calculated dynamically from task or system behavior. The two values are then combined to yield the ranking used by the scheduler.

Real-Time Liberal Granting

Priority inversions are quite common in real-time systems because a high priority task may arrive after a lower priority task has gained control of a resource. If priority inversions are not controlled, priority order cannot be maintained and critical tasks may miss their deadlines. A common scheme that remedies this undesirable situation is called priority inheritance[14]. Using this scheme, we simply set the priority of the lower priority task equal to the priority of the higher priority task. In the previous example, if a priority inheritance policy is used, the LRO would appear as follows:

LRO	7	5	2	8	3	0	Available
	1+[2]	1+[1]	1+[2]	[5]	[3]	1+[2]	2

This simple example illustrates a number of the issues that we are investigating in order to apply the Liberal Granting Algorithm to real-time resource management. First, the processes at priorities 7, 5, and 2 are blocking the priority 8 process with respect to its claim. As a result, they could "inherit" a priority of 8; however, they are not blocking the priority 8 process with respect to its requests since it hasn't made any requests, and in fact, may not make any. Thus, one implementation option would be to apply the inheritance rule as resources are requested. Of course, one now has the problem of deciding whether all or a subset of the blocking processes should inherit.

Another important point concerns the relationship between priority and the linear resource ordering. The LRO must be maintained to guarantee the safety so the LRO and priority order are likely to be distinct.

Notice that the priority 3 process has been demoted, which is an operation not anticipated by Munch-Anderson. It would clearly be a mistake to have this process inherit a higher priority as that could only degrade the solution since it holds no resources. It would also be a mistake to leave it alone. Because even though it has lower priority than process 8, it is higher in the LRO. Therefore, if it requests a resource, it can block further execution by the priority 8 process. As a result of these observations, we introduced a demotion rule that causes all lower-priority, non-blocking processes to be moved down in the LRO.

The Experiments

The experiments to determine the effect of priority inheritance on the liberal granting algorithm were greatly facilitated by the StarLite environment. The components used were the concurrent programming package, the simulation package, the probability distribution modules, the multi-thread debugger, and the profiler. Furthermore, the Banker and task generator modules were contributed back to the master library for use by the database group and the operating systems classes.

We ran numerous experiments but only report on one of them to illustrate our methods. In this experiment, we implemented the Banker's (Figure 2), Priority-Ordered Liberal Granting (Figure 3), and Priority-Inheritance Liberal Granting (Figure 4) algorithms. The task set consists of 10 periodic and 5 sporadic processes. The priorities are assigned according to the rate-monotonic rule. The sporadic tasks are quasi-periodic in that they have a listed period in the Figures, but the values represent the range [period-dev..period+dev]. The deadline column lists the deadline for each process relative to its arrival time and the hold time column lists the hold time for the resource. Also, the maximum claim and the initial request for each process are listed. Only a single resource with 8 total units was used in order to control the number of variables in the experiment. The results of the experiment include the total number of processes of each class generated, the number completed, and the number missed. Infeasible processes, which could not meet their deadline, were killed.

The scheduler always executes the highest priority task first. In addition, all system queues and locks are priority ordered. Furthermore, tasks that hold resources are assumed to execute simultaneously with respect to CPU time. This restriction was necessary to eliminate the interaction between contention for a single CPU and resource management. With the elimination of CPU scheduling, the effects of resource management decisions are highlighted.

The Banker's algorithm produced the highest resource utilization (72%), but had the undesirable effect of inducing misses in a large percentage of the high-priority tasks. This is in fact the opposite of the intended result for a real-time system. The explanation is that the Banker's algorithm gives away so many resources that when the high-frequency tasks arrive, they are blocked and miss their deadline.

The impact of the Priority-Ordered Liberal Granting Algorithm is rather dramatic. The number of high-priority misses decreases by almost a factor of four. Furthermore, the total number of misses decreases by a third and the misses are not just pushed down a level, they are transferred to the lowest priority tasks. Thus, it was well worth the effort to integrate scheduling

Figure 2. (Banker's Algorithm)

Task	Pri	Period	Dev	Dead	Hold	Claim	Req	Total	Done	Miss
1	20	5	0	5	2	6	2	180	59	121
2	18	10	0	10	3	3	2	90	46	44
3	17	15	2	15	3	3	2	61	51	10
4	16	15	0	15	4	3	2	60	51	9
5	14	20	0	20	5	3	2	45	43	2
6	13	25	3	25	5	3	2	36	36	0
7	12	25	0	25	5	3	2	36	35	1
8	10	30	0	30	5	3	2	30	29	1
9	9	35	5	35	8	3	2	27	26	0
10	8	35	0	35	8	6	2	26	26	0
11	6	40	0	40	8	3	2	23	23	0
12	5	45	8	45	8	3	2	21	21	0
13	4	45	0	45	8	3	2	20	20	0
14	2	50	0	50	10	3	2	18	18	0
15	1	55	10	55	10	3	2	17	17	0
								690	501	188

Simulation Time: 900

Total Processes in Progress = 1

*** RESOURCE UTILIZATION ***

RESOURCE	Units	Time-Used	Utilization(%)
1	8	5216	72

Figure 3. (Liberal Granting without Priority Inheritance)

Task	Pri	Period	Dev	Dead	Hold	Claim	Req	Total	Done	Miss
1	20	5	0	5	2	6	2	180	133	47
2	18	10	0	10	3	3	2	90	80	10
3	17	15	2	15	3	3	2	61	61	0
4	16	15	0	15	4	3	2	60	57	3
5	14	20	0	20	5	3	2	45	44	1
6	13	25	3	25	5	3	2	36	35	1
7	12	25	0	25	5	3	2	36	32	4
8	10	30	0	30	5	3	2	30	26	4
9	9	35	5	35	8	3	2	27	24	2
10	8	35	0	35	8	6	2	26	22	3
11	6	40	0	40	8	3	2	23	18	4
12	5	45	8	45	8	3	2	21	11	10
13	4	45	0	45	8	3	2	20	3	17
14	2	50	0	50	10	3	2	18	2	16
15	1	55	10	55	10	3	2	17	1	15
								690	549	137

Simulation Time: 900

Total Processes in Progress = 4

*** RESOURCE UTILIZATION ***

RESOURCE	Units	Time-Used	Utilization(%)
1	8	4518	62

priority with resource management.

The effect of priority inheritance on the results was somewhat less than we expected. Its main impact was on the highest priority task, which had its miss count reduced by an additional 15%. However, those misses were transferred to other tasks rather than being eliminated.

In analyzing the results of the priority inheritance experiment, we discovered that low priority processes could be killed even though their execution would not interfere with a high priority process' deadline. The

Figure 4. (Liberal Granting with Priority Inheritance)

Task	Pri	Period	Dev	Dead	Hold	Claim	Req	Total	Done	Miss
1	20	5	0	5	2	6	2	180	140	40
2	18	10	0	10	3	3	2	90	80	10
3	17	15	2	15	3	3	2	61	61	0
4	16	15	0	15	4	3	2	60	55	5
5	14	20	0	20	5	3	2	45	39	6
6	13	25	3	25	5	3	2	36	34	2
7	12	25	0	25	5	3	2	36	32	4
8	10	30	0	30	5	3	2	30	26	4
9	9	35	5	35	8	3	2	27	25	1
10	8	35	0	35	8	6	2	26	24	1
11	6	40	0	40	8	3	2	23	17	5
12	5	45	8	45	8	3	2	21	11	9
13	4	45	0	45	8	3	2	20	3	17
14	2	50	0	50	10	3	2	18	2	16
15	1	55	10	55	10	3	2	17	1	15
								690	550	135

Simulation Time: 900

Total Processes in Progress = 5

*** RESOURCE UTILIZATION ***

RESOURCE	Units	Time-Used	Utilization(%)
1	8	4504	62

priority inheritance scheme failed because it had too narrow a view of the safety property. To see the reason, consider the following four periodic tasks sharing two units of one resource type and using the rate-monotonic priority assignment, i.e., Shortest Period Length First (SPLF) policy:

Task	Period	Units Needed	Hold Time	Deadline
1	10	2	2	Next Arrival Time
2	14	1	5	Next Arrival Time
3	25	1	6	Next Arrival Time
4	27	1	10	Next Arrival Time

Assume that all four tasks start at time zero. At time 30 before task 1 arrives, the LRO is (3 2 4). However, when task 1 arrives at time 30, we have two options. If the priority inheritance policy is not enforced, the resource allocation state is:

	LRO	3	2	4	1		
Resource						Available	Total
1		1	[1]	1	[2]	0	2

As soon as task 3 completes and releases its resource, task 2 can use the resource from time 32 to 36 without causing any delay to task 1. However, if the priority inheritance policy is employed, the state becomes:

	LRO	3	4	1	2		
Resource						Available	Total
1		1	1	[2]	[1]	0	2

and task 2 has to wait until time 39 when task 1 completes. As a result, task 2 will not complete by its deadline which is time 42. Thus, priority inheritance introduced unnecessary misses.

CONCLUSIONS AND FURTHER RESEARCH

The Munch-Anderson's algorithm has the nice property that any rule can be used to assign priority. However, as a result of our experiments with the StarLite environment, it became obvious that the notion of *safety* was considerably more general-purpose than just "no deadlock".

The safety test is applied whenever the resource state changes; however, why not apply the test when any system state of interest changes? With this viewpoint, the goal of the safety test is to validate that a subset of a program's specification is enforced. As the system is always in a safe state, it is obvious that the selected invariant is maintained. Obviously, it is computationally infeasible to check all of a specification; therefore, the system designer must be judicious in assigning the safety condition. We term any algorithm that maintains such a safety property a *Specification-Ordered Avoidance Algorithm*.

In the previous example in which the priority 2 task misses its deadline, we can augment the safety test with a portion of the specification that states "a high-priority task is promoted until it can meet its deadline". Notice that this may cause blocking tasks that hold critical resources to be killed. We also point out that the safety check must have feasible solutions; thus, a statement such as "every process meets its deadline" is unacceptable. With a different safety check, the desired resource state would result:

	LRO	3	2	4	1		
Resource						Available	Total
1		1	[1]	1	[2]	0	2

As a further point, if the LRO safety check guarantees that deadlines are met, there is no reason to have a scheduling priority different from the LRO. To do otherwise would introduce unnecessary context switches when processes request resources and block. The ChangePriority action is sent to the operating system's Guard procedure by the resource manager when priority adjustments are necessary.

Specification-Ordered Avoidance has great flexibility and is computationally simple since the tests are always in terms of the Linear Resource Order. As a result, the systems engineer can include non-traditional, semantic constraints in the safety condition.

There are numerous options to the implementation that are yet to be explored. For example, we are testing a distributed version of the algorithm and we are examining its applicability to database concurrency control. These additional experiments are facilitated by the support modules for distributed programming and database operations that have been contributed to the StarLite software reuse library.

RELATED WORK

A recent paper by Belik[15] describes a very efficient technique for deadlock avoidance on single-unit resources. However, the paper does not address real-time resource management issues. A recent paper by Babaoglu,

Marzullo, and Schneider[16] also considers generalized safety conditions, including their use for database concurrency control.

References

[1] Cook, R. P. and L. Hsu, "StarLite: A Software Education Laboratory," *Fourth SEI Conference on Software Engineering Education*, reprinted in *Software Engineering Education*, Springer-Verlag Lecture Notes in Computer Science 423, Lionel E. Deimel (Ed.), (April 1990).

[2] Dijkstra, E.W., "A Class of Allocation Strategies Inducing Bounded Delays Only," *AFIPS 1972 SJCC, Vol. 40*, Montvale, N.J., AFIPS Press, (1972).

[3] Habermann, A.N., "Prevention of System Deadlocks," *Communications of the ACM 12*, (Dec. 1969).

[4] Cook, R. P., "The StarLite Operating System," *Operating Systems for Mission-Critical Computing*, Eds. K. Gordon, P. Hwang, A. Agrawala, ACM Press, (to appear).

[5] S. H. Son and C. Chang, "Performance Evaluation of Real-Time Locking Protocols using a Distributed Software Prototyping Environment," *10th International Conference on Distributed Computing Systems*, Paris, France, (June 1990).

[6] Cook, R. P. and H. Oh, "The StarLite Project," *Frontiers 90 Conference on Massively Parallel Computation*, (Oct. 1990).

[7] Roberts, E.S. and M.T. Vandevoorde, "WorkCrews: An Abstraction for Controlling Parallelism," DEC SRC Research Report 42, (April 1989).

[8] Munch-Anderson, B. and T.U. Zahle, "Scheduling According to Job Priority With Prevention of Deadlock and Permanent Blocking," *Acta Informatica 8*, 2(1977).

[9] Lausen, S., "Job Scheduling Guaranteeing Reasonable Turn-Around Times," *Acta Informatica 2*, 1(1973).

[10] Rajkumar, R., L. Sha, and J.P. Lehoczky, "Real-Time Synchronization Protocols for Multiprocessors," *Real-Time Systems Symposium*, Huntsville, AL, (Dec. 1988).

[11] Abbott, R. and H. Garcia-Molina, "Scheduling Real-Time Transactions," *SIGMOD Record 17*, 1(March 1988).

324

[12] Mok, A.K., *Fundamental Design Problems of Distributed Systems for the Hard Real-Time Environment,"* Ph.D. Thesis, M.I.T. (1983).

[13] Liu, C.L. and J.W. Layland, "Scheduling Algorithms for Multiprogramming in a Hard Real-Time Environment," *JACM 20,* 1(1973).

[14] Lampson, B.W. and D.D. Redell, "Experience with Processes and Monitors in Mesa," *Communications of the ACM 23,* 2(Feb. 1980).

[15] Belik, F., "An Efficient Deadlock Avoidance Technique," *IEEE Transactions on Computers 39,* 7(July 1990).

[16] Babaoglu, O., K. Marzullo, and F.B. Schneider, "Priority Inversion and Its Prevention," Cornell TR-90-1088, (Feb. 1990).

Index